The Railways of South America

D. Trevor Rowe

A Locomotives International Publication

Above: A Paulista Railway express passes a British style signal box at Perús station on the Santos - Jundiai line in Brazil in March 1967. The clerestory roof stock is hauled by a 3,000 hp English Electric Co-Co locomotive.

Front Cover: 760mm gauge 2-8-0 no. 68 is waiting to depart on a special working from the narrow gauge terminus at São João del Rei, Brazil, 16th October 1976.

Rear Cover: One of Ecuador's Baldwin 2-8-0 locomotives built in the 1940s climbs up to Alausi with a goods train on the Guayaquil & Quito Railway on 9th October 1979.

Title Page: North British wood-fired 2-6-0 no. 104 at Encarnación, Paraguay on 27th August 1968.

ISBN 1-900340-10-0
First Edition. Published by Paul Catchpole Ltd., The Old School House, Arrow, Alcester, Warwickshire, B49 5PJ
Edited and typeset by Paul Catchpole, printed and bound by Highland Printers, Inverness.
British Library Cataloguing in Publication Data. A catalogue record for this book is available from the British Library.

The Railways of South America

D. Trevor Rowe

Contents

Special thanks are due to:
Railway Gazette International, successors to the Railway Gazette, for permission to reproduce the maps in this book, David Ibbotson of Dorridge Travel for making available photographs from his personal collection, Chris Skow for making the Trains, Unlimited Tours photographs available, Keith Taylorson for sourcing additional photographic material and preparing the initial typescript, Paul Catchpole for extra research to create the photo captions, and Richard Campbell, 'Eddie' Edmundson, Ian Thomson, and Chris West for proof reading the first drafts. Most of all, I would like to thank my wife Mary who has given me her unflagging support over the many years of travelling and writing during which the research for this book has been undertaken.

PREFACE

Trevor Rowe was born in 1929 and grew up in Britain at a time when the British railways scene was arguably at its finest. Locomotive design was developing to new peaks of speed and efficiency, the railways were the principal means of transport, and steam reigned supreme. Not only was the scene on the home railways so good but heavy engineering companies were exporting their products all around the world, to the Empire and further afield. Very few people, however, ventured abroad for their interest in railways until the end of main line steam came to Britain in 1968 and then not as far as South America.

Fortunately though, there were people in times gone by who worked for British or American owned railways in South America who took the trouble to write and to take photographs, and to whom our knowledge of earlier South American railway history owes a great deal. To these people we can add a small number of names of those who have researched further, visiting the railways and gathering their information first-hand. Trevor Rowe is foremost amongst such enthusiasts, driven by a great affection for South America, first visited in 1967 on a visit to Brazil. In the autumn of the following year Argentina and Paraguay were explored by the author and his wife Mary while on their honeymoon.

More visits to South America (and other destinations) followed, aided by the author's career in the shipping and forwarding and in the travel industry. During the period 1966-1980 with British Caledonian Airways in particular, this enabled world-wide travel before the days of organised long distance railway trips. By the time enthusiasts were able to travel on organised tours Trevor's local knowledge and command of languages meant that he was in demand to lead them.

The first item of the author's to be published was a photo in an article covering the Tollesbury branch closure, which appeared in the July 1951 'Trains Illustrated'. His first full article was printed in the same magazine, in the April 1954 issue, and was about the Spanish Railways. Since then Trevor has contributed to and written a number of books on Spain and on narrow gauge railways around the world, published in England and Spain in both countries' languages. He has also continued to write articles for magazines, not only in Britain but in France and Spain too, and as an LCGB member has regularly contributed to the LCGB Club Bulletin in a very long running series of articles entitled 'Railways and I'.

My own first encounter with both the author and South American railways came in 1995 with my editorship of 'Locomotives International' magazine, to which Trevor has long been a contributor, followed by a visit to relatives in Chile. Patchy knowledge gained from articles in the magazine and other books on particular railways have been brought together by Trevor's work and broadened to include some areas rarely covered in the railway press.

South America's railways have always been the least well represented in print, in spite of the fact that they are some of the most spectacular in terms of scenery, engineering and motive power. This obscurity is probably because they are relatively remote - in fact some of them are extremely so, high up in the Andes mountains or buried in the jungle. They deserve a much wider appreciation and as world travel to exotic places increases perhaps they will gain more attention.

The railways in this book have included an astounding array of motive power, not only steam, but diesels and electrics which were experimented with and put to work in South America at an early stage of development. The variation of types is attributable to the wide variations in topography and traffic demands, particularly in the mountain areas where articulated steam types were required on an assortment of gauges. British and North American working practices have mainly predominated and this is reflected in the origin of much of the motive power at work throughout the history of South America's railways, however, locomotives produced by many other countries are also mentioned and illustrated in these pages, as particular railways have had affiliations with particular builders or nations over time.

Paul Catchpole, November 2000

BRITISH GUIANA
Area 90,000 Sq. Miles.
Population 300,000.
Railway Mileage 79

DUTCH GUIANA
Area 54,000 Sq. Miles.
Population 136,000.
Railway Mileage 108.

CARACAS ⊙

VENEZUELA
Area 394,000 Sq. Miles.
Population 2,560,000.
Railway Mileage 661.

GEORGETOWN

PARAMARIBO

CAYENNE

FRENCH GUIANA
Area 35,000 Sq. Miles.
Population 49,000.
Railway Mileage Nil.

COLOMBIA
⊙ BOGOTA
Area 441,000 Sq. Miles.
Population 6,600,000.
Railway Mileage 1,054.

ECUADOR
Area 220,000
Sq. Miles.
Population
2,000,000.
Railway
Mileage 413. ⊙GUAYAQUIL

B R A Z I L

Area
3,300,000
Sq. Miles.

Population
34,000,000.

Railway
Mileage
19,205.

⊙RECIFE

PERU
Area 532,000 Sq. Miles.
⊙ LIMA
Population 5,500,000.
Railway Mileage 2,081.

⊙BAHIA

BOLIVIA
⊙ LA PAZ
Area 708,000 Sq. Miles.
Population 2,800,000.
Railway Mileage 1,449.

PARAGUAY
Area 62,000 Sq. Miles.
Population 1,000,000.
Railway Mileage 517.

ASCUNCION ⊙

SAN PAULO ⊙   ⊙ RIO DE JANEIRO

ARGENTINE
REPUBLIC.

⊙PORTO ALEGRE

VALPARAISO ⊙

Area 1,100,000 Sq. Miles.

BUENOS AIRES ⊙

⊙MONTEVIDEO

URUGUAY
Area 72,200 Sq. Miles.
Population 1,700,000.
Railway Mileage 1,654.

CHILE
Area 290,000 Sq. Miles.
Population 4,000,000.
Railway Mileage 5960.

Population
10,000,000.

Railway Mileage
23,728. ⊙ BAHIA BLANCA

SOUTH AMERICA

0 100 200 300 400 500   1,000 Miles.

ENGLAND & WALES
ON THE SAME SCALE.

FALKLAND Is.

The countries of South America with statistics as published in the Railway Gazette of December 6th, 1926.

ARGENTINA

Argentina is the eighth largest country in the world, and in South America the second largest in area and third largest in population. It covers an area of 1,084,000 square miles which is equal to 29% of the area of Europe. In 1926 when the Railway Gazette published a survey of South America, 65% of Argentina's railways were British owned, representing a capital investment of £250 million. In 1945 there were 42,036 km of railway, of which 58.2% were British controlled, 11% French controlled and 30.8% State owned. By 1977 trackage had decreased to 32,000 km and the railways carried only 8% of freight and 15% of passenger traffic.

The total population of the country today is around 35 million, with the capital city of Buenos Aires accounting for over 3 million, but the population of the greater Buenos Aries area, including the surrounding districts, is estimated to be around 12 million, more than a third of the nation's inhabitants. In the early days of the railways this vast country was only beginning to be settled, and the first national census of 1869 quoted a population of 1,877,490, less than one person to every two square kilometres, while Buenos Aires had less than 180,000 inhabitants. It is therefore not surprising that railways came to Argentina later than to some other South American countries, and the first concession was applied for on 14th September 1853 and granted on 12th January 1854.

Capital was raised in Argentina but construction was entrusted to an Englishman, William Bragge, born in Birmingham in 1822 and surveyor of the first line in Brazil. The

2-2-0ST 'La Porteña' hauled a centenary special between Linieres and Once on 25th October 1957 and is now kept in the Colonial and Historical Museum at Luján.

Dom Pedro II Railway, opened on 30th April 1854. The concession for a line from the Plaza del Parque in Buenos Aires (today Lavalle) to San Joséde Flores, a distance of 20 km and work on the first ten kilometres to Floresta commenced in 1855. On a trial run in August 1857 all went well on the outward journey, made so slowly that the administrator, who was on horseback, arrived at the same time as the train, but for the return journey speed was increased up to 25 mph resulting in a derailment, fortunately without serious injury. The official opening took place on 30th August 1857, trains being worked by the locomotives "La Portena" and "La Argentina". Present at the opening ceremony were two men whose names were long commemorated as regional titles of the

national railway system, Bartolomé Mitre and Domingo Faustino Sarmiento.

The gauge was 1,676 mm (5'6"), reputedly because the material and locomotives had been bought up from stock intended for India. It is often claimed that "La Portena" had seen service in the Crimea but this has been disproved. Both locomotives were 2-2-0ST built by E.B. Wilson at Leeds in 1856, works numbers 570/571, and "La Portena" can still be seen today in the Colonial and Historical Museum at Luján, near Buenos Aires. "La Argentina" went to Paraguay in 1869 for use by the occupying Brazilian Army there after the War of the Triple Alliance (see chapter 9).

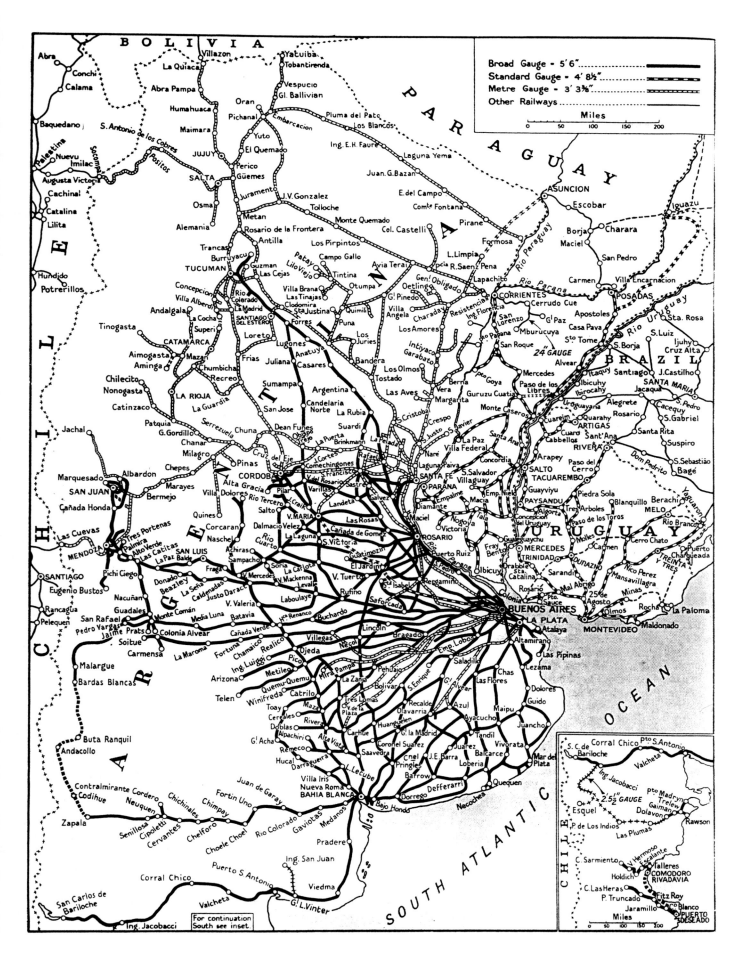

BOLIVIA

PARAGUAY

Broad Gauge - 5'6" ....
Standard Gauge - 4' 8½" ....
Metre Gauge - 3' 3⅜" ....
Other Railways ....

Miles
0   50   100   150   200

CHILE

BRAZIL

URUGUAY

BUENOS AIRES
LA PLATA
MONTEVIDEO

SOUTH ATLANTIC OCEAN

For continuation South see inset.

CHILE
S. C. de Bariloche
Corral Chico Pto S. Antonio
Ing. Jacobacci
2.5" GAUGE
Esquel
P. de Los Indios
Las Plumas
C. Sarmiento
Holdich
C. Las Heras
P. Truncado
Jaramillo
Valcheta
Pto Madryn
Trelew
Gaiman
Dolavon
Rawson
V. Hermoso
Escalante
Talleres
COMODORO RIVADAVIA
Fitz Roy
Pico Blanco
PUERTO DESEADO
Miles
0 50 100 150 200

7

During the first two weeks the railway carried 15,000 passengers, with two trains daily and three on official holidays, and the next locomotives received were two 2-2-0 tender engines built by Sharp Stewart in 1859, works numbers 1124/1125, and named "Constitución" and "Libertad". Extension of the railway continued and during the next few years Floresta to Ramos Mejía (8 km) was opened on 27th September 1858, Ramos Mejía to Morón (5km) on 6th February 1859, and Morón to Moreno (16km) on 12th April 1860. At this point the company got into financial difficulties and the Buenos Aires Government, already a shareholder, took over on 1st January 1863, extending the line to Luján on 23rd May 1864, to Mercedes in 1865 and to Chivilcoy in 1866, a total distance of 166 km. No further extensions were made for several hears until ambitious ideas of making this line, the Western Railway, the basis of a transandine Atlantic - Pacific link, caused further money to be made available in 1869 for an extension to Bragado, a further 51km which took eight years to complete. In fact, this railway was not destined to become a transcontinental main line, as will be related later.

The Central Argentine Railway

Meanwhile, an interest in railways was being manifested further north, and a concession was granted to an American, William Wheelwright, to build a line between Rosario and Córdoba, a distance of 396km. Work started in March 1863, although the concession was not ratified until a month later. Wheelwright had built the first railway in Chile some ten years earlier, and had his own plans for a transandine link (see Chapter 4), but on this project he was working for a British company formed in London as the Central Argentine Railway, and using the same gauge as the Western Railway (5'6"). President Mitre himself cut the first sod and despite difficulties, including a period of war with Paraguay, the railway crept forward from Rosario, reaching Fraile Muerto in 1866 Villa María in 1867, Oncativo in 1869 and Córdoba in 1870. Prior to the coming of this railway, 20,000 tons of freight a year was moved between these cities using 8,000 carts. The census of 1869 gives the population of Rosario as 23,169 and Córdoba 28,523 inhabitants, making them the largest centres of population outside Buenos Aires, and in 1870 the railway carried 35,042 passengers and 35,682 tons of freight between them. No further extension was made to this line until 1889 and so we will now turn our attention back to Buenos Aires.

The Buenos Aires Great Southern

In 1862 a railway was projected to link the capital with Chascomús (114 km). Unable to raise sufficient capital in Argentina the promoter, Edward Lumb, headed for London and with the support of Baring's Bank and a Mr. David Robinson, formed the Buenos Aires Great Southern Railway, contractors Peto and Betts, engineer Thos. Rumball. Work started on 7th March 1864 at the Constitución market (and as at Rosario President Mitre was again present), and the first 77km to Jeppener were opened on 14th August 1865, Chascomús being reached on 14th December that year. There were eleven stations in all, and the line was worked with 8 locomotives, 38 carriages, 177 wagons and 7 service vehicles. Profitable from its inception, the company paid a dividend of 7.89 % in 1870, in which year it carried 516,993 passengers and 54,116 tons of freight.

The Buenos Aires Northern Railway

A concession granted prior to that of the Buenos Aires Great Southern was dated 27th June 1857, and was for a horse-worked railway from Buenos Aires to San Fernando, but the original promoter having made no progress, the concession was transferred on 25th February 1862 to a British controlled company entitled the Buenos Aires Northern Railway. Sections of line were opened between December 1862 and December 1863 and the use of steam locomotives was authorised in February 1864.

San Fernando was reached in the same year and Tigre in February 1865, a total distance of only 29km. The city terminus was at first a small station at Retiro, and later the old Central station on the Paseo de Julio near Government House, a station later shared by five different companies until replaced by Retiro at the turn of the century. Another line In Buenos Aires built 1865-70 was the short Boca Railway, which grew into the Buenos Aires and Ensenada Port Railway, reaching Ensenada via Quilmes in 1872. This railway owned the Central station in Buenos Aires. All these lines mentioned up to now were of 5'6" gauge.

Expansion of the Railways 1870-1880

Argentina is quoted as having 732km of railway in 1870, over half of which must have consisted of the Rosario to Córdoba line, although virtually all the others were in the Buenos Aires region. The next decade, up to 1880, saw a steady extension of existing lines, the Buenos Aires Great Southern (BAGSR) in particular reaching southwards towards areas still troubled by Indian wars. A French writer who served with General Roca's expedition in 1879 described how, on a coach journey to Bahía Blanca, the first information given to passengers boarding the vehicle was where the rifles and ammunition were stored, and how they were to defend themselves in case of attack! In 1876 the frontier beyond which the Indian tribes prowled was little further south than Olavarría and the BAGSR was committed under the terms of its concession to push the rails, and with them civilisation and settlers, on to Dolores and Azul, reached in 1877. Dolores to Ayacucho followed in December 1880, rails then extending 332km southwards from Buenos Aires.

In March 1871 the Western Railway opened a 64km branch between Merlo and Lobos and in 1890 this passed to the BAGSR. As already mentioned, the Western reached Chivilcoy in 1866 and it also commenced construction of a branch from Luján to Pergamino, in the direction of Rosario, opening the first 30km on 30th March 1880. Meanwhile, a link between the Rosario Córdoba line and the Andes was being studied and in 1870 a contract was signed with John Simmons of London for the Andine Railway from Villa María to Río Cuarto. This 132km section was opened on 24th October 1873 and continued to Villa Mercedes, reached in October 1875. This railway was state financed, but worked by a contractor, J.E.C. Rogers, until 1st January 1880, when administration was taken over by the Public Works department of the nation.

It was also decided during this decade to build a line northwards from Córdoba towards Salta and Jujuy, powers for which had existed since 1868, and in 1873 construction was undertaken on behalf of the Government by an Italian contractor, Count Telfener, who completed the 547 km between Tucmán and Córdoba within four years. Although the Central Argentine Railway between Rosario and Córdoba was already in existence with a gauge of 5'6" the government had the new line built to the metre gauge, the first railway of this gauge in the country. The opening date was 31st October 1876, and preserved at Córdoba works is the locomotive claimed to have worked the inaugural train, Córdoba & Tucmán Railway no. 7 "Avellaneda", an 0-4-2 built by Fox Walker and one of a batch of ten locomotives (four 2-4-0s and six 0-4-2s) supplied by this builder in 1874. As preserved the locomotive has lost its name and acquired the number 1, but as the rest of the class was withdrawn 1895-96 it is fortunate to have survived at all. This railway was worked by the contractor until 10th January 1877, when the state assumed direct control under the title of the Argentine Central Northern Railway.

In 1870 a line had been authorised between Moreno, on the Western Railway, and the port of Campana on the Paraná river, but this was not built and a little later another line, this time from Buenos Aires to Campana, was substituted. The Buenos Aires and Campana Railway Company was formed in London and the line was opened on 22nd April 1876, over a distance of 77km. In 1878 the company received authorisation to extend to Rosario, thus linking the capital with the expanding system to the north, but this was not finally achieved until 1886.

The year 1873 saw the beginnings of a standard gauge railway system serving the provinces of Entre Ríos and Corrientes, isolated geographically from the rest of the country by the river Paraná. A concession had been granted in 1864 for a line linking Concordia with Mercedes, but it was not until 1875 that 155km between Concordia and Monte Caseros was opened to traffic under the auspices of the East Argentine Railway. The rapids at Salto Grande and Salto Chico on the river Uruguay prevented steamers plying north of Concordia and the railway overcame this obstacle.

The decade up to 1880 had been a period of expansion, at the end of which there were 2,516km of railway to serve a national population of 2,492,866. The railways encouraged agriculture to flourish; and while prior to 1870 the nation had not been self supporting in cereals, by 1879 huge quantities were available for export. Sugar production was flourishing in the north and a significant development in 1876 was the arrival of the first vessel

designed to transport frozen meat across the ocean. This was the French ship "Frigorifique" of 700 tons, shortly followed by the "Paraguay" similarly equipped, and although not particularly successful these experiments opened the way for further development by the British, which was to bring fame and prosperity to the pampas of Argentina. The decade closed with the Indian wars of 1879-83 pushing the frontiers of civilisation and settlement southwards to the Río Negro, in campaigns led by General Roca, whose name was commemorated in the title of the southern section of the national railways.

Developments 1880-1890

During the next ten years up to 1890 railways in Argentina were financed both by the state and by private (mostly British) companies, although it is noticeable that the British lines focused on the ports, leaving the relatively unprofitable areas to State enterprise. During this period a number of state owned lines were sold to private foreign interests, and transfers were taking place between companies as their respective spheres of influence became defined. Later, duplication of routes was to lead to more competition.

With the pacification of the south, the way was open for the extension of the Buenos Aires Great Southern Railway, and in May 1884 Bahía Blanca was reached and soon developed into a port of major importance. At the same time the BAGSR was being extended from Ayacucho via Tandil to Tres Arroyos, reached in 1886, in which year Mar del Plata was also linked with Buenos Aires by rail. Meanwhile, the city of La Plata had been founded in 1882 as the capital of the province of Buenos Aires, and was situated quite near to the terminus of the railway from Buenos Aires to Ensenada. A link with the provincial capital was soon provided and before long both the BAGSR and the Western Railway had branches serving the new city. With the Ensenada line reconstituted as the Buenos Aires, Ensenada and South Coast Railway, it took over some of the Western Railway branches in the La Plata area and was then itself absorbed by the BAGSR in 1899.

During the 1880s the provincial government decide to sell the

Lithograph of a Buenos Ayres & Campaná Railway 0-6-0 tank locomotive, reproduced from the "Engineer" of 1876.

Metre gauge F.C. Central Cordoba class S11 0-6-4T no. 162 was seen at Rosario on 28th April 1971, by which time it bore the 'Ferrocarriles Argentinos' markings and F.C. Belgrano number 2112. The loco was supplied by Kitson in 1911, works no. 4830.

Another class built by Kitson for the F.C. Central Cordoba was a series of 56 4-6-0s, five more of which were lost at sea en route. The initial identity of this example was no. 92 'San Javier' (Kitson 3266 of 1890). By the time it was seen at Concepción on 22nd April 1971 several renumberings and re-classifications had taken place, so it carried F.C. Belgrano no. 1023 as a member of class C22.

Western Railway to private bidders and the whole system, totalling over 1,000 km, was disposed of between 1888 and 1890. Most of it was purchased by British interests which formed in 1890 the Buenos Aires Western Railway, selling off branches in which they were not interested to neighbouring concerns but retaining the principal routes. Thus the line from Luján to Pergamino, with the Junín and San Nicolas branches, went to the Central Argentine Railway and the Merlo to Saladillo line went to the BAGSR, which later (1899-1901) took over the La Plata branch, together with the works at Tolosa, on the outskirts of the city. With the money realised from these transactions, the Buenos Aires Western Railway built itself a new works at Liniers, the extension into Once terminus, Buenos Aires, and further extensions to the west.

Before leaving the Buenos Aires area to see how railways in the other provinces were developing during the period 1880-90, it is convenient to mention the takeover in 1889 of the Buenos Aires Northern Railway by the Central Argentine Company, giving it a foothold in the capital. We must next turn to the Buenos Aires - Rosario Railway (formerly the Buenos Aires & Compana Railway), which extended its line to Zárate in 1885 and reached Rosario on 1st February 1886, thus linking the capital with existing railways in the north. This railway operated from the Central Station in Buenos Aires. In 1890 another link with Rosario became available when the Central Argentine Railway completed its line between Cañada e Gómez and Pergamino, thereby reaching Buenos Aires (Once) via Luján and the Buenos Aires Western Railway.

Meanwhile, the Buenos Aires & Rosario Railway did not stop at the latter city, but continued onwards via Rafaela to La Banda, in the province of Santiago del Estero, and to Iturraspe, in the province of Córdoba. Further north, the metre gauge Argentine Central Northern Railway built a 161 km branch from Frías to Santiago del Estero, reached in 1884, and a 176 km branch from Recreo to Chumbicha. These two branches, together with the main Córdoba - Tucumán line, were sold by the Government to private interests at the end of 1887; but the section beyond Tucmán, which was being pushed towards Metán and Salto during 1885-6, remained government property under the same title. The sections sold went to Hume Bros., who formed in London the Central Córdoba Railway, and this company operated the extension towards Salta until its completion in 1891.

We have already mentioned the Andine Railway linking Villa María on the Central Argentine Railway with Villa Mercedes in the province of San Luís, and this railway reached the provincial capital in 1882, Maipú in 1884, and Mendoza and San Juan in 1885. At last a railway had reached the foothills of the Andes, but it offered only an indirect line with Buenos Aires. In 1882 a company had been formed in London with the title Buenos Aires and Pacific Railway, to build a line from Mercedes (on the Western Railway) to Villa Mercedes and this was opened in 1886, with a further section from Mercedes to Palermo being put into service in 1888. This company operated a total of 690 km and reached Buenos Aires Central station over the tracks of the Buenos Aires Northern Railway.

During the 1880s a number of minor companies appeared in the Santa Fe area and constructed various local lines of metre gauge. One of theses was leased by the French Fives-Lille Company and there were also 'Western' and 'Southern' of Santa Fe railways. Across the Paraná river from Santa Fe, standard gauge railways were developing and a line from the city of Paraná to Concepción del Uruguay (286km) was authorised in 1883 and opened in 1887. Together with branches, and absorbing the 10km line which had been opened between Gualeguay and Puerto Ruiz in 1874, this system was entitled the FC Central Entrerriano. In 1891 it was ceded by the government of the province of Entre Ríos to British interests and became the Entre Ríos railway. In the same region a concession was granted to Juan E. Clark in November 1886 for a railway linking Monte Caseros with Corrientes and Posadas and this concession was transferred two years later to the British owned Argentine North Eastern Railway. The first section from Monte Caseros to Curuzú Cuatiá was opened in 1890.

Finally far away to the south, the first railway in Patagonia was opened between Puerto Madryn and Trelew in 1889, a 70 km metre gauge line built by the British owned Central Chubut Railway. This area had first been settled by Welsh immigrants in 1865, who after initial hardships had founded a self-governing colony which by 1880 numbered some 800 souls. In 1884 the territory of Chubut was declared part of the Argentine Republic and immigration from further north began to lessen the influence of the Welsh, but even today some of the older people can still speak the Welsh language, although they may well know no English.

In 1890 there were 9,397 km of railway in Argentina to serve a population of 3,377,780 but this year brought bank failures on a large scale, including the collapse of Baring Bros Bank in London. Nonetheless, the frozen meat trade was fast developing, with 278 refrigerated ships in service between Argentina and Britain in 1890.

Main Line Expansion up to 1900

During the period 1890 - 1900 a number of secondary lines were built, linking largely undeveloped areas with the existing railway system. Some were built by small companies which were soon absorbed by the larger ones, but details of these would be tedious and we will concentrate on developments and extensions to the main lines of the major companies. The Buenos Aires Great Southern Railway completed its second link with the Bahía Blanca, via Tres Arroyos, in 1891, and the following year completed the Ayacucho - Balcarce - Quequén line. As will be seen from the map, this area of the province of Buenos Aires was soon to be covered with a network of lines, the importance of which declined drastically with the development of road transport. In the mid 1890s political relations with Chile were strained and it became a matter of strategic importance to have a railway extending westwards from Bahía Blanca towards the Andes. The BAGSR was persuaded to undertake construction of this extension with all haste and pushed a line through previously undeveloped territory with remarkable speed, completing the first 171km to Río Colorado in a little over a year and reaching Neuquén (550km) in 1901. It was also in 1898-9 that the BAGSR absorbed the Buenos Aires, Ensenada & South Coast Railway, whose Central station in Buenos Aires was used by five companies until burnt down in 1897, after which the line was cut back to Retiro.

In 1887 a concession had been granted for a railway form Bahía Blanca via Toay to Villa Mercedes in San Luis province and this concession, after passing through the hands of Meiggs of Chilean and Peruvian fame, was finally taken up by a British company, the Bahía Blanca & North Western Railway, who built the line between 1891 and 1897 from Bahía Blanca to Toay, at which point it made connection with a branch of the Buenos Aires Western Railway. No further construction was undertaken but the building of this railway enabled traffic from the BAWR to reach the developing port Bahía Blanca, previously monopolised by the BAGSR.

In 1891 the Government rescinded the lease of the metre gauge Tucumán - Salta line granted to Hume Bros' Córdoba Central Railway in 1888 and took over responsibility themselves, construction actually being completed between Güemes and Salta the same year, while the section from Güemes to Jujuy was opened in 1900.

We now turn to metre gauge lines in the Santa Fe area, which were leased by the provincial government in 1888 to the French Fives-Lille company, however, the concession was transferred in the same year to the Santa Fe Provincial Railway (Compagnie Française des Chemins de Fer de la Province de Santa Fe). This concern worked the Santa Fe - Rafaela - San Cristóbal line (201 km) and built the 622 km San Cristóbal - Tucumán Railway across the arid and desolate province of Santiago del Estero in 1891-92. This latter line was taken over by the Argentine Central Northern Railway in 1896 but the French company later extended its activities further into Santa Fe province and built a main line northwards to Resistencia.

By the turn of the century there were 16,563 km of railway in service, but the next 14 years up to the outbreak of World War 1 in 1914 were to see this figure doubled.

In 1904 Kerr Stuart supplied three 30-ton 0-6-2T to the F.C.C.N., works nos. 784-786. Their most distinctive feature was a very short rigid wheelbase.
Photo: Author's collection.

The Railway Boom Period 1900-1914

In 1903 the Argentine Great Western Railway, which on its formation in 1887 had bought from the national government the line between Villa Mercedes and Mendoza, took over operation of the Andine Railway. Meanwhile, the Buenos Aires & Pacific Railway had gained control of the Villa María to Rufino line in 1900 and the 226km branch from villa Mercedes via La Toma to Villa Dolores in 1909. The interests of the two companies were becoming closely allied, and on 23rd April 1907 the BAPR took over operation of the AGWR, initially for a period of 20 years but in fact until nationalisation in 1947. In 1901 the BAPR had received authorisation to build its own line between Palermo and Buenos Aires (Retiro) and this was opened on 7th July 1912. A great number of extensions and new lines followed the takeover of the AGWR by the BAPR, but they remained nominally sepa-

rate companies.

Westwards, the broad gauge BAPR terminated at Mendoza, whence the metre gauge Transandine line was built towards the border with Chile, as far as Punta de Vacas (144km) by 1893. After several years of inactivity this line was extended by 16km to reached Puente del Inca in 1902, and a further 14km to Las Cuevas in 1903. The summit tunnel between Argentina and Chile was completed in 1910 and the first train passed through on 4th April, regular services beginning in May of the same year. This railway was worked by the Argentine Great Western while under construction, and following the amalgamation with the BAPR, by their joint administration until cancellation of their contract in 1923. From 1923 to 1932 the Chilean and Argentine sections were united under a single administration but by 1932 control of the Argentine section had passed back to the Buenos Aires & Pacific

Railway, who suspended operations for several months in 1932. After little more than a year of operation, floods in January 1934 caused such extensive damage that part of the Argentine section was closed. The Argentine Government took over the line in 1939, and wartime traffic caused them to repair the damage and reopen their section in 1944. There were rack sections on this railway, which is more fully described in the Chilean chapter, as it was so closely linked with the corresponding line on the other side of the frontier.

The only noticeable addition to the BAGSR between 1900 and 1914 was the extension of the Neuquén line to Zapala (187km) in 1913. Although the BAGSR had built the Neuquén line largely at the request of the government, this had been at a time of a national emergency, and the state itself undertook further development of the south by building the San Antonio Railway from Viedma, where it later made contact with the BAGSR across the river Negro, to San Carlos de Bariloche, a distance of 837km. The first 174km were completed in 1911.

Further south still, the state built between 1910 and 1914 long and isolated lines inland from the oilfields at Comodoro Rivadavia to Colonia Sarmiento and Puerto Deseado to Colonia Las Heras. Both were of 5'6" gauge and the first line totalled 298km with branches while the second extended for 286km. Also in this region the Central Chubut Railway was extended to Gaimánin 1909 and Dolavón in 1915. This metre gauge railway was bought by the state in 1922 and converted to 750mm gauge, extension later being made to the coast at Rawson and inland to Alto de las Plumas, the system then totalling 267km.

In 1900 two local railways in the Santa Fe area were absorbed by the larger broad gauge companies operating in the region. These were the 210km Santa Fe Western Railway and the Santa Fe and Córdoba Great Southern Railway (384km), which went to the Central Argentine and Buenos Aires & Rosario railways respectively. These two relatively large concerns themselves merged in 1902, becoming one of the largest companies in the country and soon taking over other small lines, such as the 51km Córdoba - Malagueño, built in 1895 to a gauge of 750mm, and now regauged, and also the last section of the Andine railway

from Villa María to Río Cuarto (136km) in 1909. Many new sections were opened up to 1914, including an alternative route between Rosario and Córdoba via Cruz Alta and Rafael García. The combine had taken the name of the Central Argentine Railway and in August 1915 their fine new Retiro terminus at Buenos Aires was completed, being acclaimed at the time as ' the largest and finest terminal station south of the equator'.

Next door was the metre gauge terminus of the Central Córdoba Railway and beyond that the broad gauge station of the Buenos Aires & Pacific Railway, these last two built on land reclaimed from the river. In front of these stations was the Plaza Británica, with its typically British clock tower built with materials shipped out from England and adding greatly to the British atmosphere which the railway terminal had brought to the district, site of a slave market in Spanish colonial times. The scene changed little over the years, with lines continuing beyond the terminal station into the docks.

During this period certain new companies appeared in areas already well served by railways. The broad gauge Rosario and Puerto Belgrano Railway, built by a French company between 1907 and 1911, was so constructed that any point served was nearer to Puerto Belgrano (Bahía Blanca) or Rosario than to Buenos Aires, thus abstracting traffic from its rivals.

Another French company was the General Railway Company in the Province of Buenos Aires (Compagnie Général des Chemins de Fer de la Province de Buenos Aires), linking Buenos Aires with Rosario via Villars and Pergamino (376km) and also reaching La Plata from González Catán. This system came to total some 1,269km built between 1908 and 1912. This company is not to be confused with the Buenos Aires Provincial Railway (FC Provincial de Buenos Aires), another metre gauge line built by the provincial government linking Buenos Aires (Avellaneda) with La Plata and Azul/Olavarría and Mirapampa. Construction began in 1910, and by 1914 some 575km were in operation. Also opened during 1907-11 was the metre gauge Buenos Aires Midland Railway, from Buenos Aires (Puente Alsina) to Carhué (517km). This railway was worked jointly by the BAGSR and the BGWR from inception to nationalisation.

An early scene on the Compagnie Général des Chemins de Fer de la Province de Buenos Aires with 4-6-0 no. 211 at the head of a long goods train. No. 211 was built in France by SACM (G) in 1907, works no. 5763.
Photo: Courtesy of 'La Vie du Rail'.

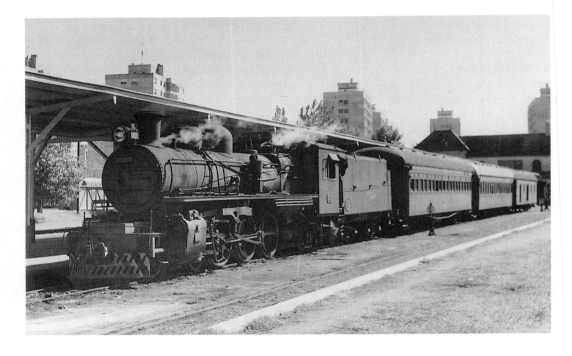

Former F.C. Provincial de Buenos Aires class H 4-6-2 no. 10353 stands at Buenos Aires Avellaneda station with the 12:50 to La Plata on 17th April 1971. Henschel built the loco in 1929 (works no. 21286), and the F.C. General Belgrano withdrew it in the early 1980s.
Photo: Richard Campbell.

Turning now to the standard gauge systems across the Paraná river, the Entre Ríos Railway and the Argentine North Eastern Railway (which in 1907 absorbed the East Argentine Railway) were extending their systems and in 1915 they came under joint management. Prior to this the North Eastern had reached Posadas in 1912, and made connection by train ferry across the river Paraná with the Central Paraguay Railway, while earlier still, in December 1909, the Entre Ríos had reached Ibicuy and inaugurated train ferry services along the river Paraná to Zárate, whence the Buenos Aires Central Railway extended to Buenos Aires.

Thus, in 1912, Buenos Aires and Asunción, capital of Paraguay, were linked by rail without a break of gauge, almost the whole journey in both countries being made over British operated railways.

The exception was the mileage of the Buenos Aires Central. This line originated in a concession granted by the provincial government in 1886 to D. Federico Lacroze who built the Rural Railway of the Province of Buenos Aires, opened in 1888. At first it was horse-worked and an illustration in 'The Engineer' shows a four wheel horse-drawn sleeping car built by the Brill Company of the USA which it states was used for journeys taking three days over this line. Steam working was introduced in 1896-67 and the company became The Rural Steam Tramway Co., then the Buenos Aires Central Railway in 1906. Apart from the 101km linking Buenos Aires with Zárate, this company built a longer line via Salto and Rojas (reached in 1909) to 4 de Febrero, a distance of 319km from Buenos Aires. The city suburban services out as far as Campo de Mayo and the San Martín branch were electrified about 1908 and worked until 1955 by double truck Brill tramcars, using tramway type overhead. The Lacroze family, whose name the Buenos Aires terminal station still bears, also owned some street tramway lines in the city and the underground railway from the terminus to the Post Office, until these were acquired by the City Transport Corporation in 1939. Before leaving the standard gauge railways, mention should also be made of the government owned Eastern State Railway, the first section of which was built in 1912 from Diamante to Crespo, where it joined the Entre Ríos Railway. The line was eventually extended north to Curuzú Cuatiá, 395km, where it made connection with the Argentine North Eastern.

The effects of the World War on the railways of Argentina meant that little new development was possible during the period 1914 to 1920, although the first Buenos Aires suburban electrification (apart from the tramcars at Lacroze) was completed in 1916 by the Central Argentine Railway. The consulting engineers were Livesey, Son and Henderson and the contractors Merz & McLennan, and according to contemporary reports, all the equipment seems to have been supplied by British companies. The section Retiro to Tigre via Victoria (29km), was inaugurated on 24th August 1916 and the rolling stock consisted of 67 motor coaches and 50 trailers supplied by the Metropolitan Carriage & Wagon Co and the Birmingham Railway Carriage & Wagon Co. It is thought that further trailers were made from the old steam stock previously in use. The third rail system, with current at 800V dc was used.

In view of the relative lack of developments during this period, I feel it is permissible to jump ahead to 1926, when the 'Railway Gazette' published two excellent special issues devoted to British enterprise in Argentina at that time. Most of the following information is taken from this source.

Broad Gauge Railways in the 1920s

The Buenos Aires Great Southern Railway

In 1926 the Buenos Aires Great Southern Railway operated 7,597km of 5'6" gauge, owning 6,169km and working since 1924 the Bahía Blanca & North Western Railway (1,230km), the Buenos Aires, Ensenada & South Coast Railway (175km), the Buenos Aires Southern Dock line (5km), and the National Government line at La Plata (18km). It was the premier line in Argentina for passenger traffic, and the second for freight. A closely knit web of tracks covered the province of Buenos Aires and the long line from Bahía Blanca via Neuquén terminated at Zápala, 1,481 km from Buenos Aires. Also at the southern extremity of the system, the Bahía Blanca - Stroeder line (174km) had been purchased from the Bahía Blanca North Western Railway in 1921, and extended 93km in 1922 to the río Negro at Carmen de Patagones, from where the national government was actively building an onward connection to its already existing line from the port of San Antonio to San Carlos de Bariloche. Naturally most of the BAGSR was single track, but there were 32km of quadruple track and 396km of double track in existence. Over 70% of the track was earth ballasted, mostly using rail of 100 lb and 85 lb per yard. Stone ballast was being increasingly used, and the railway had its own quarries, the principal one being at Tandil. Plaza Constitución terminus at Buenos Aires was in the process of being rebuilt, with 14 passenger platforms, 9 for local traffic and 5 for long distance workings. The four track approach to the capital had just been completed out to Temperley, 17km from the terminus.

Remedios de Escalera shed was photographed on 30th August 1968 without a diesel in sight. The 0-6-0ST in the foreground was ex-Bahia Blanca North Western Railway class BE no. 516 (NBL 16674/1904), later inherited by the F.C. General Roca. Photo: Richard Campbell.

The principal locomotive shops of the company were at Remedios de Escalada, between Plaza Contitución and Temperley, and these handled work on the 683 locomotives then in service, comprising 195 passenger, 189 mixed traffic, 187 freight and 112 shunting types. The suburban tank engines were mostly 3-cylinder simple oil burning 2-6-4Ts, of which 62 were supplied by British builders between 1922 and 1930. A few were still in use when I first visited Argentina in 1968 although by 1971 they had been displaced by diesels on the rush hour suburban services and were mostly on station pilot and standby duties. Long distance passenger engines in 1924 were 2-cylinder 4-6-0s which were then about to be superseded by a batch of 3-cylinder 4-6-2s, twenty of which were to be delivered by the Vulcan Foundry in 1927/28, and additional one being built by Vulcan for exhibition at the British Trade Fair in Buenos Aires in 1931 and afterwards added to stock.

Heavy goods traffic was in the hands of 2-8-0s and 4-8-0s, 25 of the latter having been delivered in 1924-25 from Armstrong Whitworth. They were 3-cylinder simples and one had been exhibited at the British Empire Exhibition, Wembley, prior to shipment. A further 50 4-8-0s were to be delivered in 1929, built by Armstrong Whitworth and Beyer Peacock.

On the coaching side there were 1,304 vehicles, including Pullman, sleeping and restaurant cars, many of the more recent having been built in the Company's own workshop in Argentina. Freight stock comprised 14,489 wagons with a total capacity of 446,227 tons.

The BAGSR also had a considerable interest in the docks at Bahía Blanca, where the port was named Ingeniero White in 1899 after the president of the local committee of the railway. These docks had developed rapidly since 1900, and by 1926 included grain elevators, the whole area being served by almost 100 km of sidings. The company also held a substantial interest in the local water works and at Buenos Aires in the Southern Docks Company, where the BAGSR had built in 1915 a transporter bridge over the Riachuelo river, which is still in existence, if unused.

Going back a few years to 1921, the BAGSR pioneered extensive 600mm gauge agricultural railway systems to act as feeders to the broad gauge. World War One surplus material was still available and the first 80km was laid in the Orense area in 1921. These systems grew to a total extent of about 400 km by 1925, much of the traffic being potatoes. Motive power was 16 ex-War Department Hunslet tank engines and 31 Simplex (and similar) petrol tractors of 20-45 hp, also war surplus. There were five passenger coaches and well over 1,000 wagons, mostly of 6 and 10 ton capacity. The light railways were a great success, but declined as road transport became more efficient. They closed shortly before World War II, but some Hunslet 4-6-0Ts were to be found on the Correntino Light Railway in 1968 and these had been acquired from the BAGSR by this formerly independent railway situated well to the north of Buenos Aires. One of these locomotives is preserved at Buenos Aires Lacroze Station and another in front of the former Railway Hospital near the port.

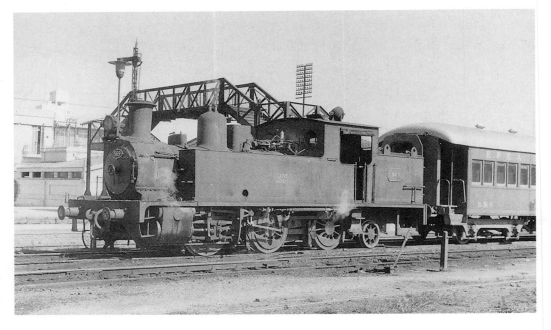

In 1948 the F.C. General Mitre inherited 50 class SS5 0-6-2Ts from the F.C. Central Argentine, 30 built by NBL in 1928/29 and the rest by Stephenson in 1930/31. No. 569 was from the NBL batch, works no. 23763, and was still active shunting carriages at Rosario in April 1971.

The Central Argentine Railway in the 1920s

We now turn to what was in 1926 the second largest broad gauge system in the country, the Central Argentine Railway, with 5,318km extending from Buenos Aires northwards to Tucumán (1,157km)and serving such important cities as Rosario, Santa Fe and Córdoba. At this time the (river) port of Rosario was second only to Montreal (Canada) in volume of grain exports. To the west, traffic was exchanged with the Buenos Aires & Pacific Railway at Río Cuarto, while northwards the metre gauge state railways offered connections from Córdoba into the provinces of

Catamarca, La Rioja and San Juan, and from Tucumán into the provinces of Jujuy and Salta, and on into Bolivia. At Santa Fe connection was made with the State railway, and the Province of Santa Fe system.

It will be recalled that the Central Argentine terminal in Buenos Aires was the exceptionally fine Doric style station at Retiro, the foundation stone of which was laid in 1909 and the first part of which was in use by 1915. The war had delayed construction and the edifice was still not complete by 1926. The Central Argentine had been the pioneer of South American suburban electrification in 1916 and 46km of extensions were energised in 1931.

Steam motive power consisted of 695 machines, including nearly 150 4-6-2s, some 4-6-0s, 2-6-0s, and 4-6-2Ts for suburban work. Freight locomotives included 90 2-8-0s and 70 4-8-0s, all of the latter built by North British in 1915 and 1920. There were a few 0-6-2Ts shunting at Rosario, where many other types were to be found derelict. Passenger stock totalled 733 vehicles, including restaurant cars, sleepers etc., and freight wagons 17,096, many of 45 ton capacity. The locomotive repair works for the system was at Pérez, 15km from Rosario and had been christened 'Gorton Works' in 1913. The carriage and wagon works was also at Rosario, which was the traffic centre of the railway. Rosario, second city of Argentina, is 303km from Buenos Aires, and in 1926 the fastest passenger trains covered this distance in 4½ hours. A special for the newspaper, La Nación, hauled by Pacific no. 191 (North British, 1914), had done the journey in 3 hours 21 minutes.

The Buenos Aires & Pacific

Next came the Buenos Aires & Pacific, which together with the Argentine Great Western and the Villa María - Rufino railways totalled 4,267km and in 1926 could claim the unusual distinction of obtaining 25% of its revenue from the transport of wine and empty casks, while only 17½% came from passengers! This system extended from Buenos Aires to Mendoza, with branches from there to both north and south and other branches, plus a secondary route across the pampas from Chacabuco to the foothills of the Andes via Malargüe to the río Grande. In 1926 the Buenos Aires terminus at Retiro was in the process of being rebuilt, the works at Junín were being enlarged and new workshops were being built at Mendoza. Motive power totalled 578 locomotives, and there were 331 passenger coaches, including a 'steam motor coach', 28 restaurant cars and 53 sleepers. Passenger traffic was not very heavy, due to the sparsely populated area served, but there was important through traffic to Santiago (Chile) via the metre gauge Transandine Railway, and the international train between Buenos Aires and Mendoza covered the 1,064 km in a little under 21 hours.

The Buenos Aires Western Railway

The remaining British owned broad gauge railway to be described was the Buenos Aires Western Railway, with 3,028km extending westwards across the plains from the capital to the various termini, and in many cases paralleling the lines of other companies. The Buenos Aires passenger terminus was Once de Septiembre station, and also two platforms at the nearby Plaza Miserere underground station, offering cross platform interchange with the metro, which at that time was owned by another British concern, the Anglo-Argentine Tramways Company. In 1926 the Buenos Aires Western Railway had a total steam stock of 346 machines and 370 coaching stock units.

Electrification of the suburban services out to Moreno (36km) at 800V dc (third rail) had commenced in 1913 under the supervison of the same companies as were also working on the Central Argentine line from Retiro. Although this was opened in 1916, work on the Once suburban lines was virtually suspended during World War One and it was not until 16th October 1922 that the first train ran through to Castelar. On 30th April 1923 the

President of the Republic, Dr. Marcelo T. Alvear, inaugurated the electrified service to Moreno, which was in full public use the next day.

The whole of the apparatus used in connection with this electrification was manufactured in Great Britain by companies such as Babcock & Wilcox, Henley's Telegraph Works and English Electric. The wooden bodied multiple unit rolling stock came from Metropolitan-Vickers and the Birmingham Railway Carriage & Wagon Co., the motor coaches having two motor bogies, each fitted with two 220 hp motors. Four or six coach trains were usual and the initial order was for 46 motor coaches, 45 trailers and one composite motor coach for the short spur line between Villa Luro and Versailles. There were also two BB electric locomotives for working freight trains through a 5km tunnel to the docks, and these were also equipped with pantographs as overhead wires were in use there. This freight link was still in use in the 1970s, by which time General Motors G-12 and GR12 diesels had taken over, though now other types of diesel may be seen too. Also a Castelar - Puerto Madero passenger service is run with diesel railcars.

Standard Gauge Railways in the 1920s

Information for 1926 shows that the Buenos Aires Central Railway from Lacroze station to Zárate and 4 de febrero had undergone little change and the motive power included six Maffei 4-6-2s of 1911 and Kerr Stuart 4-4-0s and 4-6-0s, to be joined in 1929 by six 4-8-0s from the same builder. Continuing on the train ferry up the Paraná river from Zárate to Ibicuy we come to the Entre Ríos Railway, administered jointly with the Argentine North Eastern Railway since 1915. In 1926 the former totalled 1,171km and the latter 1,210km and they held a monopoly of the area bounded by the rivers Paraná and Uruguay, except for the state owned Diamante - Crespo and Hasenkamp - Federal lines, of which 167km were in service in 1926, and the 600mm gauge Correntino Railway. The Entre Ríos had 90 locomotives and the North Eastern 65, plus 11 Drewry railcars. Three 2-6-0+0-6-2 Garratts had been delivered to the Entre Ríos in 1925 and five more were to come in 1927, along with four for the North Eastern. A series of passenger 4-4-2+2-4-4 Garratts was also due to appear in 1927-30, five each going to the two railways. Less exalted motive power consisted of 46 Neilson 0-6-0s built in 1888-89, Baldwin 4-6-0s of 1906-10, Hawthorn Leslie 2-6-0s of 1910-12, North British 2-8-0s of 1913, and a number of other classes. The Eastern State Railway had 6 Belgian built 2-6-0s and 4 Baldwin 2-8-2s, the latter delivered in 1924. Many of the old 0-6-0s were still to be seen all over the system in 1972.

Metre Gauge Railways in the 1920s

The British owned Córdoba Central Railway comprised 1,934km in 1926, two-thirds of which were accounted for by the main line from Buenos Aires (Retiro) via Rosario and Córdoba to Tucumán. The main locomotive works, built in 1912, was situated at Alta Córdoba, and motive power consisted of 301 machines (1925), of which 25 were passenger types, 59 mixed traffic, 174 freight, and 43 shunting engines. With 342 passenger coaches (including sleepers, diners, etc.), this aspect of operations was not as important as freight, which accounted for 76% of the revenue. Traffic was fairly evenly divided between general merchandise, cereals, sugar cane and forest products. The railway served eight-

Class B54 Maffei Pacific no. 614 was built in 1910 for the metre gauge Central Northern Railway (works no. 3220), and was seen on shed at Resistencia, F.C. General Belgrano, during August 1968. The class B54 lasted until the late 1970s

teen sugar factories, mostly in the province of Tucumán, and many of these had light railways of their own.

To a certain degree, the Córdoba Central Railway was in competition with the state owned Central Northern, and we have already seen how the development of these two systems was to some extent linked, particularly in the Tucumán region. In other ways the two systems were complementary, particularly as in 1926 the Central Northern did not reach further south than Córdoba and Santa Fe. With almost 5,000km of line, the Central Northern extended from Santa Fe to Tucumán, via Añatuya, whence there was a long branch to Resistencia. There was also a line westwards from Santa Fe via Deán Funes and Cruz del Eje (junction for Córdoba) to San Juan and various points in the province of Catamarca. From Tucumán the main line extended

northwards via Metán, where a branch was under construction to join the Añatuya - Resistencia line, Güemes (for Salta), Perico (for Embarcación, from where the long line to Formosa was under construction), and via Jujuy to the Bolivian frontier at La Quiaca, where connection was made with the Bolivian system. There was an 11km Abt rack section between León and Volcán, with a maximum grade of 6 per cent, and 2½ per cent grades on the adhesion sections, as from km 956 at Jujuy (1,259 metres above sea level) the line has to climb 2,183 metres to km 1,239 at La Quiaca (3,442 metres above sea level). On the adhesion sections Borsig tender Mallets were tried, while the earlier rack locomotives were three 0-8-2RTs from Esslingen in 1905. The principal workshops of the Central Northern were built in 1911 at Tafi Viejo (near Tucumán), and active power in 1926 consisted of 585 machines,

F.C. General Belgrano Pacific no. 3011 stands beside a very English style signal gantry at Tucuman. The carriages are distinctly American in style and the loco is Baldwin 55219 of 1921, originally supplied to the F.C. Central Norte.

including 4-6-2s, 4-8-2s, 2-8-4s, 2-8-2s, etc. Probably the finest machines were the Maffei Pacifics, built in 1910, while the more numerous were the 2-8-2s from North British and various German builders, 100 in all. The Córdoba Central was taken over by the state in 1938 and integrated with the Central Northern.

Other metre gauge railways in service in 1926 included the French owned Santa Fe Provincial Railway, working some 2,000 route kms, with a main line extending from Rosario via Santa Fe to Resistencia, and various branches. Motive power totalled 186 machines, including some Swiss-built 2-6-2s. Between Santa Fe and Resistencia connections were made with the extensive timber carrying railways owned by the Forestal Land Company.

Another French company, already mentioned, was the General Railway of the Province of Buenos Aires, and there was also the Buenos Aires Midland Railway, with its works at Libertad (opened 1912) and 37 steam locomotives in 1926, consisting of 19 4-6-0s by North British, 1 by Naysmith Wilson, and 6 by Kerr Stuart, plus 5 Hunslet 2-6-4Ts.

Not all railways in service in 1926 have been mentioned, but the foregoing gives a good idea of the situation on the major routes. By this date most of the railway system of Argentina had been built, and the only sections under construction were relatively minor lines. The following decade saw little change, although public works undertaken in the 1930s included extensive road building which was later to have an adverse effect on rail transportation.

Diesel Traction in the 1920s and 1930s

We now turn to early diesel traction experiments carried out by the BAGSR. About 1928 serious consideration was being given to electrification of the Buenos Aires suburban lines, but in view of the high capital cost involved the CME, Mr. P.C. Saccaggio, proposed diesel powered train sets which he considered would provide a service equal to that possible with electrification, and avoiding the capital outlay in fixed equipment. In the 'Railway Gazette' of 12th January 1951 it was claimed that the first diesel-engined rail vehicle in South America was a Beardmore 375 hp Bo-Bo unit supplied to the BAGSR in 1929. It was constructed by the Metropolitan Carriage & Wagon Co and was followed by another from the same source, but equipped with a more powerful Sulzer diesel engine. The Beardmore locomotive made the longest non-stop journey hitherto achieved in South America when it ran the 1,194km from Buenos Aires to Neuquén. Surprisingly, both machines survived until 1941, when they were stripped of their power equipment and saw further, if less exalted use as parcels vans. They gave the company and its staff experience with this form of traction which was to be invaluable when Mr. Saccaggio's diesel electric mobile power houses arrived from Armstrong Whitworth towards the end of 1930.

These two machines were equipped with Sulzer engines (2 x 600 hp each) and electric generators made by Oerlikon, while the traction motors came from Metropolitan-Vickers. They were permanently marshalled in five-coach train sets constructed at Remedios de Escalada, the bogies of the coaches being fitted with traction motors, as were two of the four fixed axles in the mobile power house. The train could be driven from either end, although in regular service this was not done. They proved so successful that three larger units of 1,700 hp were supplied by Armstrong Whitworth in 1933, and these were coupled in to eight-coach sets. They were extremely successful, and all five remained in service up to and beyond nationalisation in 1948, the later units being withdrawn in 1962, after which the carriages, stripped of their electrical equipment, saw still further service. It is unfortunate that their great potential was not able to be fully exploited as they had to be integrated with the steam workings, however, the CME had proved his point and electrification was shelved.

Main line dieselisation was also under consideration, and in 1933 a twin unit Sulzer-engined diesel-electric of 1,700 hp came from Armstrong Whitworth and went into service in August between Buenos Aires and Bahía Blanca (640km) on the heavy night expresses. These trains were worked with only one man in the cab and the locomotive was still performing this duty in 1948. It was finally withdrawn from service in 1962, worn out and lacking spare parts.

Four more diesel-electric locomotives were put into service by the BAGSR in 1937 but these had not been specifically designed for their use and in fact the first two, built by Armstrong Whitworth, had originally been destined for Ceylon. They were designed to operate together as one 1,600 hp unit, although one was soon damaged and the other then transferred to lighter duties on milk trains until it caught fire and was withdrawn in 1943. The other pair came from Harland and Wolff and were designed to test the two-stroke diesel system as opposed to the four-stroke already in use. They were not very reliable but remained in service until damaged by fire in 1941. In 1941 the BAGSR was quoted as having fourteen Drewry shunters of 100 hp, one 1,700 hp locomotive, four 900 hp locomotives, two 400 hp locomotives, five mobile power houses, and an out of use 1-C-1 diesel hydraulic of 600 hp, supplied by Armstrong Whitworth/Sulzer in 1933 .

Other early users of diesels were the BAWR with a 450 hp Armstrong Whitworth/Sulzer diesel-electric twin articulated railbus unit in October 1934 and it was followed by a 140 hp railbus which seated 57 passengers. The Buenos Aires Provincial Railway had four diesel-electric bogie railcars equipped with Sulzer 270 hp engines in 1935-36 and in 1943 these, and some similar cars on the BAWR were claimed to be the only diesel-electric railcars in Argentina. The Buenos Aires & Pacific Railway had built some Leyland petrol engined railcars in the Mendoza and Junín shops in 1931, and at the end of 1937 they received two 120 hp Leyland engined diesel-hydraulic railcars from the Birmingham Railway Carriage & Wagon Co., and also built in their own workshops six 240 hp bogie railcars using Ganz engines, three having mechanical transmission and three Voith-Sinclair hydraulic drive. Another twelve mechanical transmission Ganz railcars were subsequently acquired, and in 1944 one of the Voith-Sinclair cars was matched with a Central Argentine Railway Ganz twin-articulated railcar, twelve of which had been received early in 1938.

The tests took place on 8th September between Buenos Aires and Tucumán on the Central Argentine and the twin unit reached Rosario (303km) in 3 hours 7 minutes from Buenos Aires, at an average speed of 61 miles per hour, the maximum speed reached having been 82 mph. The CAR also had in 1937 four double

bogie diesel mechanical railcars and two tin-unit articulated sets built by Armstrong Whitworth with Sulzer engines. The largest pre-war order for diesel equipment was received by the Drewry company 1936-37, for 99 diesel mechanical double bogie railcars for the BAGSR and BAWR, and 8 standard gauge railcars for the Entre Ríos and Argentine North Eastern systems. In 1941 the Entre Ríos rebuilt a twin-unit steam railcar as a diesel mechanical train. Another company with British built twin-articulated railcar sets of 200 hp was the Buenos Aires Midland Railway, which made extensive use of ten units built in 1938 by the Birmingham RC&W Co.

The foregoing gives only an incomplete picture but does show the interest in diesel traction in Argentina which was intensified by the lack of coal supplies during the war years. The BAGSR burned locally produced oil fuel in over 80% of its steam locomotives but water supply, damage to boilers due to impure water where it was available at all, were factors influencing their interest in diesel traction. In 1946 they had 856 steam locomotives, 72 railcars, 18 diesel-electric units and 6 petrol railcars. The BAWR had 284 steam locomotives and 26 railcars and the Central Argentine 612 steam locomotives and 13 diesel railcars. Later events have tended to obscure the lead which the Argentine had established in the diesel field by 1939-41 and today it is often overlooked.

Perón and the Post-War Period

With the shortage of materials from abroad, plus increased traffic, the railways of Argentina were in a very run down condition at the end of the Second World War. They were also in a number of cases, approaching the end of 40 year concessions which had been fixed by the Mitre law of 1908, which had granted to foreign-owned railways the right to import equipment duty free and relieved them of other rates and taxes in exchange for a levy of 3% on receipts, which was to be used for such public works as building road approaches to stations, laying out goods yards etc. The end of the war also coincided with the advent of a nationalistic military government (1943) which culminated in the election of President Perón early in 1946.

Starting with the Central Bank, insurance and the North American-owned telephone system, Perón soon turned his attention to the railways, which were under pressure from depreciation of equipment and the threat of import duties being imposed on material required for re-equipment, factors which threatened their future financial stability. Also, Britain owed Argentina £130 million at the end of the war, and this debt was wiped out by the sale of the railways. While a popular opinion may be that the Dictator forced the nationalisation of the railways upon the companies, and national pride was certainly involved, the view has also been expressed that it was British government pressure which caused Perón to agree to outright purchase in January 1947.

Actually, the first railways to be taken over, on 1st November 1947, were those owned by French interests and most of the British-owned railways were transferred on 1st March 1948, although in both cases, while negotiations were in progress the companies had been operating their systems on behalf of the Argentine government since 1st July 1946. For those who are interested in the details of the takeover, the Anglo-Argentine 'Andes Agreement' on the transfer of British assets was published as a White Paper Cmd 7346 (1948). The final company to be absorbed was the Buenos Aires Provincial Railway, incorporated into the national system on 1st January 1952.

The nationalised system was at first entitled 'Empresa de los Ferrocarriles del Estado Argentino' (EFEA), shortened in 1965 to 'Empresa Ferrocarriles Argentinos' (EFA). Initially seven regions were formed, six named after prominent historical heroes (usually if not exclusively Generals), if possible associated with the regions served. A number of transfers later took place over 'borderline' routes but briefly the regions were constituted as follows.

FC Nacional General Belgrano

Former state railways of metre gauge, principally Central Northern and Córdoba Central (which had been combined in 1938), Buenos Aires Midland Railway, former French companies in the Buenos Aires and Santa Fe areas, Buenos Aires Provincial Railway, and the Rafaela Steam Tramway. Total 14,935km of metre gauge.

FC Nacional General Urquiza

Former Eastern State Railway, Argentine North Eastern Railway, Entre Ríos Railway and Buenos Aires Central Railway. Total 3,430km of standard gauge, plus 209km of 600mm gauge (Correntino Railway).

FC Nacional General Roca

Former BAGSR, part of the Rosario - Puerto Belgrano Railway, state-owned San Antonio Railway. Total 7,688km of broad gauge, plus 505km of 750mm gauge.

FC Nacional Domingo Faustino Sarmiento

Former Buenos Aires Western Railway, Bahía Blanca North Western Railway, BAGSR Merlo - Lobos branch. Total 4,486km of broad gauge.

FC Nacional General San Martin

Former Buenos Aires & Pacific Railway, Argentine Great Western Railway, Argentine Transandine Railway, San Rafael - Malargüe state line, parts of the Villa María - Rufino Railway, the former Andine Railway and two branches of the Central Argentine Railway. Total 4,785km of broad gauge, plus 179km of metre gauge (Transandine Railway).

FC Nacional Bartolomé Mitre

Former Central Argentine Railway (with certain exceptions). The Villa María - Carlota line of the Buenos Aires & Pacific Railway, and part of the Rosario - Puerto Belgrano Railway. Total 6,726km of broad gauge.

FC Nacional Patagónico

Former Central Chubut (750mm gauge) and Comodoro Rivadavia and Puerto Deseado broad gauge lines, all three unconnected with each other. This 'National Railway' did not last long as a separate entity and was soon incorporated into the Roca administration.

For a brief while in the early 1970s the military administration, taking note of a World Bank criticism calling for greater overall co-ordination, reorganised (at least in theory) the six railways into four geographical regions but this did not appear to have much practical effect and the appointment of a civilian government in 1973 saw reversion to the six original titles. Thus were the 'historic Generals' restored to their former glory while the 'present-day Generals' handed over the administration to civilians! Despite this, much was later done towards centralisation of management and administration.

Narrow Gauge Railways

Before looking at more recent developments, there are a few narrow gauge lines which deserve more attention. Starting in the north of the country, the 600mm gauge Correntino Railway extended from Corrientes to General Paz (153km), with a branch from Lomas de Vallejos to Mburucuyá (55km). Constructed between 1910 and 1914, this independent railway possessed an imposing roofed terminus at Corrientes well apart from the standard gauge, with which there was no connection. In 1926 motive power was provided by six locomotives from Orenstein and Koppel and eventually the railway was incorporated into the Urquiza system. When I visited the region in August 1968 the passenger service had just been reduced and there remained but twice weekly trains in each direction. The roundhouse at Corrientes contained some ex-First World War 4-6-0Ts with their side tanks removed and carried on a 'tender' (actually an old wagon), and some 0-8-0s, while the train on which I travelled for a short distance was hauled by a 2-6-0. Unfortunately, none of the locomotives bore works plates. The railway closed on 1st November 1969.

Across the river from Corrientes, at Resistencia, is the metre gauge Belgrano Railway, and a short distance along the cross country line towards Metán is Lapachito, from where a 750mm gauge line formerly extended to Zapallar. The railway was worked by 2-8-2s and existed for industrial reasons, although there was a passenger service advertised until closure, which took place about the same time as that of the Correntino system.

In this general area were many forestry lines connected with the tannin industry and southwards from Resistencia there were a number of systems belonging to the British owned Forestal Company. These included a line from the Paraná river to km 366 of the Resistencia - Santa Fe main line, and a long connected system touching this main line at Colmena, Margarita and another point, serving the headquarters of the company at La Gallareta. These lines, which in 1926 totalled 414km, were of metre, 750mm and 600mm gauge and at that time thirty-eight locomotives, all but four of them tender engines, were operated. The Forestal Company became Unitan S.A. and one metre gauge line remained in operation in the 1970s at Puerto Tirol. Preserved at an abandoned station in Resistencia is 0-4-0T 'Hardy' built by A. Barclay in 1882 and a survivor from the Las Palmas sugar mill. There have been many sugar plantation railways in the north of Argentina, particularly around Tucumán, where some still exist.

In 1964 Ruston and Hornsby diesel locomotives were supplied to the Cia Azucarera Mercedes S/A (750mm gauge) and the Cia Azucarera Bella Vista S/A (metre gauge) near Tucumán and since then steam has been reported on the metre gauge at Ingenio La Fronterita and Ingenio La Providencia, both in Tucumán province. Still operating in the 1980s was the 600mm gauge system at Ingenio San Martin de Tabacal (Salta province), with Orenstein & Koppel three, four and five-coupled tank engines, but this system was reported fully dieselised in 1990. Also in this area is Ingenio Ledesma S/A, about 120km north east of Salta at Liberador General San Martin, where until 1990 remnants of the once extensive (200km) 700mm gauge system still remained active. Motive power consisted of Orenstein & Koppel 0-8-0s and Henschel Luttermöller type 0-10-0s, three of the latter having been built in 1959. The mill also had Orenstein & Koppel 0-6-0Ts for use on their connection to the Belgrano railway, but was fully dieselised in 1990.

The Esquel Branch

Travelling now to the far south of the country, the 750mm gauge branch of the Roca railway from Ing. Jacobacci to Esquel (386km) is undoubtedly the most interesting sub-metre gauge line of any length on which passengers can travel in South America today. It is entirely steam worked, with a stud of around 30 oil fired 2-8-2s built by Baldwin and Henschel in 1922. The works and principal running shed are situated at El Maitén, with smaller depots at Esquel and Cerro Mesa. The bogie rolling stock is comfortable, and in the 1960s a restaurant car, seating ten, was attached to through trains and served delicious snacks, which in Argentina can mean huge steaks with chips! Over the most steeply graded sections north of El Maitén the 2-8-2s are often used in tandem and the whole journey is very reminiscent of American 'Wild West' films with horsemen meeting the train at stations apparently devoid of roads, and the sunlight making beautiful patterns on the hillsides, while there is always a strong and quite chill wind blowing of the almost treeless and uncultivated landscape.

When I travelled the line in 1969 there were three passenger trains weekly in each direction but by 1980 this service had been

Esquel branch 2-8-2s 110 and 111 head through the barren Patagonian landscape, crossing a road near Ñorquincó in October 1976. Twenty-five class 75Bs were supplied by Baldwin in 1922, plus fifty Henschels, including nos. 110 and 111, and nearly half of them remained in use until the 1990s, in fact some are still maintained for tourist and charter trains as we write at the dawn of the 21st Century.

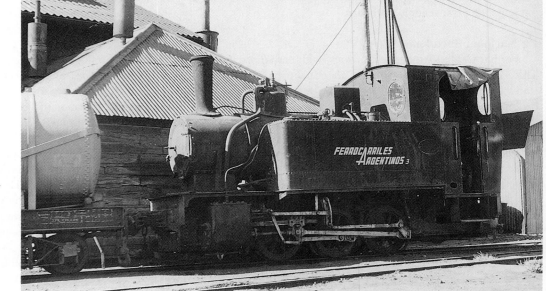

The smallest locomotive on the F.C. Patagonia is no. 3A, one of four Henschel 0-6-0T built in 1922, works nos. 19452-5. The other three were transferred to Rio Turbio around 1950. 3A was pictured at El Maiten on 28th October 1976.

reduced to once weekly in each direction, and less freight traffic was also in evidence. A correspondent reports that in 1985 he travelled in midwinter with six other passengers, only two of whom were fare paying. By contrast, a visit in January 1991 (summer in Argentina), found trains carrying 220 regular vacationers, i.e. not railfans. Political rather than economic factors seem to have precipitated the line's survival into the twenty-first century. The railway still ekes out a precarious existence with a once weekly train between El Maitén and Esquel, plus railfan specials. Once there was another 750mm gauge branch off the Viedma - San Carlos de Bariloche line of the Roca railway, extending from General Vintter to Coronel F. Sosa, but this has been closed for many years.

Southwards from here there are only the three isolated Patagonian lines already mentioned of which the narrow gauge Central Chubut closed in 1965, plus the narrow gauge tourist line at Ushuaia. The two broad gauge lines were equipped with 4-6-2s built by Haine St. Pierre and Cockerill of Belgium in 1910 and they have been closed for many years now, although there were reports in the 1960s of spasmodic steam and regular railcar operation at Comodoro Rivadavia.

The Río Turbio Line

The most southerly industrial railway in Argentina, and probably the world is the 261km long, 750mm gauge Río Turbio line, built as recently as 1951 to link coal mines situated well inland close to the Chilean border with the port of Río Gallegos. Early motive power consisted of 2-8-2s from the then fairly recently closed Central Chubut Railway but these were soon replaced by purpose built 2-10-2s from Japan in 1956, since supplemented with another batch supplied in 1963. These locomotives were of course coal fired and were fitted with mechanical stokers. The design was based on Baldwin built machines in service on the Belgrano Railway but improved by the Argentinian engineer L.D. Porta under advice from André Chapelon. They hauled 65-wagon trains of some 1,600 - 1,700 tons gross. There were plans to increase coal output from the mines at Río Turbio dramatically and to cope with this Ing. Porta designed a massive 2-12-12-0 Mallet which it was claimed could haul 10,000 ton trains, but

unfortunately this was never built! Recent developments have included the opening of a new deep water port at Punta Loyola, requiring a branch off the existing main line at km17, with a length of 35km. This opened on 12th May 1995 and subsequently six BB diesel-hydraulics were acquired second hand from Bulgaria and refurbished in Argentina with 1,065 hp Catapillar engines. It appears that they now handle all of the coal traffic, which has now been diverted to the new port, but Río Gallegos still sees some activity, though no longer with steam.

The distinction of the 'most southerly railway in the world' is held by a tourist line at Ushuaia, where an earlier 600mm gauge line served a penal settlement. The original line was closed in 1948 but an O&K 0-6-0WT and coach remain preserved in the former prison yard.

Motive Power of the Perón Era

Reverting to state railways immediately after nationalisation, a number of steam locomotives were ordered before dieselisation started in earnest. Post-war steam included 15 Henschel 2-10-0s built in 1952 for the standard gauge Urquiza Railway, thought to be the only new standard gauge steam locos purchased since the Atlantic Garratts of 1930. The Broad Gauge Roca Railway received 5 Pacifics, named after lakes, built by the Vulcan Foundry in 1949 (further examples of this type were acquired for the Mitre and San Martín Railways), and 30 two-cylinder 4-8-0s from the same builder in 1948-49. On the metre gauge Belgrano Railway additions to stock included Škoda 2-10-2s built in 1949 to supplement the earlier Baldwin (1921-26) and Henschel (1937) classes of this wheel arrangement in use around Salta. Some more 4-8-2s also came from Baldwin and Alco for use in the north of the country and again this was a well proven type dating back to 1921 (Baldwin) and 1938 (Henschel/Krupp). The Baldwin Pacifics of 1922 were perpetuated in a further series from Lima in 1948 but most exciting of all on the metre gauge was the arrival in 1954 of two Esslingen rack and adhesion 0-12-2Ts for the León - Volcán rack section near Jujuy. These were, however, extremely heavy on maintenance, and did not see much service.

During these last years of steam deliveries, two new international rail links were opened in the north of the country. The first

The 750mm gauge Rio Turbio line was one of South America's last working steam operations, with heavy mineral trains hauled by Mitsubishi 2-10-2s. No. 107, built in 1956, was seen with Porta modifications nearly 40 years later in November 1995 passing Las Buiteras.
Photo: David Ibbotson.

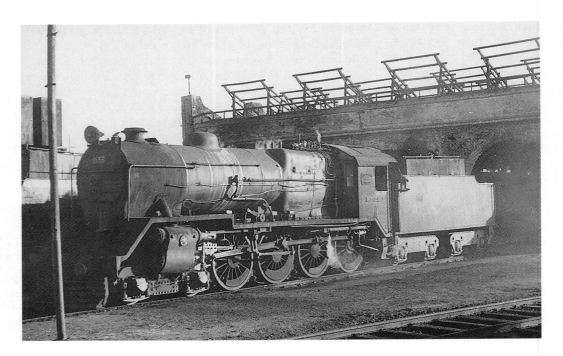

The Buenos Aires Great Southern had an initial series of eight class 15A 4-8-0s built by Vulcan Foundry in 1938, followed by thirty 15Bs in 1949. General Roca Railway no. 1555 'Orion' seen on shed at Olvarria, was one of four 15As built with Caprotti valve gear, the others and the 15B class having Walschearts.

was the Northern Transandean line from Salta to Antofagasta in Chile, the Argentinean section of which extends for 569km from Salta to the frontier at Socompa, and includes 20 tunnels, 13 viaducts, 31 bridges, and reaches a maximum height of 4,475 metres at Chorrillos. This railway was opened to international traffic in 1948. The other line forms a link with the lowlands of Bolivia and extends from Embarcación via the frontier at Yacuiba to Santa Cruz, Bolivia. By far the longest part of this railway is in Bolivia but the entire line was financed by Argentina and built between 1944 and 1957.

Despite post-nationalisation orders for steam locomotives, dieselisation soon became something of an obsession under the Perón government, and relatively small quantities of many different types were purchased. In 1949 Whitcomb supplied 75 metre gauge 675 hp Co-Co diesels and these were followed up by 95 General Electric units for delivery in 1949-50, which included some main line Co-Co units of 1,000 hp. At the beginning of 1950 the railways had 4,061 steam locomotives, 269 diesel railcars (of which only four had electrical transmission), 16 internal combustion railcars, 5 steam railcars, 64 diesel-electric locomotives, 13 other diesel locomotives, 10 electric locomotives, 285 electric motor coaches with 292 trailers, and 3,064 passenger coaches. By 1954 orders had been placed in the USA for 49 broad gauge diesel-electrics, but then others also began to arrive from a variety of sources, including 10 1,500 hp and 50 600 hp units from Holland in 1955, 26 1,000 hp metre gauge main line types from English Electric in 1955 (5), and 1958 (21), while some French Alsthom Co-Co locomotives were also received.

When the Perón government collapsed in 1955, 60 out of a total of 320 diesel locomotives were already out of service due to

1500 hp Baldwin RF-615E no. 7026 stands at Olavarria on 25th October 1976. Baldwin supplied 51 of these diesel electrics 1953-54, and the F.C. General Roca numbered them 5001-5051, but later added another 2000 to the numbers.

Buenos Aires Lacroze station was visited on 19th April 1971, when some interurban units obtained second-hand from the USA were found to be in use.

poor maintenance and lack of spares. The steam situation was even worse, as out of 4,000 locomotives 1,200 were out of service. At this time 1,500 steam locomotives were over 48 years old, another 1,500 between 24 and 47 years old, with the balance less than 24 years old.

The year 1957 saw an order for Whitcomb (who had just been taken over by Baldwin) diesel-electric locomotives, 60 of 1,300 hp and 30 of 1,950 hp Further diesel orders were placed in the 1960s, when new locomotives included Fiat metre gauge Bo-Bo diesel electrics of 1,125 hp and two single broad gauge Co-Co types of 2,250 hp and 1,500 hp, supplied in 1966-67. But the maintenance/spares situation worsened, and by mid-1968 the 'International Railway Journal' was reporting that out of a total stock of 1,180 diesel locomotives 40% were out of service; of 740 railcars only 370 were in service; and of 2,550 steam locomotives 50% were unserviceable. During this decade the railways reached

their lowest ebb but World Bank aid put them on the road to recovery, although 45% of the diesel fleet was still out of service in 1972. Subsequently, large numbers of General Electric diesels were acquired for all gauges, many of these being built in Argentina under licence. Much new rolling stock also appeared, including passenger coaches, sleepers, etc., many built by Fiat-Concord, a post-war Argentine subsidiary of the Italian Fiat group.

Steam Reconstruction by Chapelon, Porta and Vittone

Steam traction, apart from the Esquel line, has been eliminated, but it had a final fling in the late 1950s when a selection of locomotives were modified in various ways as recommended by the eminent French engineer André Chapelon, in collaboration with Ing. L.D. Porta. Improvements consisted of modifying draughting, improving the steam circuit and introducing the gas

A pair of C-C General Electric 95-ton diesels double head a Ganz rack & adhesion railcar on the Transandine Northern at Campo Quijano, Salta State in October 1991. The locos were supplied to the F.C. General Belgrano in 1953 as nos. 5101-5105, later renumbered 6701-6705, of which 6703 is seen here.
Photo: Chris Skow, Trains Unlimited, Tours.

producer technique to combustion. A total of nine types were involved, including metre gauge Pacifics and 4-8-2s, and a metre gauge 4-8-0 compound which was rebuilt from a 4-6-2 and provided with a semi-streamlined casing. Ing. J. Vittone modified the exhaust of the Henschel 4-6-2 of the Provincial Railway (before working for 5 months in the UK supervising the building of the 5 Provincial Railway diesels).

On the broad gauge all 75 of the Roca 4-8-0s of class 11c built in the late 1920s and some of the class 11b were converted by Chapelon and it was claimed that their performance was considerably improved, so much so that they replaced the more modern and powerful 4-8-0s of classes 15a and 15b on fast fruit trains between the Río Negro valley and Buenos Aires. Despite these claims little further was heard after these feats had been publicised in a paper given to the Institute of Mechanical Engineers in

Manchester on 7th March 1969, and early in 1971 the metre gauge compound 4-8-0, prominently illustrated in press reports, was lying derelict at La Plata, though it has since received a cosmetic restoration and has been placed in the museum at Tucuman.

Electrification

For many years electrification was confined to the Buenos Aires suburban services from Retiro, Once and Lacroze stations, largely worked by Japanese built multiple units, though it is worth recalling that between 1955-59 and about 1973 the Lacroze services were worked with second hand interurban tramcars obtained from the Pacific and Electric and Key systems in the USA, coupled in multiple. However, in the mid 1980s, electrification at 25kV was completed on broad gauge Roca suburban lines from Plaza Constitucion station to Temperley, including short branches to Glew and Ezeiza, in all some 45km. The work was carried out by a Japanese consortium which also supplied the rolling stock. At the time an extension to La Plata was proposed but did not go ahead.

This electrification was the last real expenditure on modernising Argentinean railways. In 1980 only 810 of the total fleet of 1,176 diesel locomotives were in service, and of the 2,000 passenger coaches only 1,193 were available, but diesel locomotives were still coming into service and new arrivals included diesel hydraulic shunters built by Cockerill in Belgium and locally under their licence. Also completed during this decade was the road/rail bridge over the Paraná river between Zárate and Brazo Largo, eliminating the long river trip for trains of the Urquiza railway linking Buenos Aires and the province of Mesopotamia, and Paraguay. By the early 1990s the international bridge from Posadas to Encarnación was at last completed, putting out of service the ancient train ferry which had long been used for passenger and freight trains alike. But all these bridges were road/rail and long distance bus travel was increasing to the detriment of rail passengers, despite the introduction of 'prestige' trains.

By the end of the 1980s the railways were losing US$ 400 million a year. Availability of locomotives was only at 50% and privatisation was considered to be the only solution. In early 1993 the government passenger subsidy was withdrawn from long-distance passenger services and provinces were invited to fund and operate their own trains, which in turn resulted in wholesale service withdrawals. Privatisation was to follow, the last report of the National Railways quoting ownership of 1003 diesel-electric locomotives, 129 diesel-hydraulics, 8 electric main line locos, 800 emu cars, 215 diesel railcars, 1,973 passenger coaches and 39,780 freight wagons. How many of these were serviceable is debatable, and although the track mileage had hardly declined since 1977, much of it was probably disused. Privatisation during the early 1990s was a complicated and confusing stratagem, with many international bids, both American and European. The Spanish RENFE in particular had already sold surplus locomotives and railcars to Argentina. There have been some successes on the freight side, mostly flows such as cereals from the interior to the ports, but much of the former system is closed or moribund, with little

Six 3-car rack and adhesion railcar units were obtained by the F.C. General Belgrano for use on the Transandine route. They were built in Hungary by Ganz 1963-64, and unit 4708 was seen in April 1989 at Polvaredas.
Photo: Chris Skow,
Trains Unlimited, Tours.

A mixed train is being worked near near Campo Quijano by one of the General Motors GT22CU diesels supplied in the 1970s. The bridge and scenery are typical of the Transandine line.
Photo: Chris Skow,
Trains Unlimited, Tours.

Crossing the Comallo River near Pilcaniyeu is a westbound F.C. General Roca passenger train with GM-EMD C-C diesel no. 9009 in charge. This class, the 2250 hp GT22CW, was supplied in 1972, and the picture dates from October 1991.
Photo: Chris Skow,
Trains Unlimited, Tours.

chance of revival. As in the UK, there was far too much duplication of routes, particularly in the Buenos Aires province, and wholesale closures, an Argentinean 'Beeching era' was inevitable. It is not intended here to follow the saga of privatisation, but to end on a happier note.

In 1994 a 6km, 500mm gauge tourist line was opened at Ushuaia. This is the 'Ferrocarril Austral Fueguino' operated by the Buenos Aires based firm of Tranex Turismo SA. Trains depart from a station 10km from Ushuaia and travel into the National Park, making use of part of the former trackbed of the penal colony railway and following the course of the river Pipo, which is crossed twice. Passengers have a bus connection from the town/harbour, no doubt much traffic being generated by cruise ships. Motive power consists of 2-6-2T no. 1 'Camila', built by Winson Engineering in 1995, and 0-4-0+0-4-0 Garratt no. 2 'Nora', built by Tranex in Argentina. There is also a diesel-mechanical of 1937 vintage (O & K built, ex-600mm Correntino Railway), two second hand Rustons, and a new 0-6-0 diesel 'Tierra del Fuego' built in South Africa by Girdlestone Rail which entered service on 5th November 1999.

The railway has been highly successful in attracting visitors and is to be extended 10 km to Ushuaia. 'Camilla' is undergoing an extensive technological upgrade and has been operational during the 1999-2000 season with the first stage of modifications complete. A new 0-4-0+0-4-0 Garratt based on 'Nora' is under construction using the latest Porta-inspired steam technology and is to be followed by a radical new 2-cylinder compound 0-6-0T whose design will be on the leading edge of steam technology.

On the world's most southerly and perhaps most remote railway, 500mm gauge 0-4-4-0 Garratt 'Nora', the F.C. Austral Fueguino's no. 2, is seen in action in November 1995. Discounting miniatures, this is (to date) the last Garratt to be built, the railway itself having only opened in 1994.
Photo: David Ibbotson.

BOLIVIA

Bolivia is the fifth largest country in South America, and is twice the size of Spain. It has an area of 424,162 square miles and has been land-locked since the war of the Pacific with Chile between 1879-1883. The terrain ranges from the high, windswept Altiplano, much of which is over 4,000 metres above sea level, to the lowland tropics, the latter accounting for 70 per cent of the nation's area, although perversely 75 per cent of the population of 7,900,000 live on the Altiplano. A potentially rich country, Bolivia is in fact one of the poorest of the South American states, due partly to the difficulty of communications, which makes exploitation of her natural mineral resources expensive. There is still no railway linking the lowlands (where much of the food is produced) with the Altiplano (where most of the population live), and many roads are unpaved and subject to washouts during the rainy season. The nation's economy has always been based on mineral wealth, which until the 1952 revolution was largely in the hands of a few wealthy families. Nowadays, oil is being produced in the lowlands, an area of phenomenal growth in the latter part of the 20th Century, not least in railway construction, which has opened up previously isolated and undeveloped territory and provided international outlets for Bolivian produce into Argentina and Brazil.

Great Britain played a prominent part in providing Bolivia with railways, the first of which was a 35km mineral line built in 1873 by the Antofagasta Nitrate & Railway Company, from the port of that name inland to Salar del Carmen. This 760mm gauge railway crept forward to Carmen Alto (1877), Salinas (1879) and Pampa Alta (1883), construction apparently continuing despite the outbreak of war in 1879, when Bolivia and Peru fought Chile for the nitrate deposits of this region. Under the terms of the peace treaty of 1884, Bolivia ceded its coastal territory to Chile and the frontier was established at Ollague, 441km from Antofagasta. A link with the sea was vital to the Bolivian economy, based almost exclusively on the export of minerals, mostly exploited by foreign companies, and in 1887 the Antofagasta (Chile) & Bolivia Railway Company Ltd was formed in London to prolong the original nitrate line toward the frontier at Ollague and thence via Uyuni to Oruro. Ascotan (366km) was reached in 1888, and Oruro (930km) in 1892. The principal Bolivian

Shunting at Uyuni in November 1977 is ENFE no. 552, a former FCAB 2-8-4T, one of two built by Hunslet (1103/1912). Photo: Chris Skow, Trains Unlimited, Tours.

protagonist of this scheme was Aniceto Arce, a leading shareholder in the Huanchaca Mining Company, and President of the Republic from 1882 to 1892. In fact the concession was originally granted to the mining company but presumably lack of capital made them turn to British interests, which leased the railway back to them for a period of 15 years, until the end of 1903, after which date the British company took over operations themselves.

In 1903 another war, this time a very local affair with Brazil over the Acre territory, resulted in the treaty of Petrópolis by which Bolivia ceded territory to Brazil and received a substantial sum of money in exchange. Part of this was put towards railway construction and , backed by further investment from an American consortium, the Bolivia Railway Company was formed

which constructed the following metre gauge lines:

Oruro to Viacha	201km	built 1906-09
Río Mulato to Potosí	174km	built 1909-11
Uyuni to Atocha	90km	built 1909-13
Oruro to Cochabamba	205km	built 1909-17

The Cochabamba line, in particular, proved very expensive to construct, and some funds were advanced by the Antofagasta (Chile) & Bolivia Railway Company (hereafter to be known by the Spanish title initials of FCAB) which took over all operation in 1908 on a ninety-nine year lease. To link Atocha with the Argentine frontier the French-financed Villazón - Atocha Railway

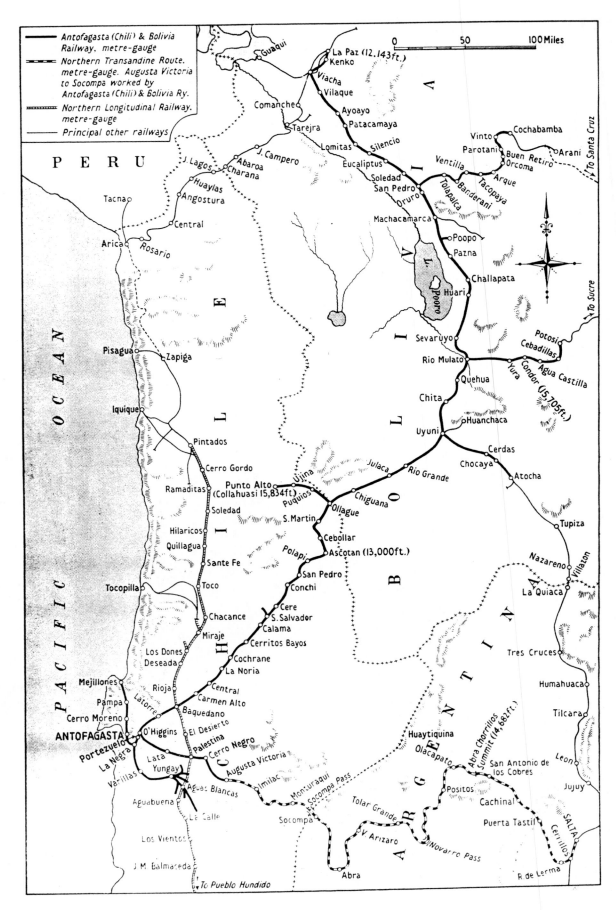

The Antofagasta (Chili) & Bolivia Railway system.

was formed but abrogated with the work unfinished. Later, American finance enabled the line to be completed and this 203km section was opened through to La Quiaca in 1925. The North Central Argentine Railway had reached the frontier in 1907 and for many years passengers had suffered an uncomfortable road journey between the two railheads, but at last through working between the countries was possible. There was some delay in reaching agreement but by 1928 there were through coaches, including sleeping cars, between Tucumán and La Paz. Buenos Aires to Tucumán was via the broad gauge Central Argentine Railway, into whose terminus at the latter city a metre gauge link existed. Later, metre gauge coaches ran through from Buenos Aires to La Paz, a distance of about 2,500km. At first the journey took about five days and it improved but little over the years! The Bolivian government sponsored the extension of the Potosí line on to Sucre, a distance of 174km, and this took thirty years to complete, Sucre finally being reached in 1936. The same year the line was continued towards Boyuibe, reaching Tarabuco in 1943. Work still proceeds intermittently on the next section! From Viacha to La Paz trains from Oruro used the tracks of the Guaquí - La Paz Railway between 1909 and 1917, when their own line was opened for traffic.

Well before all the above mentioned extensions were completed, the FCAB had come to appreciate the inconvenience of operating two gauges, 760mm and metre, despite use of a bogie changing apparatus for freight wagons at Uyuni which must have been one of the earliest examples of this practice in the world. The FCAB also owned a number of bogie combined sleeping/restaurant cars built in the early years of this century by the Gloucester Railway Carriage & Wagon Co. for the 760mm gauge, capable of accommodating ten first class passengers with the berths convertible into armchair seats and adjustable tables provided for the daytime service of meals. Conversion to metre gauge was effected from Uyuni to Oruro, together with some locomotives and stock, in 1916, but the effects of the World War delayed further progress until 1926, when a massive effort, which included complete closure of the Calama - Uyuni section for five days in 1928, completed the programme towards the end of that year. One of the last sections to be dealt with was the Collahuasi branch in Chile, which for many years could claim the highest point reached by

rail in the world (see chapter 4). Since closure of this section some years ago the record has passed to the Central of Peru, although a close second is Condor, on the Potosí line, with an altitude of 4,788m (15,705ft). With completion of the gauge conversion, the journey time from Antofagasta to La Paz was shortened from forty-two to thirty-nine hours.

The early 760mm gauge motive power included 2-8-0s with outside frames supplied by North British in 1911, while from Hudswell Clarke came two 0-6-2Ts in 1906, and two 2-8-2s in 1907. Earlier 2-8-0s had come from Hunslet in 1908, together with some 0-6-2Ts and some 2-8-4Ts about the same time but their most interesting contribution was two batches of Kitson-Meyer articulated tank engines, of 2-6+6-4 and 2-6+6-2 wheel arrangement, supplied in1908 and in 1911 respectively. In all sixty-one locomotives were converted from 760mm to metre gauge at Mejillones workshops in Chile, and a number survived in service until the final demise of steam. Thus during the 1950s Hunslet and North British 2-8-0s were noted and one of the Hunslet 2-8-4Ts, in excellent condition, was still at work at Oruro in the 1970s. The metre gauge Bolivia Railway Company started out with Alco 2-8-0s built in 1906-8, and in 1913 had a batch of six Beyer Peacock 0-6-2+0-6-2 Kitson-Meyers, which had separate tenders, carried on two 4-wheel bogies. These classes also survived into the mid-fifties.

Later metre gauge types included Hawthorn Leslie 4-8-2Ts of 1928, North British 2-8-4Ts of 1927, Henschel 4-6-2s of 1914 and 1928, and many other types. Three 4-8-2+2-8-4 Garratts made their appearance in 1929, and were most successful on the Potosí branch. Similar machines were borrowed from Argentina to help cope with increased traffic during World War II and in 1950 a further six were ordered, some of which were noted at work on the Cochabamba line in 1970, although by 1972 they had vanished, reputedly on transfer to the Potosí line. Some still existed in 1989 in the "graveyard", some 3km from Uyuni, along with five of the Kitson-Meyers, very derelict indeed! The only Villazon-Atocha Railway locomotives of which I have a record are No 5, a 2-8-2 of 1925, No 7, a 2-8-0 of 1927, both built by Borsig, and a batch of six Baldwin 2-10-2s built in 1942 and 1946 and used on trains to and from the Argentine frontier. The last two classes of steam locomotives supplied to Bolivia were nine 4-8-2s from Vulcan Foundry in 1954 and 12 2-8-2s from Japan in 1957/59.

For many years it had been intended to link Cochabamba with Santa Cruz by rail, a distance of 692km, and work started on this line in 1928, but progress has been painfully slow, with only 163km to date. Rotting away at Cochabamba in the 1970s were some old Borsig 2-6-0s of 1913 which were once used on this railway, while in service in 1972 were their 2-8-2s supplied from Orenstein & Koppel in 1929.

F.C. Cochabamba - Santa Cruz 2-6-0 no. 6 prepares for departure from Cochabamba station in March 1955. Borsig built no. 6 in 1913, works no. 87213. Photo: David Ibbotson.

At Cochabamba there was formerly a 760mm gauge railway to Vinto (19km) operated by the Empresa de Luz y Fuerza Eléctrica de Cochabamba and one of the locomotives, an 0-4-0T built by Borsig in 1905, was preserved at Cochabamba station. The company also operated a line from Cochabamba to Arani (62km), replaced when the metre gauge extension was started in 1938. In fact, the Borsig 2-6-0s mentioned in the previous paragraph were rebuilt from 760mm gauge, and presumably worked on this line. The tramway system was also their responsibility and this was in service in 1948 but apart from the preserved locomotive no other traces remained in 1970.

Before leaving this area for La Paz mention should be made of two other lines, one of which linked Uyuni with Pulacayo, is

about 40km long, and has 13km of electrified track (500V DC overhead wire). The FC Huanchaca de Bolivia is claimed to be the oldest railway in Bolivia, and is of 760mm gauge. Another mining line is the 96km metre gauge branch off the former FCAB main line near Oruro, the Machacamarca - Uncia Railway, built between 1913 and 1921 and formerly owned by the Patiño Tin Mines. Since nationalisation of the mines in 1952 the line has become property of COMIBOL, the National Mining Corporation of Bolivia. This railway had some interesting locomotives in steam days, including 0-6-6-0Ts and some others which appear to be 0-10-0s but have in fact three sets of driving wheels coupled with the pony and trailing truck wheels as well as the driving wheels, all of which are the same diameter. They are geared internally to the forward and rear driving axles respectively. These two machines were still in existence in 1972 and were built by Orenstein & Koppel in 1928 and 1930, while the two Mallets came from the same builder in 1913. There was also a Sulzer diesel electric of 730bhp, a Co-Co type machine with jackshaft drive which was built about 1948 and tested on the Rhaetian system in Switzerland, and this was noted in action in 1989. The railway was dieselised about 1969 and some of its

F.C. Machacamarca - Uncia no. 2, built by General Electric in 1948, departs from Oruro with an ore train in July 1975. Photo: Chris Skow, Trains Unlimited, Tours.

F.C. Arica-La Paz no. 3331 was one of six Ua class 2-8-2 rack tanks built by Esslingen (4127/1924), equipped with Abt rack gear for working the Central - Puquios section in Chile. It is now preserved outside Arica station.
Photo: Richard Pelham.

passenger trains worked over the State Railways into Oruro. In 1998 the line was still in existence but had no regular traffic.

Following the railway across the Altiplano from Oruro towards La Paz, we come to Viacha, a windswept junction from where two routes exist to the capital. Here we meet the tracks of the Arica-La Paz Railway, which offers the shortest route between the Bolivian capital and the sea (448km). This railway was the result of the "Treaty of Peace and Friendship" signed in 1904 by Bolivia and Chile following the War of the Pacific, and was meant to compensate Bolivia for her loss of coastline. Construction commenced in 1906 but little progress was made until 1909 when work was taken over by the British contractor Sir John Jackson. Material reached the Bolivian end via the Southern of Peru and Lake Titicaca, while construction was also pushed inland from Arica. The line was completed throughout in 1913 and originally was wholly administered by Chile, but Bolivia took over the section in her territory in 1928. The Chilean section includes about 40km of Abt rack, disused since 1967 but still partly in situ, between Central, 70 km from Arica and already 1,480m above sea level, and Puquios, 3,737m. The highest point on the railway, General Lagos (4,259m), is also on Chilean territory. Steam power used on the rack section has included Esslingen and Baldwin types, and the railway possessed Hanomag and Baldwin 0-6-6-0 Mallets, the Baldwin being supplied in 1918. Other motive power has included Borsig 2-8-0s of 1929 and a Borsig 2-10-2 of 1927.

Dieselisation commenced in 1953, but happily one of the rack locomotives was saved and is "on display" at Arica station. Nowadays the twice weekly railcars do the journey in about 11 hours. Maps show that within Bolivia there is (or was) a 9km branch from General Pando to Corocoro and at Villa Industrial there was once a narrow gauge line to a sulphur mine, (see chapter 4). Between Viacha and La Paz the old FCAB route is now used, with the Arica-La Paz track between Viacha and El Alto

abandoned. This railway is not as busy as it might be, partly because of the poor port facilities at Arica but also because of the very competitive tariffs offered by the Peruvian route via Lake Titicaca and the Southern of Peru.

Another railway encountered at Viacha is the Guaquí - La Paz (90km) and this was in fact the first to arrive there. Work commenced in October 1900 and was taken over by the Peruvian Corporation in 1902. It was opened on 1 December 1905 and purchased from the Bolivian Government by the Peruvian Corporation on 22 July 1910. In chapter 10 details are given of the services once operated on Lake Titicaca between Guaquí and Peru by the Peruvian Corporation, and this foothold in Bolivia proved to be a great asset to that concern. Until the 1970s the railway was steam worked between Guaquí and El Alto, with an interesting selection of motive power including a typical British industrial 0-4-0ST built by Peckett of Bristol in 1906. Also dating from 1906 is the oldest "road" engine and only surviving 2-6-0, built by Alco. The rest of the steam locomotives were 2-8-0s, two from Alco in 1911-12, one from Avonside in 1931, and two from Hunslet in 1948 and 1955 respectively. All except the Peckett carried the names of peaks in the Bolivian Andes. Despite the predominance of steam power the railway did experiment with diesel shunters, an 0-6-0D having been supplied by Hunslet in 1938. The railway lost its identity when taken over by the Bolivian State Railways in 1973 but the seven steam locomotives were still at Guaquí in the 1980s. As already mentioned, the Guaquí - La Paz was the first line between Viacha and the capital, its track being used by the FCAB between 1909 and 1917. Thus there were once three separate lines between Viacha and El Alto, and the FCAB line was rebuilt in 1924, partly on a new alignment.

It is only about 30km from Viacha to El Alto, from where there were two routes down into La Paz. It is well known that Bolivia's capital is the highest in the world, situated at 3,600m

The 2-8-0 became well established as suitable motive power for railways in the Andes and F.C. Guaqui - La Paz no. 8 'Sajama' is a typical example. In spite of its American appearance this loco was built in Britain by the Avonside Engine Co., works no. 2049 of 1930. The photo was taken on 25th January 1970 but no. 8 was still active in the 1990s.

Streetcar no. 10, built by Brill in 1906, gets ready to depart from the Pura Pura workshops at La Paz in July 1975.
Photo: Chris Skow,
Trains Unlimited, Tours.

above sea level. But the surrounding Altiplano is 400m higher still, with the city in a deep bowl, and this certainly presented problems for the railway builders. The Guaquí - La Paz line dived down steeply from El Alto, on a grade of 1 in 14.3 and with a centre rail for braking. This 9km section was electrified on the OHW system in 1905, the first railway electrification in South America. The Pura Pura shops of the company at La Paz have housed some interesting old electric locomotives, and also a pair of old tramcars which once ran a shuttle service between the La Paz terminal station of Challapampa and El Alto, and were latterly used as works vehicles. More recently, some railcars worked the once daily passenger service to Guaquí, but they offered poor competition to the buses operating about half-hourly for most of

the day, and since about 1973 all services have been suspended and the electrification abandoned. The station building in La Paz can still be seen and enjoys continuing use as the long-distance bus terminal.

The Arica - La Paz never had a route of its own from El Alto into La Paz, but used the FCAB tracks, which are forced to take a devious route down the mountainside involving a distance of some 17km and absorbing so much time that any passenger missing the train at La Paz could easily get a bus up to El Alto and be there before it! In steam days the weekly international train for Buenos Aires and Antofagasta was lifted up the long 1 in 33 grade by four massive 4-8-2s, but latterly the train was split into two sections, each handled by one diesel locomotive. In 1997 it was

Baldwin 2-10-2 no. 709 brings the southbound 'El Internacional' passenger train into Villazon, Bolivia in July 1975. The train will soon be turned over to the F.C. General Belgrano across the border in La Quiaca, Argentina for the journey to Buenos Aires.
Photo: Chris Skow, Trains Unlimited, Tours.

reported that trains no longer run from El Alto into La Paz, and the few remaining services started and finished at El Alto.

In 1914, the Bolivian government started construction of a very steeply graded line from La Paz towards the remote Beni province, the first part of which was to serve the Yungas, steep mountain valleys which provide most of the fruit for La Paz. Only 65km were built and the terminus was at Unduavi. Passenger services were worked by ancient home made railcars which abounded in Bolivia, often constructed from road motor vehicles and running in convoys, while for freight work the line has two Lima Shays, one of which survived until the 1970s, and has often been photographed shunting at La Paz Central (FCAB) Station and was La Paz - Beni No 2, latterly numbered 508, built in 1917.

It is thought that these geared locomotives were the only ones owned by the line, as they alone were capable of negotiating the fearsome curves and gradients involved! All services were abandoned in 1959, and it is unlikely that this line will ever proceed further, as the Beni province is planned to be opened up by a new line thrusting from the lowland city of Santa Cruz towards the Río Mamoré.

We have now covered the railway geography of Bolivia as it was up to the late 1940s, the next decade seeing a remarkable increase in track mileage serving the newly booming Santa Cruz area, previously without railways but now to be linked with both Argentina and Brazil by international lines financed by the countries concerned. Prior to completion of these projects, however,

In November 1967 F.C. La Paz - Beni shay no. 1 meets two of South America's oldest electric locomotives, built for the steep section down from El Alto, electrified in 1905.

One of the many and varied Bolivian railbuses at Atocha in July 1975.
Photo: Chris Skow,
Trains Unlimited, Tours.

came the 1952 revolution (the 179th in Bolivian history and since overtaken by other more recent ones) which saw sweeping agrarian reforms and the nationalisation of the tin mines and railways. All public railways not already the property of the State (excluding the Guaquí - La Paz, at that time the property of the Peruvian Corporation) were taken over to form the Empresa Nacional de Ferrocarriles de Bolivia, but this was not without problems, as the FCAB was still independent in 1959, when the government refused the company permission to increase tariffs and they ceased operations within Bolivia. The whole concern was offered to the Bolivian Government for £4,650,000 and within a few

months of takeover rates had been increased by 25 per cent. Efficiency decreased, however, and in 1962 the British were asked to return and manage the railway, which they did for a period of two and a half years, putting things back in order again. The final financial settlement amounted to £2,500,000, the Chilean part of the system remaining under British control.

As mentioned earlier, Cochabamba was reached by rail in 1917, although the building of the 205km line from Oruro had proved it to be the most expensive in the country and caused the FCAB to render financial assistance to the Bolivia Railways Company. At Oruro the railway is at 3,706m above sea level,

Cochabamba station in 1970 with a railcar from La Paz, ENFE no. 335.

while Cochabamba is at 2,558m, but between the two the line must climb through the cordillera, reaching a height of 4,131m at La Cumbre. Cochabamba has a fine modern station, but as the railway on to Santa Cruz has not progressed very far it is necessary to continue by bus, a journey of some 11 hours. Santa Cruz was founded in 1565 but in 1954 the population was only 25,000, connected with the outside world by many miles of poor roads and by air transport. But development of the oil resources of the tropical lowlands of Bolivia rapidly changed the situation and in 1944 work had started on a railway from Corumbá, Brazil, a distance of 643km through virgin forest where Indians are reported to have fired arrows at the first trains by way of protest! The line was financed by Brazil in exchange for Bolivian petrol and offers a through link with the Atlantic Ocean at the port of Santos. It was completed in 1955, but still sees little traffic, while the passenger facilities, are said to be extremely primitive.

At a spectacular location on the F.C. Corumba - Santa Cruz near Cochis, railcar no. 345 and trailer built by Ferrostaal of Germany are seen westbound in October 1994.
Photo: Chris Skow, Trains Unlimited, Tours.

later saw standard Bolivian Railway types. As stated earlier, there has been for many years a project to link Cochabamba and Santa Cruz by rail, thus completing a more or less direct Atlantic - Pacific rail connection and, of more practical value, joining the "old" and "new" railway systems of the country and eliminating the long detour through Argentina which is needed when stock and locomotives require transfer from one system to the other. In the 1060s work was continued on yet another railway from Santa Cruz, which striking northwards towards the Río Mamoré, via Santa Rosa, which was reached on 2nd October 1970. There are six major bridges on this section alone, the largest being over the river Piray. Track components were purchased in Britain, and the track has now reached Río Grande, 190km. The ultimate destination is Trinidad, capital of the isolated Beni province, and some 435km from Santa Cruz. Founded in 1686, and with a population of 56,000, Trinidad can at present only be reached by air, or with difficulty by river, or over poor roads.

Tales have been told of smugglers crossing from Brazil on the train, throwing their contraband overboard once over the river bridge, where it was then gathered up by colleagues and taken to the Bolivian station beyond the Customs point and returned to them for onward carriage to Santa Cruz, no doubt with some official connivance! This is probably why the twice weekly train (as distinct from the railcars) obliged passengers to alight at Puerto Suárez and cross the frontier by bus. Trains took twenty-four hours, but the railcar did the journey in half this time and crossed the frontier into the bargain! However, if you had a motor car with you, and a flat car was available, it could be transported on the train, there being no suitable road between the border and Santa Cruz. Drug trafficking is now a problem in this area.

The other international rail link from Santa Cruz is with Argentina via Yacuiba (539km), built between 1944 and 1957, and Argentine financed with repayments promised in petrol over a period of 20 years. With the coming of these railways the population of Santa Cruz quadrupled within four years and now exceeds 130,000. At first these metre gauge lines were worked with steam locomotives donated by Brazil and Argentina, but they

Until 1968, and railcars apart, Bolivia had virtually a 100 per cent steam operated railway system, although the total stock was only about 130 machines. Then a 10 million dollar aid programme was agreed with the Japanese, and on the motive power side this resulted in the acquisition of two series of diesel locomotives, main line diesel electrics of Bo-Bo-Bo wheel arrangement, 1,870hp, and weighing 82 tonnes, and secondary Bo-Bo diesel hydraulic units of 1,250hp, 55 tonnes, both from Hitachi. The initial order was for ten of the former and five of the latter, but more have been supplied since.

In 1973 the railway claimed to be operating 124 steam locomotives and 29 diesel electric units, ten railbuses, two diesel trainsets (Hitachi 1968) and 25 railcars but in 1972 only 79 of the 153 motive power units were available for service, the remainder being out of action due to lack of spares. A similar situation prevailed with railcars and other rolling stock and steam operation was quite widespread, operating about 43 per cent of the traffic. Massive international loans in the 1970s (75 million dollars between 1972 and 1977) enabled repairs to be effected and new

F.C. Guaqui - La Paz motive power included no. 5, a Peckett 0-4-0ST built in 1906, works no. 1086. Inside the shed are Baldwin 2-10-2 no. 704 and Hunslet 2-8-0 no. 9 'Mururata'.
Photo: Richard Pelham.

material obtained, and technical assistance from the French organisation Sofrerail helped to put the funds to good use by training staff, establishing new commercial policies and generally working towards a more viable transport policy. During the latter half of the 1970s steam traction was virtually eliminated, diesel locomotives and railcars being obtained from Japan, Germany and General Electric of Brazil.

In 1980 a six car diesel unit built by Hitachi operated three services a week between La Paz and Villazón and diesel electrics of 2,000hp handled freight traffic. Passenger rolling stock was also modernised, and the old wooden bodied coaches of British manufacture dating from around 1912, which were much in evidence not so many years ago, have now been replaced. Britain supplied three Pullman type coaches in 1955, and Wickham railcars built in 1960 were once in use on the Corumbá - Santa Cruz line. However, a fairly recent photograph showed an old Ford lorry, perhaps of 1930s vintage, converted to rail use and operating on the brand new line between Santa Cruz and Santa Rosa, so maybe modernisation has not quite swept away the Bolivian tradition of converting road vehicles and running them in convoys along newly built, but usually uncompleted, railways which no doubt will have great potential one day, but which tend to be something of a liability meanwhile.

Not surprisingly, there has been little progress since the 1970s on the construction of the 'new' lines referred to above, though none of the projects have been formally abandoned. On the existing network, services were subject to a continuing decline throughout the 1980s. The 1993 South America Handbook stated passenger services to Cochabamba were suspended and in the Continental Railway Journal winter edition 1994/95 two services a week were shown between Oruro and Cochabamba. There were also two railcars a week between La Paz and Sucre. There was a weekly express La Paz Villazón, plus four trains (or railcars) Oruro - Villazón, a weekly mixed Oruro - Calama (on the

Antofagasta line), and a weekly mixed La Paz - Charana on the Arica line, the through railcar service being suspended. It was claimed that the Calama train was the only international passenger train in South America apart from railcars on the short Tacna - Arica line, implying that there are no longer through railcars between Corumbá and Santa Cruz as stated earlier. Stock figures for 1993 were 56 diesel locomotives (the most recent having been delivered in 1987), diesel railbuses 13, passenger coaches 83 and freight wagons 2061. Against this only 35 diesel locomotives were serviceable in 1990.

In the mid 1990s the Bolivian Government invited bids for operating the Andean and Eastern railway networks. The successful bidder for the western network was Antofagasta Holdings, the Chilean-based mining and banking group which is also the owner of the Chilean end of the FCAB. The company now operates trains under the banner 'Andina Railroad' (Empresa Ferroviária Andina S.A.) and services in operation in 1997 included La Paz - Villazón (once a week), and Oruro - Cochabamba (3 times a week). Probably more the result of local initiative, a regular but untimetabled service run with GM-built 'Model T' type railcars offered a hair-raising service over the switchback route from Sucre to Potosi, arguably the most scenic and exciting railway journey left in the world today. Passenger services on this line are shown as suspended in Thomas Cook's November-December 2000 Overseas Timetable, but the actual local situation may still be as mentioned and freight traffic still operates. Passenger services are suspended between Viacha and Arica, and Rio Mulato and Tarabuco. The eastern system is now operated by the FC Oriental, with three trains a week running between Santa Cruz and Yacuiba and six between Santa Cruz and Corumbá.

Freight traffic continues to be buoyant and, due to Bolivia's still primitive road network, her railroads seem, in contrast to other South American countries, to be continuing to fulfill a useful function and to have a reasonably secure future.

BRAZIL

Brazil is the fifth largest country in the world and has the sixth largest population. It is almost as large as the USA and bigger than Australia. Half of the total population of South America, nearly 160 million people, live in Brazil, the only country on the continent which uses the Portuguese language.

A comparison between Brazil and Australia is valid not only in terms of land area, but also in political structure and railways. Brazil is now a federal country composed of large states, each as large as a European country and having a degree of autonomy. However, responsibility for granting the initial railway concessions and for building those lines which did not attract private investors lay in the 19th Century with the Provinces (now States), rather than with the then Imperial government of Brazil. This led to the establishment of a number of separate railway systems differing in gauges, equipment and braking systems, and often separated by large tracts of territory without railways. In some cases, such as the Leopoldina, private companies established large systems serving more than one state, but the more usual pattern was one railway system for each state.

Not until the early 1930s did the Federal government take an active part in railway development, producing a plan to link up hitherto separate systems, and this Plan of National Communications (revised in 1959, 1964 and 1966) determines the course of new construction today. The new lines are built by a Federal agency, the National Railways Department (Departamento Nacional de Estradas de Ferro) which, although it has legal authority to control the federal railways, limits itself in practice to planning and supervising construction of new lines and works. The 1934 plan also introduced a measure of gauge unification, the broad gauge (5ft 3in or 1,600mm) being retained in the Rio - São Paulo area and the metre gauge used elsewhere. Of the 37,000km of railway in Brazil in 1952, nine tenths were of metre gauge. There have been many closures since, but some new lines, and today the figure is nearer 23,000km, probably not all of which is in use.

In 1957, railways under the control of the Federal government were grouped into the Rêde Ferroviaria Federal SA (RFFSA), a joint stock company of which the government held 87.2 per cent, the States 10.2 per cent, and municipalities 2.6 per cent. In 1967 there were twenty-four major Brazilian railways and more than half of these, with three-quarters of the national route mileage, were included in the RFFSA. At first the railways retained their individuality and were more or less autonomous in all normal operations, with budgets submitted to the RFFSA, which purchased all capital equipment, replacement material etc. Its operating income was derived from railway revenues and subventions of the Federal government, with construction of new lines remaining under control of the National Railways Department, a not particularly satisfactory situation.

After some years, and gradual but logical transfers of certain lines between the railways, the old company names began to fade from use and were replaced by geographical regions which by the 1980s were six in number, based at Recife, Belo Horizonte, Rio, São Paulo. Curitiba and Porto Alegre, plus a "Greater Rio" suburban division. These were responsible for in all some 23,649km. In 1984, with long distance passenger services declining dramati-

cally, the CTBU (Companhia Brazileira de Trens Urbanos), was set up as an RFFSA subsidiary to be responsible for urban services in the larger cities.

In São Paulo the responsibilities were shared with the Ferrovias Paulistas SA (FEPASA), which had been set up in 1970 to consolidate operation of five railways owned by the State of São Paulo. These were the Paulista, Araraquara, Sorocabana , Mogiana and São Paulo a Minas, all of which will be described later under their titles. In 1980 FEPASA, with 1,647km of broad gauge and 3,649km of metre gauge, despite carrying heavy freight traffic, had made more effort than the RFFSA to retain long distance passenger traffic, refurbishing all their long distance passenger stock by 1989 and starting tourist train operation in 1987. The São Paulo suburban lines carried around 99 million passengers in 1988. Figures for 1978 showed FEPASA having 147 electric locomotives and 351 diesels (EMUs and DMUs unspecified) and an electrified route length (all at 3,000 V) of 493km broad gauge and 657km metre gauge. Many changes have taken place during the last decade but as this work is intended to be mainly historical and I want to steer clear of modern political developments, suffice it to say that privatisation of the RFFSA (and probably by the time this is published FEPASA also), has been effected.

In July 1993 the CPTM (Companhia de Trens Metropolitanos) was created to take charge of the São Paulo metro system and also take over FEPASA suburban routes, which it did from January 1994. FEPASA retained the longer distance routes and developed both the passenger and freight sides of the operation.

In this necessarily long chapter, each (former) main railway system in Brazil will receive mention, going firstly northwards from Rio de Janeiro to the Amazon and then southwards from Rio to the border with Uruguay. In an attempt to preserve continuity, the railways will be followed geographically as far as is possible, history, locomotives, and anything of special interest being mentioned in accordance with space limitations. Inevitably this is to a large extent a look into the past, as most of the company identities have now been lost and the tracks of many smaller ones have vanished altogether. The privatisation of the late 1990s has created a further set of new companies. As may be expected with such a large country, the railway history is complicated, many small companies having amalgamated or been taken over, and it would become tedious to mention all the constituents and changes of ownership since the early days.

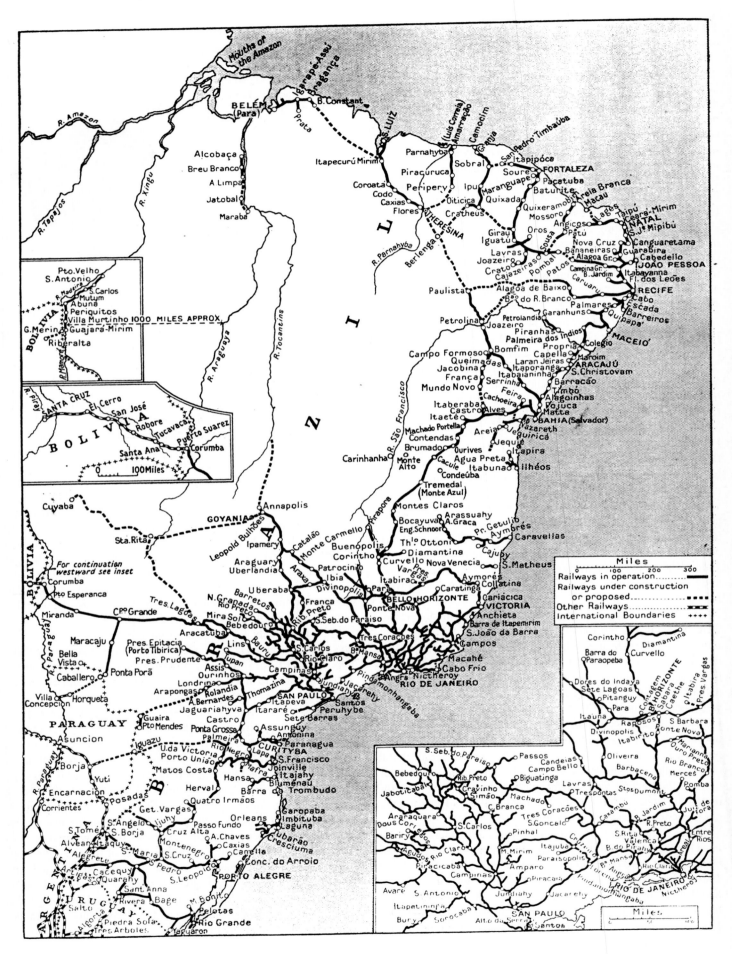

The Leopoldina Railway

The first railway to have been built in Brazil later became part of the metre gauge Leopoldina Railway. The original line, of 1,600mm gauge, was promoted by the Baron de Mauá, who obtained a concession from the province of Rio de Janeiro in 1852 for a railway to Petrópolis, the first section of which was opened to traffic on 30th April 1854. The locomotive which hauled the first train was named 'Baroneza', a 2-2-2 well tank, one of a series of four built by Fairbairn of Manchester in 1851 for the Midland Great Western Railway of Ireland. The other three reached Ireland but for some reason unknown to me 'Baroneza' went to Brazil. It has been preserved at the Centro de Preservação da História Ferroviária at the Engenho de Dentro Museum in Rio de Janeiro. The FC de Mauá passed to the Companhia Principe do Grão Pará in 1889, when the gauge was altered to metre. A curious geographical feature of Brazil is the Serra do Mar, a mountain wall some 15-50 miles inland and 7,000 to 8,000 feet high, which runs parallel with the coast for 300 miles. The original line terminated at Vila Inhomerim, at the foot of the Serra, and a Riggenbach rack section was opened from there to Petrópolis on 20th February 1883

In 1886 another line was authorised in this region, and the first section of the Cantagalo Railway opened in 1860. This line, initially built to a gauge of 1,600mm also had to ascend the Serra and used the Fell centre rail system on a gauge of 1,100mm. It was opened between Cachoeiras do Macacu and Nova Friburgo in December 1873. Some of material used came from the Fell line over Mont Cenis in Europe, including French

The lines of the Leopoldina Railway, 1926.

locomotives manufactured by the Gouin Company. The Fell section extended 12.5km from Boca do Mato (mouth of the forest) to Teodoro de Oliveira, and at Nova Friburgo the track ran along the main street of the town. In the opposite direction this line reached Niterói, across the bay from Rio, at the same time as the Fell section was opened to traffic. Both of these railways,

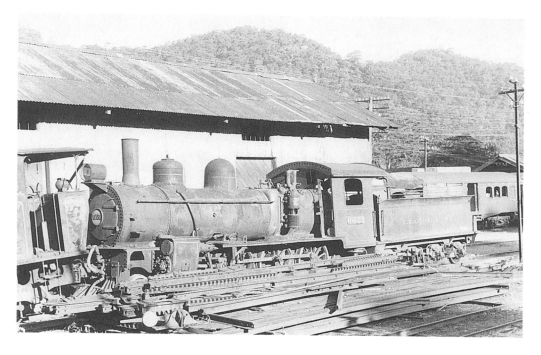

Leopoldina Railway 2-6-0 no. 1059, built in 1925 by Armstrong Whitworth, was found out of use on 28th March 1967 at Villa. Inhomerim, located at the foot of the Riggenbach rack system to Petrópolis.

converted to metre gauge, became part of the Leopoldina Railway, formed in 1872 and expanded by takeovers and new construction until it extended over 3,000km in the states of Rio, Minas Gerais and Espiritu Santo. The Leopoldina was originally a Brazilian company, but after some shady activity by certain directors liquidation took place in 1897 and the company was reconstituted with British capital. It was nationalised in 1949, and in common with most Brazilian lines, was subsequently 'rationalised', closures including the rack and Fell lines described. Today two principal main lines remain, the Linha do Litoral, from Rio to Vitória via Campos (638km), and the Linha do Centro from Rio via Recreio to Manhuassu (575km). There are also suburban services from Barão de Mauá station in Rio and General Dutra station in Niterói.

The steam locomotive stock of the Leopoldina was most varied, ranging from small tank engines to Garratts. On the Petrópolis rack section 0-4-0Ts from Esslingen and SLM, built 1905-28, worked traffic until closure; the later ones were superheated, and a few were still around derelict at the foot of the incline in 1967, while one is preserved at Petrópolis. The locomotive history of the Fell line is more obscure; the first locomotives were built by the French firm of Gouin (ex-Mont Cenis), and Fairlies were also tried before the line was reconstructed, as were Baldwin 0-6-0Ts received between 1883 and 1900. These only used the centre rail for braking. Although Mallets were proposed they do not seem to have appeared, but a Kitson-Meyer 2-6-6-4 was tried in 1908. More 0-6-0Ts came from North British in 1929

and 1946, and another was reputed to have been built by the Leopoldina itself in 1938. This was no. 109, which was cut up at Nova Friburgo in 1967. In 1981 one of these locomotives was found derelict in a cement works near Niterói and it may have been preserved.

Other unusual Leopoldina types were two geared locomotives, a Heisler of 1914 and a Shay of 1921, while pre-1900 tank engines included 2-4-2Ts, 2-4-4Ts and 0-4-2Ts from Baldwin. There were plenty of 2-6-0s and 2-8-0s from the same builder, along with some 4-4-0s, both American and British built. Later types included Armstrong Whitworth 4-6-0s, some Beyer Peacock 4-6-2s of 1925-28 and fine suburban 4-6-2Ts from the same firm between 1928 and 1937. Four of the last batch were lost at sea and subsequently replaced. The Leopoldina had sixteen 4-6-2+2-6-4 Garratts built in 1929, 1937 and 1943 and used on passenger trains between Campos and Vitória, where they were capable of hauling a 75% greater load than the Pacifics they replaced. There were also four 2-4-2+2-4-2 Garratts supplied in 1943 for the Cantagalo branch, and these were wood fired. The final steam locos supplied appear to have been Baldwin 2-8-2s in 1945-47.

Having commenced this survey with the Rio de Janeiro area, we will now travel northwards and mention other lines along the Atlantic coast. Thanks to relatively recent construction one could in theory travel a considerable distance by rail, although it is doubtful if many people actually did so, and nowadays passenger services over almost all of the sections have been withdrawn.

A northbound freight on the Leopoldina Railway, triple-headed by three of the RFFSA's General Electric of Brazil diesels, moves out of Santo Eduardo in Rio de Janeiro State, November 1977.
Photo: Chris Skow,
Trains Unlimited, Tours.

The Vitória a Minas Railway

From Vitória, the Vitória a Minas Railway extends inland to Belo Horizonte. It is of metre gauge and nowadays exists to transport iron ore from the mines in the Itibara area to the coast. The first stretch was opened from Porto Novo do Cunha to Cataguazes, and a branch reached the city of Leopoldina in 1877. Construction to connect the port of Vitória with Minas Gerais State was progressed from 1903 to 1942 and the link to Itabira was made shortly afterwards. Connection with the Central of

Brazil was made at Nova Era, whence one could travel to Belo Horizonte by broad gauge, but in 1992 a 50km link was built from Costa Lacerda on the VM to reach the RFFSA metre gauge line at Corinto (the former Central of Brazil Linha do Centro to Monte Azul) and this revived passenger traffic, with a daily through train between Belo Horizonte and Vitória. In my old late 1960s timetable there was a daily fast train taking 13 hours, plus a combination of two stopping services daily giving a short overnight break en route (restart about 04:00 hrs), thus taking about 22 hours in all. There is now a daily train in both directions taking about 15 hours, but the railway exists for freight. In 1991 94.2 million tons of goods were carried of which 72.9 million tons were iron ore. Other traffic includes Fiat cars. At one time the railway ran through the main street of some towns, but no doubt has been realigned.

Nowadays the motive power consists of over 200 diesel-electric locos, the most recent built in 1996, while the final steam power included French built 4-8-4s supplied in 1954, superb machines with a 13 tonne axle load, 26,000 lb. Tractive effort and mechanical stokers. Their maximum speed was 80 kph, but they had a short life as the railway was completely dieselised soon afterwards. From General Motors G16 1,800 hp diesel-electrics, the railway progressed to Krauss-Maffei 3,600 hp diesel-hydraulics and to General Motors DDM 45 Do-Do diesel-electrics of 3,900 hp, twenty of which were delivered in late 1969. Examples of trains worked with this equipment are 140 90-tonne wagons hauled by a pair of Krauss-Maffei locomotives or four General Motors G16 diesel-electrics. A train of 200 90 tonne wagons was successfully tried and 114-tonne wagons are now in service. More recently General Electric DASH 8 and 9 Bo-Bo-Bo-Bos have been introduced. During the last decade most of the main line has been doubled and a Japanese computerised train control system installed, bringing the capacity of the line up to 100 million tonnes a year. Electrification and possibly partial gauge widening have been under consideration for some years by this progressive railway, which is owned by the Companhia Vale do Rio Doce, itself formerly a government-owned mining organisation, but now privatised.

North of Vitória, two lines formerly existed, one extending inland from São Mateus to Nova Venezia, and the other, much longer, the Bahia & Minas Railway, from Caravelas to Aracuai. Both of these appear to have closed around 1966-67.

Railways in the State of Minas Gerais

Returning to Rio, we will now consider travelling northwards via Belo Horizonte. The broad gauge (1,600mm, 5'3") Central of Brazil links the two cities, a distance of 640km. Belo Horizonte is the capital of the state of Minas Gerais, one of Brazil's richest, once described as having 'a heart of gold and a breast of iron'. Half of the nation's mineral production comes from this state, and it has the only two working gold mines in Brazil. From Belo Horizonte a metre gauge line of the Central Railway extends to Monte Azul (718km), from where the Viação Férrea Leste Brasileiro continues a further 877km to Salvador (Bahia). The Leste Brazileiro totals 2,533km, with lines reaching out from Salvador to Paulistana (Piauí) and northwards through Sergipe state to Aracajú and Propriá (552km). Salvador is the capital of Bahia state and is the third city of Brazil. In the 1970s it was seventy hours from Rio by rail but only twenty-five by bus, the sort of comparison which is only too common in South America and explains the decline of rail passenger traffic. The population is over two million and until 1763 Salvador was the capital of Brazil.

Railways in the State of Bahia

The history of railways in the State of Bahia goes back to 1855, when the Bahia & São Francisco Railway Company was formed in London. After eight years Alagoinhas (124 km) was reached, but the railhead did not reach the São Francisco river until 1896. This railway was broad gauge (1,600mm) and was converted metre gauge in 1909. In the south of the province the Central do Bahia started construction in 1873, reaching Bandeiro do Mello in 1887 on the 1,067 mm (3'6") gauge. Other railways in the region included the Petrolina - Teresina and the Santo Amaro.

After amalgamation, much of the mileage passed into the hands of the Federal government, who leased it to a French concern the Compagnie des chemins de fer de l'est Brasilien, who completed the Monte Azul link with the Central Railway, though unfortunately the two concerns used different braking systems, air and vacuum. A northern line was also built to Propriá, where connection is made across the São Francisco river with the Nordeste Railway at Colegio. The contract with the French company was rescinded in June 1934, and the Santo Amaro Railway was taken over in 1939. The isolated 324km metre gauge Nazaré Railway was bought from the Bahia state authorities by the Federal government in 1962 and subsequently closed.

Another isolated metre gauge railway in this area was the former Bahia South Western Railway Co. Ltd., a British concern which was purchased by the Federal government in 1949 and became the EF de Ilhéus. In 1969 the stock was shown as 12 steam locomotives, 27 carriages and 49 wagons. This railway extended from Ilhéus inland via Itapira to Conquista (128km) and after takeover was administered by the VFF Leste Brasileiro until closure.

Steam power on the Leste Brasileiro was not so exciting as that of the Leopoldina. Early locomotives of the constituents included 2-4-0s and 4-4-0s and there were five Baldwin Atlantics of 1913. Later types included 2-8-0s and 4-6-0s from America and Europe, a few Pacifics, some 2-8-2s and 4-8-2s and one Henschel Garratt from the VFRGS in southern Brazil. Three British-built 450 hp diesel locomotives were supplied in 1938 and some early American ones in 1941 and 1944.

Rede Ferroviaria de Nordeste (North East Railway)

Crossing the São Francisco river by the road/rail bridge opened in 1972, we join the metre gauge tracks of the Rede Ferroviaria de Nordeste for the 588km journey to Recife, capitol of the state of Pernambuco and principal city of northern Brazil, with a population of almost 1½ million. The Nordeste is another system which was formed from numerous small companies of diverse gauges, such as the Recife - Olinda - Beberibe line, built in 1871 with a gauge of 1,200mm , and the Recife - Carango, built in 1867 to a gauge of 1,400mm. One of the earliest railways in Brazil was the Recife - São Francisco, started in 1855, the same year as the Bahia - São Francisco and built to the same (broad) gauge. The first section, from Recife to Cabo (35km) was opened on 8th February 1858 and extensions continued until by the end of 1862 some 125km were in use. By 1882, however, a further extension was being built to the metre gauge and the original section was converted in 1910.

The Great Western of Brazil Railway

In 1872 a British group met in London to incorporate a company to exploit the concession for a line from Recife to Limoeiro and formed the Great Western of Brazil Railway in 1873. The concession was transferred in 1875 and work started in

1879. The 49km to Oau d'Alho were opened on 24th October 1881. This company started out on the metre gauge and had soon swallowed up most of the others in the area.

An exception was the EF Sampaio Correia (formerly the Central do Rio Grande do Norte), extending for 381km around Natal, and linking up with the Great Western of Brazil at Nova Cruz. This railway retained a separate identity until nationalisation of all railways in the area in 1950, when, together with the GW of Brazil and other companies, it became part of the Nordeste, serving the states of Pernambuco, Paraíba, Rio Grande do Norte and Alagoas, with a total extent of 2,802km.

Great Western of Brazil Railway motive power was, as might be expected, largely British, with Manning Wardle 0-6-0Ts, Sharp Stewart and Hunslet 2-6-2Ts, a Black Hawthorn 4-4-0T and some North British 4-4-0s of 1906. There were a number of North British 2-6-0s between 1904 and 1914, 4-6-0s and 2-8-0s from both American and British builders, and some British 4-8-0s. A series of 2-8-2s came from Alco in 1941 and there were two Armstrong Whitworth 2-6-2+2-6-2 Garratts built in 1929, plus six 4-8-2+2-8-4 Garratts built by Henschel in 1952.

There is a small railway museum in the station buildings at Recife and in 1977 one of the Henschel Garratts was being restored in the station yard for exhibition, together with a North British 2-6-2T of 1906. Rotting away at that time on the sea front at Boa Viagem, a suburb of Recife, was 2-4-0T no.3, built by Robert Stephenson in 1881 and now no longer in existence. Other GWBR steam was then still active in sugar factories, for example two North British 2-6-0s of 1910 at Barreiros, one of which is now abandoned and the other reputedly in good condition but never used.

The Great Western of Brazil Railway, 1926.

Mention should also be made of another isolated railway which appears to have faded away about 1966-67. This was on the São Francisco river and linked Piranhas with Petrolândia, running parallel with the river to bypass the Paulo Afonso falls which formed an obstruction to navigation. This was worked by the Great Western of Brazil Railway.

The Great Western of Brazil had some 2-6-0s built by North British. Upon retirement some of these were sold off to sugar mills, hence NBL 19651 of 1911 was found at Barrieros Mill running as no. 34 "Jundia" where it remained active until at least 1987.

Great Western of Brazil 2-6-2T no. 17, seen on display at Recife Central Station in November 1977, had been rebuilt from a North British locomotive originally supplied in 1906.

The Rêde Viação Cearense

From Recife to Souza over the Linha Norte is 538km, and thence by the Rêde Viação Cearense to Fortaleza, a further 577km. This metre gauge system extends for 1,735km and was formed in 1910 by the amalgamation of the Baturíté and Sobral railways, originally unconnected but now linked by a line from Fortaleza to Sobral, from whence another link has been built to join the former São Luís-Teresina Railway, which extends 458km from Teresina to the coast at São Luís. This metre gauge line was built to promote agricultural development of the Itapecura Mirim and the Parnaiba valleys in the state of Maranhão. Another isolated railway linked Campo Maior (not far from Teresina), with the coast at Atalaia (Luís Correia) 258km. This metre gauge line, formerly the Central do Piaui, became part of the Rêde Viação Cearense when it was linked with the rest of the system in the 1960s.

As can be seen from the foregoing much linking up of formerly isolated lines has been achieved and in the absence of news from this isolated area one wonders how much survives and sees use today, freight only, as even when the links were built it is doubtful if any passenger services materialised.

A totally new construction has been the 900km Carajás Railway, broad gauge, linking mines well inland with the port of Ponta do Madeira, across the Baia de San Marcos from São Luís. This is mainly a mineral railway, largely financed from outside Brazil, and built between 1978 and 1985. A goods train runs with 204 wagons, reputed to be the world's longest train. A passenger service is provided thrice weekly between São Luís and Parauapebas (850km) and stock is quoted as 85 Co-Co diesel locomotives.

E.F. de Bragança

We now come to Belém, port of the mighty Amazon river, 145km from the sea and with a population of over a million. From here the EF de Bragaca formerly extended to the town of this name, traversing an area sparsely settled by Japanese growers of jute and black pepper. The metre gauge main line totalled 247km with a further 47km of 600 mm gauge. By 1960 the narrower gauge had gone, and by 1968 the railway had been condemned as uneconomic, and it was closed soon afterwards. At the time of closure the motive power consisted of fourteen steam and six diesel locomotives, and all useful items of rolling stock were transferred to the Ceará Railway.

Across the mouths of the Amazon, some 350km from Belém is Porto Santana, from where the Amapá Railway extends 196km to manganese mines at Serro do Navio. This is the only 4'8½" gauge line in Brazil and is owned by the Bethlehem Steel Corporation of the USA, through its subsidiary, Industria e Comercio de Mineras SA of Brazil. This railway was opened in January 1957 with a stock of four diesel locomotives, one railcar, three coaches and 117 wagons.

Up the river Tocantins from Belém there was until fairly near the end of the 20th Century an isolated 117km metre gauge line built to bypass the falls of the river between Tucuruí and Jatobal. It was owned by a government company, the Fundação Brasil Central, but is thought to have been destroyed by the construction of a hydro-electric scheme.

Although we have faithfully followed the railway tracks all the way from Rio de Janeiro to the far north, the journey is one better contemplated on paper than in actuality. According to a 1967 timetable it would have taken ten days of almost continuous travelling to reach Fortaleza from Rio, a distance of 4,550km, but since then most passenger services have been withdrawn.

Steam traction has vanished from the tracks of the RFFSA and also now from the sugar mills around Campos and Recife but lingered on at the Usina Serra Grande sugar mill in Alagoas State until 1999. Until the 1980s a few former main line locomotives were still in action during the harvesting season on these often quite extensive systems, most of which are of metre gauge.

The Madeira-Mamoré Railway

We have traced the isolated lines beyond Fortaleza to the mouths of the Amazon, but to find our next railway we must travel 2,500km up the river and its tributary, the Madeira, to the borders of Bolivia. The journey by boat from Belém (possible but very time consuming) takes six days to the old rubber boom city of Manaus (which had electric trams but no railway or road link with the outside world), and at least four days more to reach Porto Velho and the Madeira-Mamoré railway. This famous railway closed in 1971, but a few kilometres are retained for weekend tourist operations and there is a small railway museum at Porto Velho station. Brazil's most isolated and unlikely railway attained a certain notoriety as the line which cost a life for every hundred sleepers laid. Enterprising journalists occasionally visited it and a few connoisseurs from the railfan community have also sampled its delights. It was a railway many hundreds of miles from any other, extremely inaccessible until the age of the aeroplane, which until recently was the only really practicable means of reaching it. The Madeira is navigable upstream as far as Porto Velho, but access to a further thousand miles of navigable river, stretching into Bolivia, is obstructed here by a series of rapids.

A company was formed in 1867 to make a navigable channel past the rapids, but this was soon found to be impracticable, and a railway was proposed instead, a company being formed in London in 1872. The first attempt at construction failed miserably, and a subsequent expedition in 1874 fared little better. Conditions in the 'green hell' of the jungle were appalling, and the men died from attacks of Indians, malaria, yellow fever, and other natural hazards such as deadly snakes, alligators and piranha fish. The third expedition was made in 1878, by Messrs. P & T Collins of Philadelphia. They managed to build four miles of metre gauge track and import a Baldwin 4-4-0 before their supply steamer was sunk in a storm, with the loss of some eighty lives. This was the company's only firm link with civilisation and many of the workers came close to starvation, the lucky ones struggling almost two thousand miles down river to Belém. Of the 941 Americans, at least one third failed to return and most of those who did were in very poor shape. The railway company, its assets exhausted, was dissolved and the contractors were bankrupted.

In 1883 the Brazilian government had the route surveyed, but the whole team became ill and had to be evacuated before much serious work had been done. For twenty years the jungle grew over the Baldwin 4-4-0 before local political troubles revived the lost cause of the railway. During 1900-1903 there were disturbances by Brazilian rubber pickers in the lower Acre region of Bolivia, resulting in a transfer of territory ratified by the Treaty of Petrópolis in 1903. Bolivia received financial compensation for the territory ceded to Brazil, and the promise of an outlet to the Atlantic ocean by means of the Madeira - Mamoré railway. It was the period of the fabulous Amazon rubber boom and money was no object. The railway company was reconstituted in 1907, and lured by the offer of high wages, workers flooded into the area from the Panama Canal and the West Indies. By 1912 the 366km line between Porto Velho and Guajará Mirim was complete, although at the cost of some two thousand lives. Once more the original 4-4-0 was recovered from the jungle and put back into service, along with nine 2-6-0s and two 2-8-0s from Baldwin 1908-09.

Unfortunately no sooner was the railway fully operational than a certain Britisher smuggled out rubber seeds, which it was found flourished in Malaya, where plantations were established, thus knocking the bottom out of Brazilian production, where wild trees were tapped in the jungle. Traffic faded and in 1950 local administration by the Federal Territory of Guaporé was transferred to the Brazilian government, who operated the railway with an engineering battalion of the army. For many years the passenger service consisted of a weekly railcar which covered the line in twelve hours, plus a twice weekly steam train taking two days with an overnight stop at Abunã. Around 1965 the railcar was withdrawn and the locomotive-hauled train speeded up to do the journey in eighteen hours.

All the locomotives were wood burners and, with the exception of one 2-8-0, all were still in existence when the line closed

On a visit to the metre gauge Madeira Mamoré Railway in 1967 wood-burning 2-6-0 no. 7 was photographed taking water. This is one of the locos supplied by Baldwin in 1925.
Photo: G. Todd.

in 1971. The 4-4-0 of 1878 has been restored for preservation and bears the name "Coronel Church", who was the president of the 1867 navigation company which had first proposed a railway in the area. Later additions to the locomotive roster included three Baldwin 4-6-0s of 1913, two Alco 2-8-2s of 1941, and three German 2-8-2s of 1936, obtained second hand from the Santa Catarina line in the south in 1961. The railway is now replaced by a road, which uses its bridges and connects with the trans-amazónica highway, driven at immense cost through the virgin jungle to connect with the road system of Peru. This 5,000km road has been described as 'traversing pre-history to prepare the future'. It may not be generally realised that the Amazon region accounts for 47% of Brazilian territory, a large portion of it virgin jungle. Statistically speaking, one tree out of every three on this planet grows in Amazonia and the Amazon basin is the largest in the world, providing one fifth of all the fresh water on Earth. Great concern has been expressed about the ecological effects of the development of this region.

The Railway to Corcovado Peak

Returning (by air of course) from the wilds of the Amazon jungle to the sophistication of Rio de Janeiro, we will pause for a moment to consider a railway of a different type to those previously described. Many people are familiar with illustrations of the bay of Rio, dominated by the huge figure of Christ on Corcovado peak, 2,300 ft above the city. To facilitate access to this summit a 4km Riggenbach rack railway was opened on 1st January 1885. This metre gauge line has a ruling gradient of 1 in 6 and of 1 in 3.3 at the steepest point. It was originally steam worked, electrification on the three phase system being carried out in 1910. It has now been taken over by a National Trust type of conservation organisation entitled Empresa Incorporadas á Patrimonio Nacional and equipment, including rolling stock was modernised in 1978.

Two postcard views of the rack railway up to Corcovado summit, Rio de Janiero, upon which stands the famous statue of Christ. The first card shows one of the trains used from electrification in 1910 until modernisation in 1978 and the second illustrates a steam train on the Ponte do Sylvestre in early days.

The Central Railway

It is now time to consider Brazil's 'premier line', the Central, which links the nation's two principal cities, Rio and São Paulo. It formerly carried heavy traffic and produced almost double the revenue of any other system in the country, in fact about a quarter of the revenue of all the railways in Brazil. The broad, 1,600mm gauge totals about 1,500km and the metre gauge about 1,100km, although there have been many closures and some conversions from metre to broad gauge, particularly in the Belo Horizonte area. The Central Railway originated in 1855 as the Dom Pedro II Railway, with most of the shares owned from the beginning by the government. The first 48 km were opened from Rio to Queimados in 1858 and soon after commenced the climb up the Serra do Mar, culminating in a 2,237m tunnel. Construction was retarded by the difficult terrain and Barra do Pirai (109km), in the valley of the river Paraíba, was not reached until 12th July 1863. Expenses had been heavy and the company became bankrupt in 1865, direct operation being taken over by the government. It was the first case of its kind in Brazil, to be followed by many others in later years! In 1889, with the formation of republic, the railway was entitled Central do Brasil. At Barra do Pirai is the junction of the Belo Horizonte and São Paulo main lines and the government administration pushed on with both routes, São Paulo being reached in 1891. The Belo Horizonte line has to climb the Serra do Mantiqueira, reaching a height of 1,117m, and was opened to Juiz de Fora in 1874, subsequently being extended to Belo Horizonte. The high cost of the broad gauge sections of the Central Railway encouraged future construction on the metre gauge. Ironically, nowadays the more important metre gauge routes have difficulty offering a service competitive with other forms of transport.

Broad gauge steam locomotives used on the Central have included numerous series of 2-8-0s, and some fine Alco and Baldwin Pacifics, a few of which could still be seen on standby duties between Rio and São Paulo in 1967, at which time a typical American 4-6-0 of 1917 was working the Lorena - Piquete branch, and two 4-4-0s which a few years earlier had been reported working local trains were derelict at Saudade. Until the advent of dieselisation large locomotives abounded, the Central having been the first Brazilian railway to use Mallets, three 0-6-6-0s being supplied by Alco in 1907. They later had some 0-8-8-0s from the same builder, while on the metre gauge sections there were series of 2-8-8-4 simple expansion Mallets, super-heated and stoker fired, built by Henschel in 1937. Other metre gauge types included 2-10-4s built in the 1940s and some French 2-8-4s of 1954, which together with a series of 4-8-4s, were imported by the government and saw service on various railways throughout the country. Today the Central is dieselised, but in 1980 Baldwin Pacific no. 353 of 1927 was restored for special workings.

The intensively used Rio suburban services presented a problem as far back as 1904, when electrification was first proposed, however, no positive action was taken until 1935, when Metropolitan Vickers Electrical Co. Ltd. were awarded the contract. By 1938 19km of the main line to Nova Iguassú were completed, plus 10 km of the Santa Cruz branch from Deodoro junction to Bangui, the system chosen being 3,000V dc. To work these sections the contractors supplied nine 1-Co-Co-1 passenger locomotives and fifteen Bo-Bo freight locomotives, plus six smaller Bo-Bos for mixed traffic, and 78 three-car sets of suburban stock, consisting of one motor coach with two driving trailers, accommodating 132 first class and 296 second class passengers per set. These could be worked in multiple as six or nine car trains.

Unfortunately, the outbreak of World War II caused the British contractor to withdraw, and the work was taken over by the Electrical Export Corporation of America. Towards the end of 1943 main line electrification continued and it reached Barra do Pirai in 1949, then to Saudade to serve the newly opened steelworks of Volta Redonda. For heavy freight work connected with the steelworks, General Electric of America supplied some 3,900 hp 2-C+C-2 locomotives in 1948 and six 4,400 hp Co-Cos came from the same builder in 1963, together with some express passenger machines. Meanwhile, in 1956, Metropolitan Vickers had made a comeback with an order for a further 50 three-car sets and 50 motor coaches, plus 100 additional sets of electrical equipment for trailer cars. To complete the picture, other Central railway electrification is from São Paulo (Roosevelt) station out into the suburbs at Mogi das Cruzes (50km), completed in 1958 and worked, as at Rio, by multiple units providing intensive services at a one-rate fare. There are also some suburban electrical workings around Belo Horizonte, all at 3,000V dc.

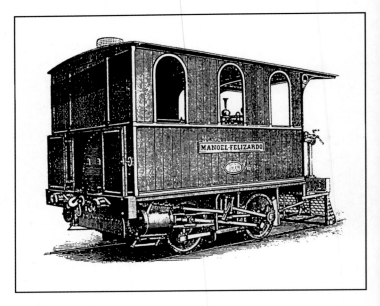

"Manoel Felizardo", an 0-4-0 tram locomotive built in 1862 by Sharp Stewart for the Tijuca Railway, a formerly horse-drawn roadside tramway operating between Rio de Janeiro and Tijuca.

To revert to Volta Redonda, this steelworks is now the largest in South America and a totally new broad gauge 'steel railway' was built during the 1980s linking it with the mining and industrial areas around Belo Horizonte. This 309km link was completed in 1989 and carries 20 million tonnes a year, mostly iron ore, steel products and cement. 90-wagon trains can load up to 8,200 tonnes, headed by four 3,000 hp diesel-electric locomotives. The railway was constructed through difficult terrain and includes seventy tunnels with a total length of 50km, plus ninety-two bridges and viaducts totalling in all 30km. The railway is single track, CTC controlled, and electrification is planned for the future.

Some 25 years ago great efforts were made by the Central to compete with air and road services for the Rio - São Paulo passenger traffic. Budd lightweight railcars gave way in 1972 to Ganz-Mavag four-car diesel trainsets, which took five hours for the 499 km, but the railway was fighting a losing battle and a 1981 timetable showed the one daily train taking 8½ hours, with the overnight sleeper taking slightly longer. Passenger services have since been severely pruned, the railways being dedicated to heavy freight haulage, particularly iron ore.

Travelling along the Central from Dom Pedro II station in Rio, the track is quadruple to Deodoro, thence double to Barra do Pirai, and in places the trains can be worked in the same direction on both tracks if required. Just before Barra Mansa (154km), the Volta Redonda steelworks is passed. The steelworks is a source of rails for Brazil.

At Barra Mansa the metre gauge tracks of the former Viação Ferrea Centro Oeste are crossed, and these too are linked with the steelworks. The VFCO's principal constituent was the Mineira de Viação Railway, which had itself originated as the Oeste de Minas, a 760mm gauge system opened between 1878 and 1881. Most of the system was converted to metre gauge, which came to a total of 3,728km. There was heavy freight traffic through Barra Mansa, and the original 1,500V dc electrification, which dates back to 1927, was extended to the coast at Angra dos Reis in 1958, and inland to Pestana, a distance of 135km, while a further 222km on to Lavras was energised at 3,000V dc. Maybe these sections were unified at 3,000V, but I have heard nothing further about this electrification for many years and feel that by now it must have fallen into disuse, as possibly have the tracks of the former VFCO railway in this area. The main line of the VFCO continues inland across the state of Minas Gerais to Goiânia and Anápolis. Since 21st April 1968 a 240 km branch has been open from Pires do Rio to Brasilia, the capital's first rail link with the outside world.

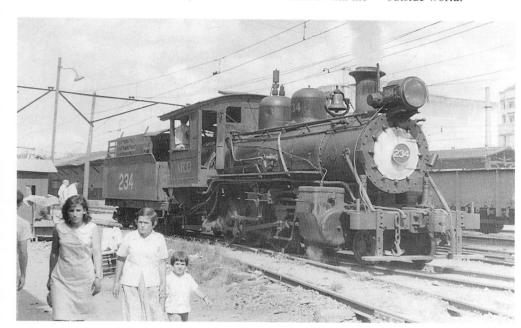

Performing station pilot duties at Barra Mansa in March 1967 was metre gauge 4-6-0 no. 234 of the Viação Ferrea Centro Oeste, built by Baldwin in 1920, works no. 54056.

Metre gauge Pacific no. 300 of the Viação Ferrea Centro Oeste was also seen at Barra Mansa. This locomotive carried two builder's plates, Schwartzkopf 8799/1926 and 8898/1927.

The once busy 760mm gauge terminus at São João del Rei with 2-8-0 no. 68 preparing to depart with a passenger train on 24th November 1981. A fire had gutted the nearby roundhouse in 1977, but restoration took place in the 1980s and several narrow gauge locomotives have been preserved.

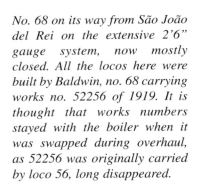

No. 68 on its way from São João del Rei on the extensive 2'6" gauge system, now mostly closed. All the locos here were built by Baldwin, no. 68 carrying works no. 52256 of 1919. It is thought that works numbers stayed with the boiler when it was swapped during overhaul, as 52256 was originally carried by loco 56, long disappeared.

Travelling inland from Barra Mansa the first junction is at Rutilo (95km), where the line extending from Santa Rita de Jacutinga across to Sapucai, inland of and parallel to the Central Railway, is crossed. This line in turn has branches, one of which reaches Cruzeiro, on the Central main line to São Paulo, while at Sapucai and Juréia there are connections with the Mogiana Railway. This part of the system originated as the Sul Mineira Railway. The next junction is at Lavras, 285km from Barra Mansa, where the 760mm gauge section across to Divinópolis (156km) was converted to metre gauge in the late 1960s. Other 760mm gauge sections, for example between Divinópolis and Barra do Paraopeba, have been closed, however, the branches from São João del Rei to A. Mourão and A. Carlos on the narrower gauge remained operational until closure in the 1980s with a fleet of Baldwin steam locomotives, 4-6-0s, 2-8-0s and two 4-4-0s, all built around the turn of the century. These 200 or so

kms were the last in Brazil to see regular steam-hauled passenger working and enthusiasts flocked from all over the world to travel on the system, of which a few kilometres only now remain as a tourist attraction, operated by the Center Atlantic Railway.

The next junction on the main line is Garcas de Minas (495km), where the line from Belo Horizonte via Divinópolis comes in. This is electrified at 3,000V dc between Divinópolis and Belo Horizonte (151km). Finally, there is a branch from Ibiá across to the Mogiana Railway at Uberaba before Goiândira is reached. The Centro Oeste carries heavy bulk freight traffic, 50% of which is limestone, coal and pig iron. A number of steam locomotives survived at Barra Mansa depot until about 1978 and old Metrovick electric locomotives of 1920 vintage were also to be found there, but these have now long gone.

Continuing along the broad gauge Central Railway from Barra Mansa, we pass through Cruzeiro, where the wagon works was reported as having steam Sentinel shunters in the 1970s. At km 326 Pindamonhangaba is reached, from where the metre gauge electrified Campos de Jordão Railway extends 47km to Emilio Ribas. The electrification is on the overhead wire system at 1,500V dc and the line carries about a million passengers a year

to the mountain spa, but has little freight traffic. It can claim the distinction of reaching the highest point attained by rail in Brazil, 1,734m, at Caique. Mogi das Cruzes heralds the approach to São Paulo, and the outer limit of the suburban electric services.

The RFFSA Rede Mineira B-B electrics at Barra Mansa were supplied by Schwartzkopf in 1934 for the 1,500V dc system in the area.

The São Paulo Railway

The State of São Paulo has an area of 95,461 square miles, and a population of 33 million. It is about the same size as Great Britain (including Northern Ireland). Along the coastline is a narrow belt of tropical lowland which rises in an unbroken slope to the Serra do Mar, some 8,000m above sea level. On the upland plateau of the state grows much of the world's supply of coffee, the major part of which is shipped via the port of Santos, which handles almost half of Brazil's external trade.

São Paulo city is the largest in Brazil, and indeed in the whole of South America, having outstripped Buenos Aires in the 1970s. With a population of over eleven million, it is the fastest growing city in the world and due to its elevated position on the serra it enjoys a less torrid climate than prevails on the coast. Through this city come the coffee exports from the interior, while in the other direction travel streams of imported goods bound for São Paulo and beyond. Much of this traffic is handled by the former São Paulo Railway, a 1,600mm gauge system retitled the Santos - Jundiaí Railway for some years until it became a division of the RFFSA.

As far back as the early 1830s the establishment of a railway had been considered here but a scheme submitted to Robert Stephenson in 1839 came to nothing and it was not until 1856 that a concession was granted, one of the promoters being the Baron de Mauá. Conditions stated that the line had to be built within eight years for a total expenditure of £2 million. The well known British engineer, James Brunlees was engaged and in his turn he sent to Brazil one of his former pupils, Daniel Fox, who at the time was only twenty-six years of age. The difficulty of this

young man's task was immense, the Serra do Mar presenting an apparently insuperable barrier vocered with thick virgin forest into which he was forced to plunge in an attempt to find a suitable route for the railway. His numerous expeditions into the rain-soaked forests left him pale-skinned from lack of sunlight and months were spent in vain searching before a possible route was discovered. Although only five miles long this section had to overcome a difference in level of 760 metres and so the the young engineer decided on a drastic solution, cable haulage, with four separate sections, each having a grade of 1 in 10 and separated by almost level bankheads on each of which stationary winding engines were to be situated. Fifteen months were spent on these plans, which were then submitted to James Brunlees in London for approval.

Construction of the first section from Santos to the foot of the Serra was not too difficult, although embankments were required to lift the line above the marshy ground and several bridges spanned rivers and the arm of the sea which makes Santos an island city, although this is hardly noticeable to the casual visitor. The climbing of the serra through virgin forest and granite rock, with heavy rainfall and frequent landslips, defies description, but it was done and the rest of the railway to Jundiaí completed ten months ahead of schedule, thereby earning a bonus of £43,750 from the Brazilian government.

Most remarkable of all, this amazing feat of engineering was soon found to be incapable of dealing with the traffic offering, and between 1895 and 1901 a second set of inclines was constructed, this time with five sections, thus reducing the grade to 1 in 14. The improvement was extremely expensive, as while the old inclines had required one tunnel and two bridges, the new ones took no less than thirteen tunnels and sixteen viaducts, all within a distance of five miles! The older route remained in use, but was restricted to freight traffic.

Each of the sections has an independent traction cable system, which provides motive power for the movement of trains through a stationary 1,000 hp steam engine. Cable gripper locomotives, resembling steam trams were attached to each section of train and these also provided adhesion power on the short, almost level, sections between inclines. Workings were counterbalanced on each incline, so over the five new sections ten trains were in motion at once. The track is of course double at the bankheads but interlaced on the inclines, except for a passing loop situated at the half-way point. On the new inclines, running time between bankheads was 7½ minutes, over a vertical rise of 160 metres, with 1½ minutes spent at each bankhead. The total train weight was only about 130 tons, including the locomotive, so considerable marshalling of trains was needed to break them up into sections of 2-3 coaches or up to 6 wagon units. The whole process was immensely costly and time-consuming, and for many years an alternative was debated. Finally, electrification of the older incline was decided upon, and this was completed during the early 1970s. Hitachi of Japan supplied eight 90 tonne rack and adhesion locomotives in 1972. One of these was destroyed in an accident but a further four were built in 1979-80. Two of these units working together can take 500 tonnes up or down the incline and all passenger traffic, minimal nowadays, is worked over the electrified rack line.

To travel from Santos inland on the SJ when steam was in use on the inclines was to experience at first hand one of the 'Railway Wonders of the World'. Santos itself is of interest, as although a great port it also has fine beaches, modern hotels, and indeed offers many of the attractions of the famous Copacabana beach at Rio, at more plebian prices. The docks are served by dual gauge tracks, as the metre gauge Sorocabana Railway also reaches Santos. The port authority has its own fleet of locomotives, which in 1967 were diesels on the metre gauge but Krauss 0-6-0Ts on the broad gauge. There is a funicular to Montserrat, and in 1967 there were trams (now gone), one route running through the docks alongside the railway tracks.

From the tidy little former SJ station at the back of the town, passenger trains soon crossed the level ground to the foot of the Serra. Here they were split, and up the inclines they went, counterbalanced by descending freight wagons. The heat of the coast gave way to dampness and mist, which swirled around the winding stations and mingled with steam from the power houses perched precariously on the hillside. Each bankhead has its row of houses for employees who (on the steam worked incline) travelled on the balcony ends of the gripper locomotives. For many years these were the only steam motive power on the SJ, which was otherwise electrified at 3,000V dc.

The steam locomotive history of the São Paulo Railway, which was the first British line in Brazil, is interesting, not least because every locomotive was supplied by British builders. It was an early user of Garratt locomotives, the first being supplied in 1915 for the Santos - Piassaguera section, where they hauled 1,000 ton loads over level but lightly laid track. The Garratts which made history were, however, those used between São Paulo and Jundiaí, the first to be designed as express passenger locomotives with 5ft 6in driving wheels. As stated in 'The Garratt Locomotive' by A.E. Durrant, 'Their presence enabled trains of 500 tons to be scheduled at an average speed of 40 mph over a

Two trains have just passed on a short level double-track section at one of the winding stations. The start of the fearsome gradient can be seen in the background where the line climbs past staff bungalows.
Photo:
Author's collection.

distance, start to stop, of 37 miles, during which 60 mph was attained, these being the first articulated locomotives in the world scheduled to runn regularly at such speeds.' Both these series of Garratts survived until electrification and dieselisation took place in the early 1950s.

Apart from the Garratts, there were some early Sharp Stewart 0-4-0STs, followed by 2-6-0s and 2-8-0s from the same builder, most of these prior to 1900. North British built a series of 2-8-4Ts between 1912 and 1947, and for passenger work there were Sharp Stewart 4-4-2Ts, built in the 1890s and superseded by some North British 4-6-4Ts in 1936. Other tank engines included 0-6-2Ts from Beyer Peacock and Kitson in the 1930s. Tender engines included eight 4-4-0s from Sharp Stewart built 1896-1900 and some 4-6-0s from North British in 1907 and 1915. The 0-4-0T 'gripper' locomotives for the inclines came from Kerr Sturart in 1900 (12 locos) and Robert Stephenson (8 locos) in 1900 and 1902-31.

Electrification of the railway was decided upon in 1946, when

a contract was signed with the English Electric Export and Trading Co. Ltd. Government purchase of the railway did not affect this project, the first section of which was completed in 1950 and the balance soon afterwards. The fifteen 3,000 hp Co-Co locomotives supplied by English Electric were at the time the most powerful completed in Britain. They are equipped with regenerative braking and can be operated in multiple. The mechanical parts were built by the Vulcan Foundry and subsequently a similar series, but of 3,600 hp, was produced by the same builders for Spain. English Electric, in conjunction with the Birmingham Railway Carriage & Wagon Co. Ltd., also supplied some three-car suburban multiple unit sets but others came later from Japan or were built locally. The overhead equipment was also supplied from Britain.

Reverting to a journey along the old SJ, at the summit of the inclines the train is quickly reformed and soon becomes entangled with the frequent suburban multiple unit services of São Paulo. The SJ carries 60 million passengers a year and has by far the greatest operating density in Brazil, 2 million tons/km per route km. It remained in British hands until nationalisation in 1946. Braz station, São Paulo, is alongside the Roosevelt terminus of the Central Railway and then the fine 19th century station of Luz is reached. Trains for the 'interior' started from here and when I first visited the area in 1967 these were made up of Paulista Railway stock hauled by SJ locomotives. A through coach of the Araraquara Railway might also be provided, giving an impression of what pre-grouping days were like in Britain.

Also in 1967, Armstrong-Whitworth diesel-electric articulated trainsets were in use between Santos and São Paulo and as these did not need to be split for the inclines, they offered a faster service than the locomotive hauled trains. The first of these was a 450 hp three-car set 'La Cometa', introduced in 1934, and it was

Armstrong Whitworth articulated trainset "La Cometa" at Santos station, used by the Santos - Jundiaí Railway for through express services between Santos and São Paulo.

Santos port authority broad gauge Krauss 0-6-0T no. 16 "Julio Barreto", shunting at Santos Docks on 3rd April 1967.

followed in 1939 by two 600 hp four-car sets named 'Estrella' and 'Planeta', on one of which I travelled in 1967. But the 1981 timetable showed only two daily through passenger trains, which were worked over the electrified rack incline and a similar service remained in 1994. Travelling inland from São Paulo, there are still some stiff grades to surmount and the track is double, while the high station platforms betray their British origin.

At Perus a 600mm gauge railway extended from the cement factory to Cajamar and this remained entirely steam operated by an interesting assortment of American built motive power until closure in the 1980s. At Campo Limpio the since closed Bragantina Railway offered in 1967 the sight of its five original

2-6-0s built by Kitson in 1881. This railway was of metre gauge and extended to Vargem, with a branch to Piracaia, a total distance of 107 km. It was owned by the São Paulo Railway and had a Garratt even earlier than the parent company, the first coming from Beyer Peacock in 1913, with another in 1936. These were 2-6-0+0-6-2s, but another is noted as of 2-4-0+0-4-2 wheel arrangement, assembled in the São Paulo Railway shops in 1919. Two Beyer Peacock 4-6-0s of 1911 complete the known steam stock of the Bragantina, a total of ten locomotives. There is also an oil pipeline laid between Santos, São Paulo and Campinas, parallel with the route of the railway.

Two foot gauge 2-6-2 no. 7 of the Companhia Brasileira de Cimento Portland Perús with a loaded stone train en route to Perús in 1967. The locomotive was built by Porter (7914/1945), for the Estrado do Ferro Perús - Pirapóra, as this line was known, though it was never actually built as far as Pirapóra.

The Paulista Railway

We will now consider the last major Brazilian broad gauge system, the Paulista Railway. The São Paulo Railway was only 115 km long from Santos to Jundiaí and it possessed powers to extend further inland, however, it was unwilling to do so, much to the indignation of those whose estates were beyond the limits of the line. These worthy (and wealthy), landowners convened a meeting and formed in 1868 the Companhia Paulista de Estrado de Ferro de Jundiaí a Campinas. The first train reached Campinas (44 km) on 11th August 1872, and the line was extended to Rio Claro exactly four years later. Further extension was planned, and at first authorised by the government on the broad gauge, but the intervention of the Conde do Pinhal caused the revocation of the concession on a technicality and when later put up to tender the contract went to a company controlled by. . . . the Conde do Pinhal ! The line was built to metre gauge and after nine years it passed to the British controlled Rio Claro Railway Co., who made considerable further extensions.

By 1892 the Paulista had managed to obtain control of the Rio Claro company but was then in the position of operating on two gauges. In 1916 a start was made on improving the situation and the metre gauge section Rio Claro - Analândia - Itirapina (70 km) was replaced by a more direct broad gauge route between the first and last points totalling only 44 km. Extensions brought the main

line to the Rio Grande at Colombia (567 km), with various branches, the most important being from Itirapina via Bauru to Panorama, on the Paraná river. A number of the branches remained of metre gauge until closure of all Paulista lines of this gauge on 1st January 1969.

Metre gauge steam on the Paulista, apart from the early Rio Claro Railway British built types, was almost entirely supplied by Baldwin, and consisted of the usual 2-8-0s and 4-6-0s. Other more modern locomotives may have appeared later and there were certainly some diesels in use at closure in 1969. On the broad gauge, Baldwin locomotives again predominated and included 4-4-0s of 1890 vintage, 2-8-0s, 4-6-0s, 4-8-2s and 2-10-2s. From Alco came other series, including some 4-6-2s and one or more 2-8-8-2 superheated compound Mallets in 1916. A few earlier locos were British built, and a Dübs 4-4-0 of 1890 was noted in use near Campinhas in 1967. An interesting sidelight on steam locomotive operation in Brazil is afforded by the high cost of imported fuel which caused the Paulista in 1904 to plant its own forests of Australian eucalyptus trees, and until the end of steam some of the surviving locomotives still burned wood fuel.

The first main line electrification in Brazil took place on 1st July 1922, when the Paulista electrified from Jundiaí to Campinas, to be followed by the section on the Rio Claro in 1926 and to Rinção in 1928 (268 km in all). This electrification at

A Paulista Railway express runs into Araraquara station behind broad gauge 2-C-C-2 electric no. 390 on 5th April 1967. This locomotive was one of a batch supplied by General Electric in 1940.

2-Do-Do-2 no. 6451, originally built by General Electric for service in Russia, but not delivered for political reasons. It was seen running eastbound light engine at Louvera in São Paulo State in July 1975.
Photo: Chris Skow,
Trains Unlimited, Tours.

3,000V dc, was continued along the branch from Itirapina to Bauru (167 km) between 1941 and 1948. Paulista main line electric locomotives have tended to be large, 2-C-C-2s and 2-D-D-2s, the latter of 5,000 hp. More modern electric types include a series of 5,200 hp Co-Cos from General Electric, USA. Of particular interest are five 2-Do-Do-2 locomotives bought from General Electric in 1950. These were part of an order for twenty placed by the Russian Government in 1946, which had been built in 1948-49 but never delivered due to a deterioration in international relations. The rest of the series, converted to standard gauge, went to various US railroads. The Brazilian locomotives, FEPASA 6451-6455, are now withdrawn and in fact de-electrification of much of the system is under consideration.

At the former Paulista Jundiaí works a small museum has been set up and the exhibits include a fine 4-4-0 plus some early electric locomotives.

The only other broad gauge railway in the area was the Araraquara, extending from the town of that name in the north of São Paulo state, on the Paulista Railway, to Presidente Vargas on the Paraná river, a distance of 440 km. This railway was originally of metre gauge, and in 1939 had some 4-10-2 locomotives, but was subsequently converted to broad gauge and dieselised between 1957 and 1960.

There are two large metre gauge systems in the state of São Paulo, the Mogiana with 1,722 km and the Sorocabana, with 2,848 km. The main line of the Mogiana extends from Campinas, where it shares the main station with the Paulista Railway, via Riberão Prêto to Araguarí (723 km), where it joins the Centro Oeste, whose through coaches for Brasilia were formerly to be found on certain trains from Campinas. There were various

Fepasa Goods engine no. 6413, seen at Jundiaí in October 1993, had been built by Westinghouse in 1927 for the Paulista Railway. Photo: Chris Skow, Trains Unlimited, Tours.

branches, and some were originally of 600 mm gauge, although these had vanished by 1970. Many branches have been closed, the system having by the 1970s been reduced even further and very few, if any, of its passenger services now remain.

The Mogiana Railway

Early Mogiana steam power was mostly British, with Sharp Stewart 4-4-0s and 4-6-0s followed by Beyer Peacock locomotives, mostly of the same wheel arrangements but including South America's first Garratts, two of which were built in 1912 and three in 1914. They were of the unusual 4-6-0+0-6-4 wheel arrangement, not repeated by Beyer Peacock, and are thought to have survived until after World War II. About the same time Henschel and Baldwin supplied 2-6-6-2 Mallets, with others from Alco in 1916-20. Other American locomotives included Alco and

Baldwin 2-8-2s in 1924-26 and 1946, and some 4-6-2s between 1917 and 1926. In the guide book issued by the company in 1939 the locomotive stock was given as 205, 84 being passenger types, 113 freight and 8 shunters. Eight were of 600 mm gauge. According to this guide, three Conslidation type locomotives had just been assembled in the company works, making a total of twenty built by them, which were, to quote, 'in no way inferior, in aspect or action to those imported from abroad'. At this time the company had 324 passenger coaches and owned extensive eucalyptus plantations, which they were extending as a source of fuel supply. Pullman cars were included in trains from Campinas to the spas of Pocos de Caldos and Prata, which were well publicised and illustrated in the guide.

At Bento Quirino, near Riberão Prêto, the Mogiana made connection with the São Paulo e Minas Railway, which was orig-

A relic of the Mogiana Railway was located at Usina São José sugar mill at Campos in October 1976. This metre gauge Sharp Stewart 4-4-0 (3790/1892) was no. 5 in the sugar mill's roster.

inally a British concern of 600 mm gauge. By 1946 it had been converted to metre gauge and passed into Brazilian ownership, but it still remained an independent concern until absorbed into FEPASA, along with the Mogiana and Sorocabana systems.

The Sorocabana Railway

The Sorocabana started out in 1875, as coincidentally did the Mogiana, and grew into the largest system in the state of São Paulo. From Julio Prestes terminus in São Paulo the main line extends to Presidente Epitacio (843 km), on the Paraná river, paralleling to the south the broad gauge Paulista line to Panorama. There is a branch to Bauru, where connection, although not physical, is made with the Paulista, and of more importance, with the metre gauge Nordeste Railway, which alone of the railways pushing out through the state of São Paulo crosses the Paraná river into the state of Matto Grosso and extends in all 1,353km to Corumbá, where connection is made with the Bolivian line to Santa Cruz. There is also a branch from Campo Grande to Ponte Pora, opened in the 1950s, as was the Corumbá - Santa Cruz (Bolivia) Railway, which was Brazilian financed.

Reverting to the Sorocabana, there are branches touching Jundiaí and Campinas, the latter offering physical connection with the Mogiana Railway, although the Sorocabana had its own station in Campinas. The interior is linked with Santos over the metre gauge, a route serves to bring metre gauge traffic from a wide to and from Santos docks without transhipment. From Santos, the Sorocabana also works the Linha do Litoral to Junquiaí (179km), which was formerly the Southern São Paulo Railway, opened 1914-15. There are a number of other branches and from São Paulo to Ipero, beyond Sorocabana where the railway works are situated, the main line is double track. Soon afterwards comes the junction of the main line and the southern trunk route to Itararé (406km from São Paulo), where a connection is made with the Paraná - Santa Catarina Railway to Curitiba, a further 436km.

These distances have been shortened in recent years by means of a cut-off line avoiding Itararé.

By courtesy of the shedmaster at Santos, I was able to inspect the Sorocabana stock list for 1950, and this included some early Baldwin 4-4-0s, a batch of 0-8-0Ts from Henschel in 1936, Baldwin 2-8-0s, and a subsequent batch of this wheel arrangement, stated to have been 'built in Brazil'. There were 2-6-6-2 Mallets from Henschel, Baldwin, and Alco between 1910 and 1916 and these were similar to those of the Mogiana. In the 1920s 2-8-2s, 4-6-0s and 4-6-2s were all supplied by American and European builders, and 4-8-2s came from Baldwin and Alco in 1927-27 (these were marked 'sold' in the 1950 stock list I perused). In 1929 five 4-10-2s came from Alco, followed by others from both Alco and Henschel in 1935-39 and a final batch from Alco in 1940, a total of twenty-two locomotives of this wheel arrangement. By 1967, when I was in Brazil, all that remained in service were some 2-8-2s and some Baldwin 4-6-2s, behind one of which I had my only steam hauled main line passenger run, from Jundiaí to Piracicaba.

The sugar factory at this latter town once had an 0-4-0+0-4-0 Garratt built by St. Leonard of Liège, Belgium, but unfortunately I was unaware of this at the time, when my object was to visit the Piracicaba tramway system, consisting of only four cars working three routes! The trams had long since gone when I returned ten years later, and so had the Garratt, only a Baldwin 2-6-2ST remaining in the now derelict factory. A Baldwin built 2-4-2ST of 1893 from this factory is preserved in a school playground at nearby Monte Alegre, and another similar machine from the Santa Barbara Sugar Factory is on show at the works of Dedini SA in Piracicaba. This type of preservation is quite common in Brazil, and two further metre gauge locomotives, one ex-Paulista and one, a Beyer Peacock, ex-Mogiana Railway, can be found in Campinas.

Electrification of the Sorocabana main line commenced in

Sorocabana Railway metre gauge 4-6-2 no. 333 was a Baldwin product of the 1920s, works no. 38700, photographed by the author, taking water at Elias Fausto on 7th April 1967.

1944, at 3,000V dc and was gradually extended along the main line to Botucatu (269km). Forty-six 1-Co+Co-1 locomotives came from General Electric, USA, and these were still in use in 1980. The intensive suburban services are handled mostly by Japanese and Brazilian built multiple units, and the original electric locomotives were supplemented by thirty Bo-Bos built at the Campinas works of General Electric of Brazil in 1968. Electrification now extends to Assis (554km). Just beyond Botucatu is Paulo Souza, where the Votorantim Railway served a cement works. This was a 14km metre gauge line, electrified in 1928 at 600V dc, and has used tramway type material for passenger workings. It was still operating in the mid 1970s.

Before turning our attention to railways south of São Paulo two preservation projects are worthy of mention. At Mairiporã, reached by bus from the station of Franco da Rocha, near Perus on the Santos - Jundiaí line is the Fundação Mairiporã de Ensino, (a school), the owner of which is a railway enthusiast and has preserved in a purpose built depot in the grounds a quantity of metre gauge rolling stock and locomotives, including Beyer Peacock 4-6-0 no. 18 (built 1937) and a Kitson 2-6-0 no. 4 (built 1881) from the nearby Bragança Railway, and Sorocabana Railway 2-6-2T no. 4 (Baldwin 1906). A short length of track allows steaming on special occasions, one of which is the 15th October, annually. Another Bragança Railway Kitson 2-6-0 is also preserved in the nearby town of Atibaia.

A more ambitious project by the Brazilian Railway Preservation Society (ABPF) is the Viação Férrea Campinas - Jaguariúna, a section of metre gauge line formerly part of the Mogiana Railway route from Campinas to Mogi Mirim. This line has been diverted to serve a new steel-making plant and the 24km between Anhumas (only 10km from central Campinas) and Jaguariúna are available. At one time it was hoped to extend a further 3km towards the city but nothing further has been heard of this. Much preserved material is stored, and in the process of restoration at the latter station, the majority ex-VFCO and other 4-6-0s, 2-8-0s, 4-6-2s and 2-8-2s, American built. There are two British exhibits, a North British built 0-6-0T of 1946 ex-Leopoldina Railway and a Sharp Stewart 0-6-0ST of 1867, from the São Paulo Railway, this latter loco being broad gauge, of course. Locomotives reported as being active since preservation include two 4-6-0s and two 2-8-0s.

To travel southwards from São Paulo to Curitiba by rail a great swing inland is needed and although a recently opened cut off between Itapeva and Ponta Grossa has shortened by 90km the original distance of 842km, it is still a journey made much more directly by road. Bus travel in Brazil is highly organised and opposite the Sorocabana terminal at São Paulo the bus station offers facilities such as hairdressers, a shopping centre and restaurants, in addition to booking offices for sometimes very long distance coach services, often of several days duration, to destinations such as Brasilia, Montevideo (Uruguay) and Asunción (Paraguay).

A 1962 model Budd diesel railcar of the Rêde de Viação Paraná - Santa Catarina passing over a bridge near Curitiba on the line to Paranagua running a tourist service in October 1993.
Photo: Chris Skow,
Trains Unlimited, Tours.

Rêde de Viação Paraná - Santa Catarina

The Rêde de Viação Paraná - Santa Catarina had 3,054km of metre gauge track serving the area around Curitiba. A particularly scenic section links Curitiba with the coast at Paranaguá (111km). Construction of this line was started in 1883, work being carried out by a French financed company formed in 1875 under the title of Compagnie de Chemins de Fer Brasilien. Other lines in the region were constructed by small local companies, most of which later came under the control of the São Paulo - Rio Grande Company, formed in 1910 and responsible for the line from Itararé to Marcelino Ramos, where the Rio Grande do Sul system is reached. The RVPSC has been in the hands of the Federal Government since 1930, but the original route to the south has been overshadowed by a new line through Mafra and Lajes to

Porto Alegre, which was opened in 1969. This is part of a planned 'southern trunk route' linking Brasilia with the south of the country and the infrastructure allows for conversion to broad gauge at a later date if required.

Other sections of the Paraná - Santa Catarina system include a line roughly along the border of these two states, from the coast at São Francisco do Sul through Mafra to Porto União da Vitória, on the 'old' main line southwards through Marcelino Ramos. There is also a line inland from Ponta Grossa to Ourinhos, on the Sorocabana line to Presidente Epitacio. From Ourinhos another line extends back into Paraná state and this splits at Apucarana into two routes, the more southerly one of which reached Ponta Grossa in 1976 while the other heads towards the Paraná river where a short line is shown on maps as linking Guaira with Porto Mendes, parallel with the river and not so very far from the Iguassú Falls, where Paraguay, Argentina, and Brazil meet. Ultimate prolongation of this line into Paraguay is projected, where it will link up with the standard gauge Asunción - Encarnación line at San Salvador. The addition of a third rail on to Asunción would make the Paraguayan capital accessible by metre gauge and of course divert to Brazil some of the traffic now handled via Argentina.

Very little information is available on the steam stock of the Paraná - Santa Catarina system, although they did have some of the French 2-8-4s supplied in 1954. Sixty-six of these were built, along with 24 of the 4-8-4s which were described in the section on the Vitória a Minas Railway. There were also some American 4-8-2s of 1945, various series of 2-8-2s, and some 2-6-6-2 Mallets built in 1945-46. In 1964 it was stated that ninety-eight remained in service, and a visitor in 1970 noted a few 2-8-2s, a 4-8-2, and some Baldwin 4-6-0s of 1910 at Ponta Grossa, where a Baldwin 2-6-0 of 1891 was shed pilot, while at Curitiba was a La Meuse 0-6-0T of 1905 and several other steam locomotives in store. The same visitor travelled on the Paranaguá - Curitiba Budd railcar set and stated that this service is geared to tourism, the fare including free Brazilian champagne! He noted evidence of former electric installations on the most steeply graded section, but although electric traction was still employed in 1968, this had fallen into disuse by 1970 and there was no sign of the ten 1,072 hp Bo-Bo mixed traffic locomotives supplied by English Electric in 1950 for 3,000V dc operation. The whole section is now diesel worked and no doubt the electrics were transferred elsewhere in Brazil.

Travelling southward (by road) along the coast from Curitiba via São Francisco do Sul, through the state of Santa Catarina, one reaches the port of Itajaí, where a metre gauge line formerly extended inland via the German-settled city of Blumenau to Trombudo, a distance of 165km. Until closure about 1970-71, this railway was steam operated with oil burning 4-6-2s of 1925, aided by a 2-8-2 of 1952 and a pair of 4-6-0s built in 1940 and 1948, all Baldwins. There were two railcars, and passenger services were operated, while the port authority at Itakaí also had two diesel shunters.

EF Dona Teresa Cristina

Continuing southwards along the coast another isolated railway is encountered, and happily this is still in existence, although not nearly as active as it used to be. Now a division of the RFFSA, it was formerly the EF Dona Teresa Cristina, linking various coal mines with the port of Imbituba, and en route the Capivari power

station, via the town of Tubarão. There was a passenger service between Tubarão and Criciúma until about 1969, worked by Baldwin 4-6-2s built in 1925, and the extent of the system, including branches and before closure of the Laura Müller line was 242 km. Steam traction survived into the 1990s, and included three Baldwin 2-6-6-0 Mallets of 1950 (two of which are reported as having been preserved elsewhere), though these were inactive towards the end of steam traction. The mainstay of the railway was some fifteen 2-10-4s built by Alco and Baldwin in 1940 and 1947. They were joined in the early 1980s by a batch of ex-Argentinian 2-10-2s and on a visit in late 1981 two of these had been placed in service, with a third being reconditioned in the works at Tubarão. At Capivari power station there were a pair of Jung 2-8-2s, built in 1954. Imbituba docks also had steam locomotives, which lay rusting away for many years when diesels arrived, and included a Manning Wardle 0-6-0T of 1916 and a Henschel 2-4-4T of 1912. Tubarão was on the itinerary of every railfan tour of South America in the 1980s and has been well documented since, but it was unknown to me when I first visited Brazil in 1967. I understand that nowadays steam operation and coal exports have ceased, the only traffic being diesel hauled to the power station.

The Railways of Rio Grande do Sul

We are now on the border of the state of Rio Grande do Sul, where fairly recent railway construction has very considerably shortened the journey between the rest of the country and Porto Alegre, though no doubt nowadays for freight only! The 'old' main line through Marcelino Ramos remains but the new 'southern trunk route' through Lajes was opened in 1970. The Viação Ferréa Rio Grande do Sul operated 3,649km of metre gauge when incorporated into the RFFSA, and had been formed in 1920 by the Federal Government. It had several constituents, the earliest being the English financed line from Porto Alegre, opened as far as São Leopoldo in April 1874 and later extended to Novo Hamburgo.

About the same time a more ambitious line was planned by the Brazil Great Southern Railway from Porto Alegre to Uruguaiana on the river Uruguay, but this proceeded very slowly and was not completed until 1907. Before this, in 1897, a short isolated line had been built parallel with the river linking Uruguaiana with Barra do Quarai, across the river from Cuareim, which had been reached by the north Western of Uruguay Railway (of standard gauge) in 1887. From the port of Rio Grande a line was built inland to Bagé, and by the time this was completed in 1884 it was under the control of a French company, la Compagnie Imperiale des Chemins de fer de Rio Grande do Sul. This line extended in 1900 to Cacequi, where it connected with the railway from Porto Alegre. Another French company in this area was the Sud-Ouest Bresilien, the first sector of which was opened in 1898. This railway reached the border of Santa Catarina state at Marcelo Ramos in 1910, thus establishing a through rail connection between the most southerly state of Brazil and São Paulo. About the turn of the century these small companies were grouped into French/Belgian financed concern entitled the Compagnie Auxilière des Chemins de fer de Bresil, which built further sections of line and completed those already under construction, forming the basis of the present day Rio Grande do Sul system. There are links with Uruguay at Rio Branco, Rivera and Barra do Quarai, although of course through working is prevented by the difference in gauge.

On the EF Doña Teresa Cristina in November 1981, American built metre gauge 2-10-4 no. 304 hauls a loaded coal train headed for Tuberão.

Czechoslovakian built EFDTC 2-10-2 no. 401 was obtained second hand from the Argentinian FC General Belgrano in 1981 and is seen back in service in November of that year. Ten such locomotives were obtained in order to be overhauled and placed back in traffic, plus a number of others for spare parts. No. 401 was built by Škoda in 1949, works number 1977.

The steam stock list of the Rio Grande do Sul system shows early 4-4-0s from Baldwin and Borsig (1890-1908), 2-6-0s from the same builders and others (1882-1908), 2-8-0s again from Baldwin and Borsig (1893-1909), followed by 4-6-0s in 1910-11 and 2-8-2s from 1921, again from both American and German builders. The first Mallets, all 2-6-6-2s, came from Alco and Henschel in 1910-11, with others in 1924, while Garratts were represented by ten 4-6-2+2-6-4s from Henschel in 1931. A large number of 4-8-2s were supplied from Germany in 1937 and 4-8-4s from Alco in 1945, while the only 4-6-2s noted are four from Alco in 1920.

Finally, from Palamares do Sul, near Porto Alegre, an isolated line, presumed to be of metre gauge, formerly extended northwards through Osorio (53km) to Maquine. This was operated by the VFRGS but I have no further information on it. To illustrate

the difficulty of obtaining accurate information on railways in Brazil, this line appears in 'World Railways' 1954-55, and on Guía Levi maps for 1966-67, although without any timetable, in spite of its description elsewhere as a 'tourist railway'. There is no sign of it, however, on the large scale map of the state, dated 1966, which details all other railways, even those in neighbouring Uruguay and Argentina!

The RFFSA and Recent Developments

Although the RFFSA had existed since 1957, ten years later each railway operated very much as it had always done, with rolling stock in different liveries, motive power numbered in the original series, etc. By the 1970s this individuality had gone, and great strides had been made towards a national integrated network, however, from 1986 the Federal government reduced the subsidies for long-distance passenger trains. Consequently the Federal Railways were forced to cut more and more services back from daily to 1-3 times a week, and to 'suspend' some services completely. On the RFFSA in 1989 only 5 million passengers were carried, as against 60 million in 1956, and during 1989 some 3,315 route kilometres lost their passenger service. The 1990s saw some reintroduction of services, primarily with an eye to their potential for tourism, but much of the equipment was old, and the permanent way suffering from a backlog of maintenance. By 1996 only a few RFFSA long-distance services remained, all covering distances below 500km, plus some short distance workings. Little has changed since privatisation.

Mention was made almost at the beginning of this chapter of the CBTU, set up to take over the mostly electrified suburban services in the larger cities. As it was an RFFSA subsidiary privatisation led to responsibility for such services passing to other organisations, backed by the States in which they were situated. In São Paulo State this has involved setting up the CPTM (Companhia Paulista Trens Metropolitanos), created in July 1993 and combining ex CBTU and FEPASA suburban services, operation of which was to be more closely integrated with the city metro system. There are basically two systems in the São Paulo area, the 'East' system taken over from CBTU and comprising the old SJ broad gauge between Paranapicicaba and Jundiai (192km), and Roosevelt to Estudiantes (50km), with a 32km loop line. The 'West' system, taken over from FEPASA in February 1996 comprises metre gauge routes from Julie Prestes (São Paulo), totalling some 78km or so. I understand that there have been some recent extensions to these ex Sorocabana Railway services. All are e.m.u. operated and will be unaffected by the proposals to de-electrify longer distance ex-FEPASA routes in the area. On 1st January 1998 the State of São Paulo sold FEPASA to the Federal Government, this sale being a method of reducing debts owing. RFFSA briefly took over operation but privatisation should not have taken place.

Rio de Janeiro area suburban services, latterly worked by CBTU, are now under the control of Flumitrens. Most are operated over the long-electrified ex-Central Railway tracks totalling 228 km, while there are also around 152 km of more recent electrification on metre gauge ex-Leopoldina routes.

Two other cities, almost at opposite ends of the country, have acquired electrified suburban lines. At Porto Alegre TRENSURB operate 27.5km of broad gauge and at Recife a broad gauge system extends 20km over former metre gauge routes (or maybe alongside them as I presume the metre gauge still reaches the city). The last information I have is of the Recife system being

CBTU operated, but this was never so for the Porto Alegre operation. Both are e.m.u. operated.

On the freight side some quite massive projects are being pursued. One such is the privately financed Ferronorte line, broad gauge 1,038km between Cuiaba and Santa Fe do Sul. The first section, between Aperecido do Tabuado and Inocencia (110km), was opened in 1998 and onwards to Alto Taquari the following year, making a total of 410 km opened so far. To connect with ex-FEPASA (now 'Ferroban') tracks at Santa Fe a bridge over the Parana river has been built and is used by grain trains made up of of 90 120-ton capacity wagons hauled by pairs of Dash 9 diesels. A feasibility study is under way to investigate using the new line as the first stage of a railway reaching to Porto Velho and construction of 800km to Rondonópolis is believed to be awaiting finances at the time of writing. This is probably the biggest railway construction undertaking in the world as at the turn of the Millennium.

Another such project is the Ferroeste (now Ferropar and owned by a Brazilian/South African consortium). This was commenced in 1992 and completed by 1996 over the 248km between Guarapuava and Cascavel, the object of this metre gauge extension being the transport of grain to the port of Paranagua. Projects also exist to extend a further 171km towards the Paraguayan border at Guaira, the railway being financed by the state of Paraná. This opens up the possibility of a link up with the line from Apucarena, mentioned earlier when describing other recently constructed lines in this area, or it could of course replace the other extension. Although of metre gauge, this line is constructed to allow conversion to broad gauge later if required. Another project linked partly to this work is the construction of a totally new 97km line linking Paranagua to Curitiba, as the existing line is already working up to capacity due to port expansion.

One can conclude that while railways in Brazil have a future as bulk carriers over specific routes, mainly linking the interior with the ports, there is less hope for the north-south links, and virtually none at all for long-distance passenger traffic.

Brazil has a locomotive and rolling stock building industry which has probably expanded beyond future domestic needs. General Electric of Brazil have supplied large numbers of diesels, mostly standard American designs, and have exported some of these to other South American countries. Rolling stock builders Mafersa and Cobrasma, both of São Paulo, have built 3-car multiple unit sets for Rio and São Paulo suburban work and stainless steel passenger stock. Their future probably is with metros and light rail, both of which modes are likely to expand in South America.

CHILE

Chile can claim the distinction of being one of the most curiously shaped nations in the world. This long, narrow land extends for 4,236km along the Pacific coast of South America, while at no point is the inland frontier more than 400km from the sea and indeed the average is more like 200km. The length of Chile is roughly equivalent to a line extending from Copenhagen to Lagos! Naturally enough, for many years coastal navigation was the answer to Chile's transportation problems, and indeed south of Puerto Montt for some 1,800km it still largely is, as the narrow land strip is mostly impassable with deep fjords, islets and mountain masses.

The north of Chile is rich in minerals, and the first railway in the country (sometimes incorrectly claimed to be the first in South America) was built to convey copper and silver to the coast. Commenced in 1850, the section from the port of Caldera to Copiapó (81km) was opened on 25th December 1851 and from there branches extended into the mountains, some reaching points in excess of 1,000m above sea level. The total extent of the system was 242km of standard gauge single track, subsequently converted to metre gauge. The first locomotives (one of which is depicted on a Chilean postage stamp issued in 1954 to mark the centenary of "the first railway in South America") were 4-4-0s built by William Norris of Philadelphia, and one is preserved at Copiapó. The man responsible for getting this railway built was William Wheelwright, born 1798 in Newburyport, Massachusetts, and a former US consul in Guayaquil, Ecuador. He had been concerned with organising coastal

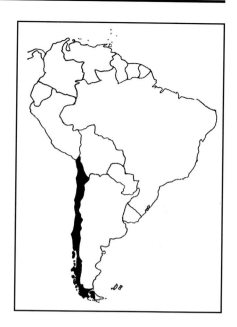

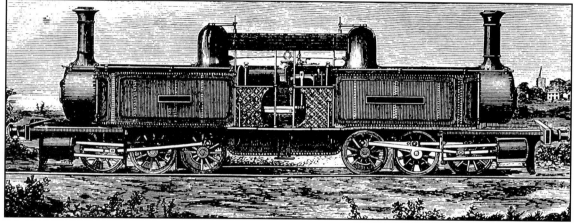

Fairlie locomotives in South America were used more on the railways of the nitrate mining region of northern Chile than in other areas. "Tarapaca" was an 0-6-0+0-6-0T of the standard gauge Iquique Railway, built by the Fairlie Engine & Steam Carriage Co. in 1870.

shipping, and although his railway, built by American contractors, was highly successful, he had much greater ambition for it than the purely local transportation of minerals to the coast. It formed the basis of his proposals for the first transandean rail link, described in detail in his paper "A proposed railway route across the Andes from Caldera to Rosario" which was read to the Royal Geographical Society in London on 23 June 1860. The route would have linked the Atlantic and Pacific oceans, and crossed the Andes by the San Francisco pass at a height of some 4,800m. However, finance was not forthcoming and Wheelwright, along with his contractors, Alan and Alexander Campbell, became less successfully involved in the Valparaíso to Santiago Railway.

Valparaíso is the port for the Chilean capital of Santiago, only 88km distant as the crow flies but double this distance through the mountains by rail. Work started on this 1,676m (5ft 6in) line in October 1852 but by the end of 1855 only 8½km to Viña del Mar had been completed. The line crept on Limache (43km) in 1856 and Quillota, another 13km, in 1857, but here funds ran out and work stopped. It later continued but only spasmodically until in 1861 there appeared on the scene a flamboyant character who was

later to make his name famous in Peru. Henry Meiggs was born in New York State in 1811, and left the USA after some shady deals in San Francisco. He had arrived in Chile in 1855 and when he took over the Valparaíso to Santiago Railway things really began to move. He had contracted to build the line in three years for a fixed sum, with a bonus for every month gained, and in fact the railway was completed in two years and three days, raking in a handsome profit. Prior to this Meiggs had been engaged on the Ferrocarril del Sur, a company formed in 1855 to build a line southwards from Santiago. The first section was opened in 1858 by President Montt (who is commemorated today in the name of the town which is the southern terminus of the railway) and extended to San Bernardo. The railway reached Curicó on 25th December 1868, and in 1873 the Government acquired all the stock of the company. Rails were pushed on southwards through Chillán and the important branch line serving Concepción and Talcahuano was opened on 10th June 1879. Temuco became part of the system in 1893 and the southern terminus of Puerto Montt was finally reached in 1913.

Thus the line from Valparaíso and Santiago southwards

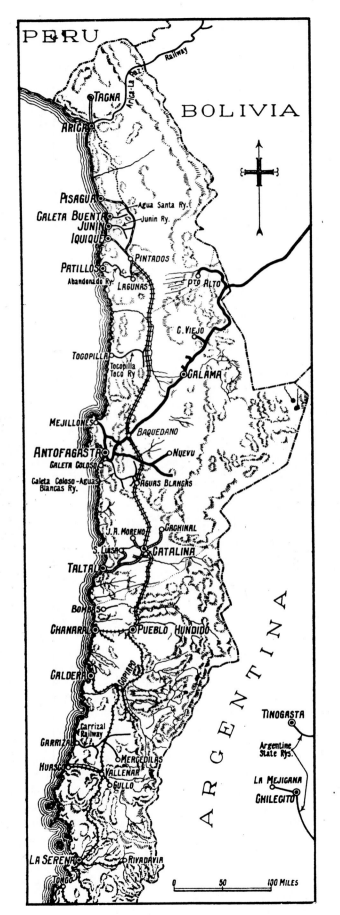

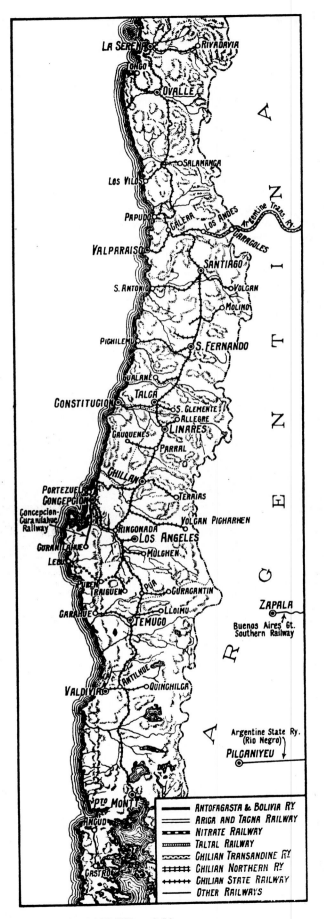

Map of the Railways of Chile, showing approximately 6,000 Miles of Line.

▬▬▬	Antofagasta & Bolivia Ry
═══	Ariga and Tagna Railway
▪▪▪	Nitrate Railway
▒▒▒	Taltal Railway
∿∿∿	Chilian Transandine Ry
┼┼┼	Chilian Northern Ry
╈╈╈	Chilian State Railway
───	Other Railways

formed the basis of the present day broad gauge system, serving the well-populated area known as the Chilean heartland, south of the capital. Chile is one of the few South American countries to have realised early the advantages of a nationally planned railway system and the State Railways (EFE - Empresa de los Ferrocarriles del Estado) were founded in 1884, the Balmaceda plan formulating future developments from 1888. However, despite this foresight, mining companies in the north built to different gauges, and this caused inconvenience when their lines were gradually taken over by the state between 1884 and 1913, and unified into the metre gauge northern system, the Red Norte.

The Broad Gauge System of Southern Chile

We will begin by examining the broad gauge artery extending from Valparaíso via Santiago to Puerto Montt, a distance of 1,265km. There is double track between Valparaíso and Limache

(43km) and between Santiago and San Fernando (134km). Valparaíso - Santiago was electrified at 3,000V dc as early as 1924, using American equipment, and since 1963 electrification has been pushing southwards down the main line, Concepción and Talcahuano being reached in 1973, and Temuco in the mid-1980s. Further progress has been hampered by political upheavals, but it was the intention ultimately to complete electrification to Puerto Montt. An Italian consortium supplied 34 3,600hp Co-Co and 22 2,400hp Bo-Bo locomotives for main line work. Three and four car train sets were supplied from Italy and Germany for suburban work, and English Electric supplied twenty sets of power equipment for two car sets in 1970. Six fully air conditioned long distance four car trains came from Japan.

There were two terminal stations in Santiago; Mapocho was built to serve Valparaíso and Alameda (which nowadays tends to be called Estación Central) was the station for the south. At San

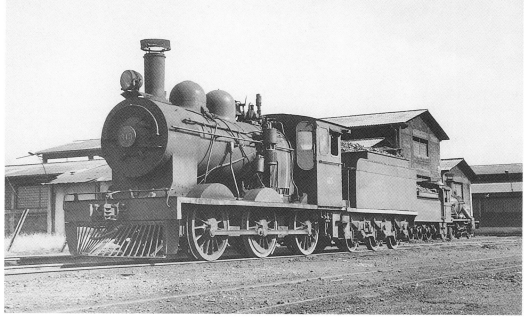

A class 47 inside cylinder 0-6-0 of very British appearance on shed at Osorno on 31st December 1968. No. 415, originally named 'I.A. Alamaza', was built by Borsig in 1905 during that company's 'British period' of styling, works no. 5945.

For general freight and passenger work there were 114 2-6-0s of class 57, many of them built in Chile, others supplied by North British and Henschel. No. 620 was built by the Compañía de Maestranzas y Galvanizaciones in 1913 and has survived in the Temuco roundhouse. She was photographed by the author working on the Lonquimay branch.

In Santiago Estación Central is EFE class 90 no. 903 built by Krupp in 1935, works no. 1465. This is now the last survivor of fifteen such 2-8-2s supplied for Chile's broad gauge southern system.
Photo: Paul Catchpole.

Bernardo, 16km from Santiago, was the works for steam locomotives. The land for this was bought in 1914 and the works was in service by 1920. When it opened the broad gauge steam fleet comprised 579 locomotives of 63 classes, with only 11 classes having more than 10 members. By 1942 there were 522 of 27 types and in 1958 509 of 28 types. By 1979 this had been reduced to 196 of 10 types and the last steam in regular use expired in 1983. The works handled steam repair and assembly of some locomotives imported in kit form. It also dealt with metre gauge steam, "W" class 2-8-2s from the northern network being loaded onto broad gauge well wagons at La Calera after some 500km of travel, either under their own steam or hauled, from the far north. Locomotives repaired here could be identified by the letters MSB (Maestranza San Bernardo) added to the brass front number plates. In latter years diesel locomotives were repaired, and some

work done on the electric fleet, but the workshop had been devoted to steam and declined with the reduction of this mode of traction. A diesel workshop was added in the late 1950s, but the works were rather moribund when I last visited them in 1981 and the "preserved" locomotives which had been exhibited there were in the process of being moved to the "Railway Museum Park" in the Quinta Normal, a leisure park situated quite near to Alameda station, Santiago. Most of the exhibits are broad gauge, but a metre gauge Kitson Meyer from the Transandine line is included. Sadly, the works closed in 1995, but it was hoped that some of the historic buildings could be incorporated into a new commercial/industrial development on the site.

Travelling southwards, the next stop of interest is Rancagua (82km) where connection was formerly made with the 74km railway of 760mm gauge extending via the mining town of Sewell to

5'6" gauge class 80 no. 822 at Concepción. Most of these impressive 4-8-2s were supplied by Baldwin from 1937 onwards, no. 822 dating from 1940, works no. 62424. Nos. 837-839 were delivered in 1947 in kit form and assembled at San Bernardo works and nos. 840-869 were built by Mitsubishi. The 52 sq. ft. grate was hand fired! They were among the last steam locos at work in Chile and several have been preserved.

El Teniente copper mine, reaching an altitude of 2,113m. This line was built in 1911 and before nationalisation (of the copper mine) was the property of the American Braden Mining Corporation. In 1970 it had 14 diesel-electric locomotives, 13 petrol railcars and 6 steam in reserve, and passenger services were worked principally for the staff. The railway closed about 1979, but two of the "Shay" steam locomotives are preserved. Rancagua was also the junction for a 34km branch to Coltauco, and soon afterwards comes Pelequen and then San Fernando (134km), the latter being the junction for a branch to the coast at Pichilemu. It should be noted that not all branches are being mentioned in the text, and most have been closed, or at least had passenger services withdrawn, during the last two decades.

At Curicó was the first metre gauge branch, an 84km line to Licantén, latterly diesel operated as was another metre gauge branch from Talca to the coast at Constitución (88km). After Chillán (397km), a line diverges to serve Concepción via Tomé, but this route is used by local trains, the main line service continuing southwards to San Rosendo (499km) and then following the course of the Bío Bío river to Concepción, a further 71km, before finally terminating at the Talcahuano naval base 15km beyond the city. In 1968 at the time of my first visit to Chile, Chillán was the first steam depot encountered travelling southwards from Santiago, and San Rosendo, an almost complete roundhouse, was the largest steam depot in the country. There was also a steam depot at Concepción, which is Chile's third largest city, but by 1981 there was little steam activity in the area.

From Concepción, there is a railway to Curanilahue (91km) via Lota, which crosses the Bío Bío river on the longest railway bridge in Chile. This bridge, opened in 1889, is claimed to be exactly 1,889m long, although other lengths have been quoted and one version claims opened 1887 and 1,887m long! The line serves a coal producing area and was built by the Arauco Coal & Railway Company, a British concern but by no means the largest of the regional coal companies. Much of the coal passed through Coronel, which prior to the opening of the Panama canal, was one of the most important ports on the South American seaboard, and off which a naval engagement between British and German warships was fought on 1st November 1914. In 1898, the company had a concession to supply coal to the State Railway and no doubt much of this crossed the Bío Bío bridge, construction of which had been an entirely British enterprise and cost £75,000. It is a tribute to those Victorian engineers that the bridge was undamaged by the earthquake of 1960 (one of the most violent tremors recorded in the world) which closed for a few weeks the road bridge, constructed in 1943! The railway's early locomotives were supplied from Britain, Fowler, Stephenson and Manning Wardle, while coaches came from the Lancaster Carriage &

On the metre gauge branch from Talca to Constitución Dt-4001 skirts the north bank of the Maule river with a special train for railfans in November 1993. This Bo-Bo diesel built by General Electric in 1945 was the first diesel loco on the national railway system in Chile. Photo: Ian Thomson.

Wagon Company. The company remained British until in 1919/20 control passed to the rival Compañia Carbonífera e Industrial de Lota, described in "World Railways" as a "coalmining company which also manufactures crockery and chinaware".

It is the coal obtained in this region which was a decisive factor in the retention of steam power in the area into the 1980s. From Curanilahue it is only about 30km by road to Lebu, terminus of a railway which started life as the British owned Chilean Eastern Central Railway, and then passed through various hands, including those of the Cía Carbonífera e Industrial de Lota, before being acquired by the State Railways in 1928. The line extended 142km to Los Sauces, from where the main line was reached either northwards via Renaico or southwards via Púa. Near Los Sauces was formerly the 600mm gauge branch linking Saboya with Capitán Pastene (35km). This was steam worked with three small tank engines, and due to lack of freight traffic causing mixed train cancellations my wife and I were marooned in 1968 in the small village at the far end of the line from 14:00h until the following morning at 05:00h. We then had some difficulty in finding our way along an unlit footpath to the station, where the train stood in total darkness until near departure time. When the crew arrived they replaced the carriage light bulbs, removed the previous evening to be placed under lock and key overnight! Sadly, this

Making its way past the coaling stage at San Rosendo on 26th December 1968, broad gauge Co-Co diesel no. D16011 is in charge of a passenger service made up of varied bogie stock.

Today's motive power for shunting and light freight work on the Red Sur is represented by Fepasa D-6114, seen at Temuco roundhouse in April 1996. The roundhouse is now a national monument, retained complete with 16 steam locos and a rake of coaches.
Photo: Paul Catchpole.

delightful line closed soon afterwards.

Púa is also the junction for a branch to Curacautín and Lonquimay, which is part of a proposed transandean route into Argentina, where it was intended to link up with the Roca Railway at Zapala, offering by far the best transcontinental route of all, and the most practicable one of unified gauge throughout. But to pierce the Andes needed what would be the longest tunnel in South America, 4,526m, and this project has not proceeded further. This steeply graded and scenic branch still offered, in 1982, the sight of steam hauled passenger/mixed trains working hard and despite the lack of paved roads in the area a number of fine action photographs could be obtained by those who had a car available. Trains worked to and from Victoria, and were usually hauled by 2-6-0s, although a 2-8-2 was also noted. More recently,

a few steam tourist trains have used the line.

Temuco

Back on the main line again, the next place of importance is Temuco, a city of some 225,000 inhabitants, and capital of the Cautín province. It is in this region that the remaining Araucanian indians live, and their handicrafts can be purchased on Temuco station. There was a branch line to Carahue (56km) and the branches from Freire to Toltén and Cunco were worked from Temuco, which had a large steam locomotive depot. In 1982 it still had a large allocation, but the locomotives there saw little use. Temuco is 690km from Santiago, and the main line continues southwards to Antilhue, which is the junction for a short branch down to the coast at Valdivia, capital of the province and a city of some 140,000 inhabitants. The small steam depot still saw some activity in early 1982. Further south along the main line, Los Lagos was formerly the junction for a metre gauge line to Riñihue. At Osorno there was another steam depot, and the final section is to Puerto Montt on the coast, 1,079km from Santiago. The nightly sleeping car express "flecha nocturna" ("night arrow") covers this distance in 19 hours, and was latterly the only through train over the whole distance. When I visited Chile in 1968 a public train timetable was published regularly, and the frequency of services in the south was very commendable. Perhaps not surprisingly in view of the subsequent unsettled political situation rail services declined, and in 1981 no timetable was available, many branches had closed or had their passenger services withdrawn and there appeared to be very little traffic on the main line south to Temuco, with many trains running late, and locomotives and stock in a very decrepit condition. Efforts have been made to improve the situation, but road competition is fierce on the parallel Pan American Highway, which is the subject of considerable investment, no doubt to the further detriment of the railway.

Although almost one-third of Chile lies to the south of Puerto Montt, further progress is only possible by sea or air, the land being covered by impenetrable forest and indented with deep waterways for almost 1,060km to Punta Arenas. A concession was granted in the early 1920s for a metre gauge line beyond Puerto Montt to Puerto Toledo (40km) and Río Frío, a further 55km, but the railway was never built. Beyond this point the few small settlements there can be reached by road only from Argentina.

A little to the south of Puerto Montt is the island of Chiloé, a pleasant day's outing and until the earthquake of 1960 the site of a 600mm gauge railway linking the island's two principal towns of Ancud and Castro (88km). There was formerly a line at Punta Arenas, known as the Loretto Mine Railway or the Magallanes Railway, which was 10½km long, of metre gauge, and served the coal mine, the local electricity company and a meat packing plant. In 1929 it had four locomotives, by Koppel and Baldwin. In 1946

this figure was unchanged but by 1960 it had been closed, as had another isolated line situated 290km north west of Punta Arenas, which had been built in 1893 to link the town of Natales with another meat freezing factory. This line was only 4.8km long and owned by the Sociedad Explotadora de Tierra de Fuego. Two German built 0-4-0WTs remain preserved at Punta Arenas. For those who travel to southern Chile, a highly recommended journey is the tourist trip through the lakes into Argentina at San Carlos de Bariloche, which is conveniently situated for a visit to the steam worked Esquel line (see chapter 1).

Broad Gauge Motive Power

As we must return to Santiago to describe the northern part of the country we will take a look en route at the steam motive power used on this route, a few examples of which were still to be seen in action in 1982. Some of the early locomotives supplied to the Chilean broad gauge were Hawthorn Leslie and Avonside 4-4-0s of 1866-76, but by the 1890s American 4-4-0s and 4-6-0s were arriving, followed by a large influx of British and German locomotives in 1906-13. These comprised 2-6-0s, 4-6-0s, 2-8-0s and a large batch of inside cylinder 0-6-0s of very British aspect, many of which remained in service almost until the end of steam. Later power includes the 70 class 2-8-2s built by the Montreal Locomotive Works in 1919, and Alco in 1921-25; the 80 class 4-8-2s built by Baldwin in 1929/37/40/47 and Mitsubishi of Japan in 1952-3. Class 90 2-8-2s came from Krupp and Esslingen in 1935, and amongst the largest locomotives used were ten 4-8-4s from Henschel 1935-6, used on main line expresses southwards from Santiago until electrification but then withdrawn and scrapped. Tank engines were always few in number, and one 0-6-0T was in use as shed pilot at Temuco in 1981. Other survivors included examples of classes 70 and 80 but the most numerous were the 2-6-0s. All locomotives were coal burners, and in very poor external condition.

Most of the diesel locomotives in service are standard American types, although 49 Brisonneau & Lotz (France) 825hp Bo-Bos were delivered in 1963/64. There are also a few

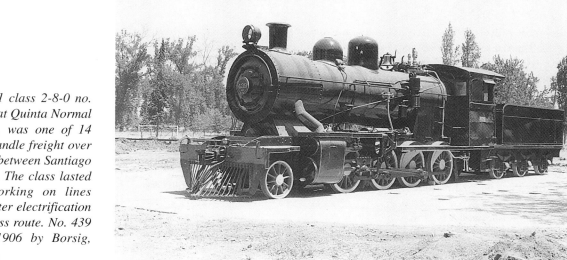

Broad gauge 51 class 2-8-0 no. 439, preserved at Quinta Normal Park, Santiago, was one of 14 locos built to handle freight over the Tabón pass between Santiago and Valparaiso. The class lasted until 1974, working on lines further south after electrification of the Tabón pass route. No. 439 was built in 1906 by Borsig, works no. 6042.

'Golden Snake' electric 2903 heads south near Ilay-Ilay with a two coach train of clerestory roof wooden-bodied stock in October 1992. These giant 2C-C2s were built by General Electric in 1949. Photo: Chris Skow, Trains Unlimited, Tours.

Ferrostaal forty seat railcars with MAN engines and matching trailers, but at the time of my visit most local services beyond the electrified area were worked by low-powered diesels hauling three or four ancient clerestory-roofed carriages.

An amusing story has recently come to light regarding a MAN three car diesel electric train set ordered by Chilean State Railways and built, but not shipped, from Germany at the outbreak of World War II. It remained in store in Germany until in mid-September 1944 it was placed on standard gauge bogies and moved to Switzerland for safe-keeping, where it was stored near Chiasso until the end of hostilities. Such regard for their customer's property at a time of national disaster reflects great credit on the builders; one wonders if they had been paid before delivery, and also if the set was duly delivered after the war, several years late!

Ferrocarril Militar de Puente Alto a El Volcán

Back at Santiago, a short bus trip to Puente Alto brings one to the site of the former 600mm gauge Ferrocarril Militar de Puente Alto a El Volcán, a distance of 60km. This railway was operated by the Army but with passenger services available to the public, who booked tickets at a window set in the wall of the barracks at Puente Alto and actually had to enter military premises to reach the platforms and board the train! Steam locomotives were in use until 1954, when diesels were obtained, and there were also five railcars to handle most of the passenger workings. The railway formerly offered connection with the metre gauge Llano de Maipú Railway, from Puente Alto to Providencia station, Santiago. This 22km line was known as the Ferrocarril a Pirque when built in 1893, and was the first part of a transandean scheme (like many others) which never materialised. It had been authorised in 1889 and was to have extended to San Carlos, near Mendoza, in Argentina. The railway was privately owned, and after electrification at 600V dc in 1925 Siemens had a financial interest in it. Closure took place about 1960. I rode on the military railway on Christmas Eve 1968, the railcar being packed with travellers who had apparently been into the mountains to acquire Christmas trees, large numbers of which were tied to the front of the vehicle, almost obscuring the driver's view ahead. The roof of this railcar was so low it was impossible to stand upright in it, and as military personnel generously gave their places to civilians one was treated to the amusing sight of these men doubled in peculiar postures far removed from those of the parade ground! I understand that this railway has been closed for some years now.

The Transandean Railway

We next come to Chile's first rail link with the Argentine, built across the Andes to afford direct rail connection between the capital cities of Santiago and Buenos Aires, through a region snowbound and often impassable by road. One would have thought that it offered great traffic potential, but due to the very difficult terrain and the necessity of using frequent rack sections it was built to the metre gauge, although the railways with which it connected at either end were of the same broad gauge. At the time of construction a broad gauge railway was not thought practicable, and would certainly have been of prohibitive cost if attempted. Although the longest section is in Argentina, the steepest grades are in Chile, and we will deal with the whole railway in this chapter. Work started on the Chilean section on 5 April

1889, two years after the commencement of work from Mendoza in Argentina. Boring of the 3,166m long Cumbre tunnel at an altitude of 3,191m commenced from both ends in 1889, but the tunnel was not completed until 1910. On the Argentine side, although the grades were less fierce, the railway had to negotiate a very difficult section where it was obliged to share a narrow gorge with the very erratic Mendoza river, liable to violent flooding at certain times of the year. Unusually, the Transandean railway used the three bar Abt system, instead of the more usual two bar rail, as originally small locomotives hauling relatively light loads were envisaged. Later, when extremely heavy machines were introduced, the two bar rack system would have been preferable, but by then it was too late to change.

All was going well until political unrest in both countries suspended operations for twelve years (1891-1903), bankrupting the original concessionaires, the Clark Bros, whose name the railway was to have borne (at least they had a station named after them). New capital was raised in Britain and America, and in 1906 the section from Los Andes to Juncal was in service, followed by a section on to Portillo in 1908. Early in 1910 the British firm of C H Walker & Co. completed the Cumbre tunnel and the railway was opened throughout on 5 April 1910. The rack sections were between Rio Blanco in Chile and Punta de Vacas in Argentina, there being six in Chile and seven in Argentina, totalling about 35km with grades of 1 in 12.5 and 1 in 16 respectively. When the line was rack worked, the steepest adhesion grade was 1 in 40. The length of the whole railway is 250km, of which only 76km are in Chile, the actual frontier being crossed in

Rio Blanco station on the Chilean Transandine, complete with 'the Gondola', a 1926-built General Motors 25 seat railcar equipped with a Cummins diesel engine, seen on 5th December 1993. Photo: Richard Pelham.

F.C. Transandino Chile metre gauge Kitson-Meyer 0-8-6-0T no. 3349 is exhibited at Quinta Normal Park Museum in Santiago. (Kitson 4664/1909). All the locos of this type originally had a rack engine driven by cylinders placed beside the smokebox, but these were removed from the Chilean examples. Sister loco 3348 is preserved at Los Andes (Kitson 4598/1908). Photo: Paul Catchpole.

the Cumbre tunnel. In Chile, the metre gauge tracks commence at Los Andes, reached by a 48km broad gauge branch off the main Santiago-Valparaíso line at Ilay-Ilay. Electrification commenced in 1927 and was completed in 1942, the original locomotives supplied being three 1,060hp rack-adhesion articulated 1-C-C-1 jackshaft drive machines from SLM and Brown Boveri of Switzerland. Two more modern machines came from Brown Boveri in 1960. Only the Chilean section is electrified, as although Argentina planned in 1955 to use 27,000V single phase current at the industrial frequency of 50 cycles, this was never actually put to the test.

Locomotives of the Transandean Railway

The steam locomotive history of both sections is of considerable interest. To take Chile first, the construction work started out with two Hawthorn Leslie 0-6-0Ts for the adhesion sections only, and these were joined in 1904 by a Lima Shay which was able to work over the rack section by adhesion alone, making it a great asset during construction but too slow to be of much use thereafter. The first rack and adhesion locomotives came from Borsig in 1905, a 2-6-4T and two 2-6-2Ts with Joy valve gear. It was soon realised that more powerful machines were needed and Kitson-Meyers, a type already in service in the north of Chile, were proposed. Two were built by Kitson at Leeds in 1907-8, with the 0-8-6-0T wheel arrangement; they were very complicated machines, heavy on maintenance and the track, but could handle 140 ton trains. A further Kitson was supplied in 1909, but prior to

this the German firm of Esslingen came up with a similar machine, but of 0-6-8-0T configuration and supplied another in 1911. The Kitsons were the more successful, but these articulated machines were expensive to maintain and it is not surprising that electrification was ultimately adopted. On the Argentine section the first locomotives were six adhesion only 2-6-2Ts from Dübs of Glasgow in 1887, and two slightly larger firm in 1901. The first rack and adhesion locomotives were 0-6-2Ts from Beyer Peacock between 1890 and 1899, followed by Kitson-Meyers identical to those in Chile, three of which were supplied in 1909, one in 1911, and another two in 1912. Further adhesion only power came when the Vulcan Foundry supplied three 2-8-4Ts in 1909, and in 1929 four Beyer Peacock Garratts of the 2-6-2+2-6-2 wheel arrangement came to the line, working on the adhesion section between Mendoza and Zanjón Amarillo (130km).

During construction, the Argentine section had been administered by the Argentine Great Western Railway, which was taken over by the Buenos Aires & Pacific Railway in 1907. The Chilean section was operated by the Chilean Transandine Railway Co until 1934, when day to day working passed to the State Railways, while the Argentine government purchased the section on its territory in 1939. Despite the fact that a single administration for the two sections was set up in 1923, international difficulties had reached a peak in 1932, when all traffic was suspended for much of the year. Soon afterwards, on 10 January 1934, nature took a hand and washed away a considerable portion of the Argentine section, marooning two of the Garratts at Zanjón

Argentina: General Belgrano 2-10-2 no. 1327, a Baldwin product of 1926, at the Tucuman workshops in July 1997.
Photo: Chris Skow, Trains Unlimited, Tours.

Bolivia: 2-8-4T no. 553 seen at Oruro is the second of a pair of tank locomotives built by Hunslet for the FCAB in 1912.
Photo: D. Trevor Rowe.

Brazil: The Usina Serra Grande still uses steam on feast days and other special occasions. The locomotives maintained in working order are former Great Western of Brazil 2-6-2T no. 7 (SLM 2805/1922), and 0-4-2T no. 1, Kerr Stuart (928/1907). Photo: Eddie Edmundson.

Brazil: 4-6-2 no. 50 deep in the tropical rain forest on the E.F. Madeira - Mamoré with a train from Porto Velho to San Antonio on 16th September 1988. Photo: Uwe Bergmann.

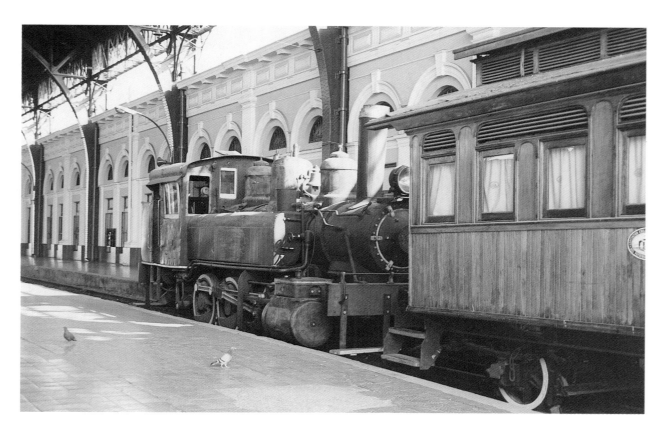

Chile: 5'6" gauge EFE type 56 0-6-0T no. 489 is now preserved, as seen here in Santiago Estación Central in April 1996. Although it is catalogued as Baldwin 31947 of 1907, it is thought that the loco was actually assembled in Chile from parts shipped out. Photo: Paul Catchpole.

Paraguay: Wood-burning 4-6-0 no. 237 of the F.C. Presidente Carlos Antonio Lopez on a Railway Travel & Photography Society special service at Aregua on 2nd December 1981. Photo: D. Trevor Rowe.

Peru: *Visitors to Machu Picchu will very likely arrive from Cuzco in a railcar built in 1966 by Ferrostaal of Germany. No. 216 of the Cuzco & Santa Ana Railway was seen northbound on 14th August 1997. Photo: Chris Skow, Trains Unlimited, Tours.*

Uruguay: *A train of timber arrives at Montevideo in October 1996 hauled by AFE Bo-Bo no. 824 built by Alsthom in 1965. Photo: Chris Skow, Trains Unlimited, Tours.*

Amarillo until the pressure of traffic brought about by World War II caused reconstruction to be pushed ahead and the line reopened in 1944. Since then traffic declined, although the introduction of containers helped for a while to solve in part the break of gauge problem. Though passenger workings have long been withdrawn, these were formerly handled by three car diesel electric sets supplied by Ganz Mavag of Budapest in 1955 and 1963. They incorporated English Electric traction equipment and operated by adhesion only, although they had rack braking equipment. Kitson Meyer 3348 still exists and, as previously mentioned, 3349 is on display in the Quinta Normal park at Santiago. It is possible that Esslingen 0-6-8-0T (note the wheel arrangement is reversed in the Esslingen examples) 3350 is still in store in a shed at Río Blanco.

We have now dealt with the Chilean heartland, and between Santiago and Puerto Montt live almost 80 per cent of the population, leaving very few inhabitants for the northern deserts where the bulk of the nation's mineral resources are to be found. We have already noted that the first railway in Chile was here, as are other lines mainly devoted to mineral traffic.

Railways in Northern Chile - Ferronor

The long metre gauge northern main line of the Chilean State Railways (now Ferronor) is composed of various early companies, welded together by 1913 to extend from Calera to Iquique, a distance of 1,880km. Constituents included the Coquimbo, Serena and Rivadavia Railway, which was built in 1883-5, only to be destroyed by floods in 1888; the Serena, Coquimbo and Ovalle Railway, built 1886-73 and taken over by the state in 1895; the Ovalle - San Marcos Railway, built 1889-96; the Los Vilos Railway; the Huasco Railway and of course the original Caldera-Copiapó line, taken over by the state in 1911. Two other constituents were the Tongoy Railway, which passed to the state in 1901, and the Chañaral Railway, built in 1872 and purchased by the state in 1888. Many of these railways were in poor condition, and considerable work was needed to form them into the northern section of the State Railways. The section north of Pueblo Hundido originally belonged to the Chilean Northern Railway and for many years was worked by the Antofagasta (Chili) and Bolivia Railway. Connection is made with the broad gauge at Calera, between Santiago and Valparaíso, and facilities exist to transfer (by means of changing bogies) metre gauge wagons to the broad gauge, but these are little used.

The metre gauge has been entirely dieselised for many years now, using standard American types, and long distance traffic, if any, is confined to freight. In 1968 there was only one passenger train twice weekly (without sleepers) between Calera and Iquique, taking two and a half days, so it is not surprising that the railway had been forsaken for road or air travel. There were once two rack sections (two-bar Abt racks), with Esslingen and Baldwin locomotives, one installed from just beyond Polquico at km 105 (measured from La Calera), to km 164, just short of Socavon. This section was a switchback, but the other was a 'straight up and down' between Matancillas (km 229) and Pama (Km 259). This section was by-passed 1934-36 and the other section was eliminated in 1943. Discrepancies in distances which discerning readers may spot can partly be accounted for by pre- and post-alignment measurements.

Starting out from Calera on the long haul northwards the journey is of little interest at first. The train runs via Ovalle and serves Coquimbo, a port with a population of around 80,000, then at approximately 475km from Calera reaches La Serena, which has some attraction as a tourist resort. From here there was a branch line up the Elqui river valley to Rivadavia (72km), a pleasant journey where mining activities mingle with agriculture, peach and walnut farms and orange groves. Not far from La Serena and over on the coast was an isolated independent industrial line owned by the Bethlehem Chile Iron Mines and linking El Tofo with the port of Cruz Grande. It was 25km long, electrified at 2,200V dc and was of 4'8½" gauge. Closure took place in December 1973.

Continuing northwards from La Serena, various branches mostly connected with the mining industry diverge on both sides before we join the old mining line linking Copiapó with Caldera (see the beginning of this chapter) and continue through Copiapó to Pueblo Hundido (1,072km), where the Northern Longitudinal Railway connects with the Potrerillos Railway, a metre gauge line of 98km owned by the Andes Copper Mining Co. The State Railways operate a branch from here to the coast at Chañaral and

An early postcard scene of Plaza de Armas de Coquimbo showing a train of mixed stock arriving behind a metre gauge tender loco. Author's collection.

the Potrerillos Railway trains are worked over this line with their own motive power, nowadays diesel. The line northwards from Pueblo Hundido was completed by Chilean Northern Railway in 1914 and from 1919 until recently it was worked by the Antofagasta (Chili) and Bolivia Railway, although it is now an integral part of the state system. It originally terminated at Pintados (710km from Pueblo Hundido) but was extended to Iquique, a further 98km, in the early 1930s. North of Pueblo Hundido, at Catalina, the tracks of the Taltal Railway are crossed, but there is no physical connection as this railway is of 1,067mm (3ft 6in) gauge.

The Taltal Railway Co was originally a British concern carrying nitrates to the coast. The railway was opened on 20th October 1882 and eventually extended some 250km, owning a stock of 46 locomotives. some of the first passenger coaches were built by the Lancaster Carriage & Wagon Co in 1881 and were bogie vehicles. Steam locomotives, all British, have included eight Nasmyth Wilson 0-6-0Ts built in 1881, 2-6-2Ts and 2-6-0Ts from the Vulcan Foundry in 1889 and 1893, North British and Beyer Peacock 2-6-0Ts in 1904 and Kitson-Meyer 0-6-6-0Ts built 1904-1907. Some further locomotives originated with the Tocopilla Railway to the north and three noted in 1977 originated with the FCAB, having started out on the 2ft 6in gauge, been converted to metre gauge by that railway, and then to 3ft 6in gauge to operate at Taltal! A visit in 1977 by the late Mr A E Durrant revealed that the railway had closed in 1976 but a Kitson-Meyer was specially steamed for him and full details of his visit, and locomotives seen thereon, are to be found in Continental Railway Journal No 35 (Autumn 1978). Locked in a shed at this time was a Drewry railcar of 1924 vintage, built by Baguley Cars Ltd at Burton on Trent as an ambulance car. The British company sold out to Chilean owners on 7 February 1956 and the company was then retitled FC Salitrero de Taltal SA.

The Northern Transandine

Back on the metre gauge at Palestina the longitudinal is crossed by the line from Antofagasta to Augusta Victoria and the Argentine frontier at Socompa. This is known as the Northern Transandine Line and the section from Antofagasta to Augusta Victoria is the property of the FCAB. The Chilean government financed the construction of the section onwards to the frontier which was completed in 1948 and worked by the FCAB until June 1963, when their contract terminated and direct working by the State Railways was instituted. Over the Northern Transandine Line there was until 1982 a weekly passenger train which carried a sleeping car for Buenos Aires, about a four day journey. The Argentine section was until 1972 steam worked by 2-10-2s, a few of which later enjoyed a new lease of life on the Tuberão coal line in Brazil. The history of the FCAB is dealt with in chapter 2; at the moment the Chilean part of the system remains a private British registered concern and freight services, with diesel power continue to operate.

In 1908 the FCAB took over the 760mm gauge Aguas Blancas Railway, a 230km system serving the port of Coloso, 10km south of Antofagasta. This railway was first opened in 1902 as the Caleta-Coloso Railway, and reorganised in 1909 with all stock held by the FCAB. It had seventeen locomotives in 1930 but the port was closed in 1932 and the system contracted until it appears to have faded away in the 1960s.

Antofagasta is 1,488km from Calera and is the largest town in northern Chile, with a population of some 200,000. The railway continues beyond the city to the port of Mejillones, which offers a good natural harbour rather better than the more exposed one at Antofagasta; both ports handled heavy bulk traffic, such as nitrates, copper and tin from Bolivia. In 1970 a visitor to Antofagasta noted the derelict remains of some 0-4-2Ts which had been the property of the port administration.

Although we are not dealing in detail with the FCAB in this chapter, it is now necessary to follow the course of their line towards Bolivia, across the desolate and rainless Atacama desert to Chiquicamata, site of the world's largest open pit copper mine, with a annual capacity of 300,000 tons. Before nationalisation this was owned by the Chile Exploration Co, a subsidiary of the Anaconda Copper Co of New York. Formerly it had a 168km 4ft 8½in gauge railway system at least part of which was electrified at 650V dc with third rail conductor. In 1963 General Motors were advertising that they had supplied twenty-four diesel electrics seven years previously and six more were on order, which would seem to indicate that the electric system was out of use by then, and indeed all rail operations are said to have ceased in 1966. Before leaving the FCAB it is worthy of mention that the branch from Ollague (on the Bolivian border) to the copper mines at Collahuasi attained at Punto Alto, between Montt and Collahuasi, a height of 4826m above sea level, the highest point reached by any railway in the world. However, this part of the branch has now been closed, leaving the present day record in Peruvian hands.

The FC Tocopilla al Toco

Returning towards Antofagasta, we can continue northwards from the junction of Baquedano, where some steam was in store a few years ago, towards Iquique. At Miraje and Toca Chica contact is made with the railway system of the Anglo-Lautaro Nitrate Corporation. The situation here is rather involved as there were three distinct railways serving different mines, each formerly separately owned and operated but interconnecting; two of them, the FC Mina María Elena and the FC Pedro de Valdivia, feed into the FC Tocopilla at Toco. All these railways, which at their maximum extent totalled around 500km, are of 3ft 6in gauge and so there is no physical connection with the State Railway, although there is some interchange of traffic. The two nitrate fields of María Elena and Pedro de Valdivia have a combined productive capacity of 1,200,000 tons of natural nitrate a year, and produce about 65 per cent of the world's supply of iodine. Parts of these railway systems are electrified at 500/1,500V dc and General Electric box cab electric locomotives dating back to 1927/8 are still in use, as were until the early 1970s some old Los Angeles tramcars, a few bodies of which are still around today.

The most difficult part of the FCTT is the 47.5km up the steep escarpment from the port of Tocopilla to El Tigre, electrified in 1927. This section has a maximum gradient of 1 in 24 as it lifts the line up from sea level to the desert plains which lie at altitudes of 1,200-1,400m above sea level. Opened in 1890, an extremely interesting fleet of steam locomotives was used until electrification, when it migrated to other parts of the system. The first locomotive superintendent was Robert Stirling, and some of the earliest steam types were Kitson-Meyers with Walschaerts valve gear, built in 1894. A further series came in 1905 but the water-

A Ferronor northbound special for railfans in the almost surreal landscape of the Atacama desert in August 1997. The train is starting the steep descent into Iquique behind a General Motors GR12 diesel, a type also to be seen on the FCAB.
Photo: Chris Skow, Trains Unlimited, Tours.

less character of the whole area (at first water was distilled from the sea and later supplies were piped down from Bolivia) and the steep grade out of Tocopilla made a good case for electrification of at least this section, and Brian Fawcett states in "Railways of the Andes" that in 1939 0-6-6-0 Mallet compounds originally built for Russia were still in use. These had been built by Baldwin in 1916 for the Vologda - Archangel railway which was of the same gauge when they were ordered but was converted by the Russian government to broad gauge for strategic reasons, the order then being cancelled. A 1995 publication has fully detailed the history and locomotive stock of this railway, listing the modern electric and diesel motive power in use today (alongside a few of the 1927/8 electrics in 1995). The total route length in operation in 1995 was 120km of which 57km were electrified but some doubt exists over the future of the spectacular electric operation "up the hill" as the equipment is life expired and this may

well be de-activated if suitable diesel traction is developed. Meanwhile, there are even "tourist trains" worked over this section for enthusiasts! In June 1968 these railways (and other nitrate lines) came under the control of the State organisation Sociedad Quimica y Minero de Chile SA but during the 1980s this organisation reverted to private ownership. Tigre to El Toco closed around 1975.

Back at Miraje on the northern network, the metre gauge continues across fairly level desert to Pintados, where connection is made with the extensive 4ft 8½in gauge Nitrates railway. It will be recalled that the metre gauge terminated here in 1919, but was later extended down the coastal escarpment to the port of Iquique, 1,880km from Calera. This section was known as the FC Tarapacá, and reversal is necessary at Pintados, with a steep drop down the final section to the coast. The two gauges are believed have separate routes between Pintados and Iquique, though it is

A Ferrocarril Pedro de Valdivia nitrate train arriving at Pedro de Valdivia being pulled by no. 937, one of the ex-Canadian National (Newfoundland RR) rebuilds, now called a GR12g.
Photo: Chris Skow, Trains Unlimited, Tours.

possible that the Pintados-Las Carpas section is now a single mixed gauge line. In 1951 the Nitrates Railway came under government control and is now merged administratively with the metre gauge to form the Iquique sector of the State Railways.

Motive Power in the North of Chile

Before leaving the northern longitudinal line a few words about motive power are needed. Steam locomotives have included 2-6-0s from Henschel and Orenstein & Koppel built 1911-12, 2-8-0s from German builders, built 1912-13, some earlier American types, with Britain represented by some Hunslet 0-6-4Ts of 1910. Mainstay of the system and by far the largest class was the 'W' series of 2-8-2s supplied by Baldwin between 1921 and 1941. The railway is now completely dieselised but reports in the "Continental Railway Journal" in 1976/7 highlighted the strange state of affairs prevailing at Iquique. Official statistics showed that 18 metre gauge locomotives were repaired in 1973 and subsequent investigation showed this to be the case; following a rapid fall-off in traffic there was no work for the locomotives but repairing them provided employment for the workers, who were also building models and restoring old rolling stock!

The Nitrate Railway

The standard gauge Nitrate Railway, full title FC Salitreros de Tarapacá, was commenced in 1865, and at its full extent operated some 618km, about half of which could be termed "main line", the remainder being branches to various nitrate establishments. Out of Iquique the steep climb up the coastal escarpment requires a reversing station and grades of 1 in 25, with one section at 1 in 23.3 and another where curvature makes the grade equivalent to 1 in 21. By Las Carpas, where the metre gauge is encountered, the line has climbed some 3,000m in about 30km. At Central is the junction for the line southwards to Pintados and beyond, and the route northwards to Pisagua, another nitrate port on the Pacific coast. The main works of the railway are at Iquique, with running sheds (in steam days) at various points including Pisagua, Pozo Almonte and Zapiga. The approach to Pisagua is also steeply graded, requiring three reversing stations and grades between 1 in 21 and 1 in 40.

Although of course principally an industrial system the Nitrate Railway also carried a large number of passengers in its heyday (over 20,000 in 1934) and as much as 900,000 tons of nitrate has been handled in a year. In 1951 the operations of the Nitrate

2-8-0 no. 3087 is a Rogers product of 1901, one of ten which worked on the northern network, mainly on freight. In later years they were believed to have also worked on some of the more southerly branches, lasting in traffic till 1974.

Railways were integrated with those of the EFE metre gauge which also linked Iquique with Pintados. At first the standard gauge route was in the ascendancy but from 1960 the standard gauge operation was wound down by means of a third rail being added so that metre gauge trains could be worked over it. Nowadays the nitrate business has declined in the face of artificial substitutes and by 1976 traffic had dropped to two trains a week between Huara and Iquique; these were, however, worked by a metre gauge 2-8-2 steam locomotive, though there were diesels on the system.

As mentioned earlier, construction of the railway commenced in 1865, at which time the provinces of Tarapacá and Antofagasta were in Peru and Bolivia. The reasons for the War of the Pacific (1879-83) were not unconnected with possession of the great mineral wealth in this area which passed to Chile with these provinces in 1883. In the first instance the railways at Iquique and Pisagua were separate concerns, linked by a third known as the Nitrate Railway, but the whole system was integrated in the 1870s, being known by 1873 as The Nitrate Railways Co Ltd, a British concern with a head office in London.

As with the other nitrate railways of northern Chile, motive power has been varied, with articulated types being used for the steeply graded sections. Fairlies were popular here, eight 0-6-6-0s being supplied 1871-2, six more in 1874 and another in 1880, all by the Avonside Engine Company of Bristol. Other locomotives included Baldwin 2-8-2s, Porter 2-8-2Ts, Yorkshire Engine Company 4-8-4Ts and six 187 ton superheated bar frame Garratts, built by Beyer Peacock in 1926 and 1928. There were sixty-seven steam locomotives in 1934, plus three Sentinel steam railcars, and in 1958 some twenty steam locomotives remained in service, including two Garratts. Dieselisation was completed in 1959. The port authority at Iquique has on display standard gauge 0-6-0ST No 3, built by Avonside in 1902, but their operations are also now dieselised.

The 760mm gauge Agua Santa Railway and Junín Railway

Connecting with the Nitrates Railway between Iquique and Pisagua there were formerly two lines of 760mm gauge. One was the Agua Santa Railway, from Agua Santa to Caleta Buena, for which the concession had been granted in 1889, in order to challenge the monopoly of the Nitrates Railway. This line was owned by the state, and leased to a Chilean company. It operated a total system of about 145km, including a three stage inclined plane 2,133m long and worked by gravity, between Alto de Caleta and

From 1921 onwards the class W 2-8-2 formed the backbone of the motive power department. They were an outstanding improvement over earlier types in all respects and handled all types of traffic on the metre gauge northern network. until the 1950s. Most were built by Baldwin, with one batch of six built by Borsig and seven assembled at San Bernardo from parts supplied by Baldwin. Preserved class member no. 3511 is seen northbound in the Atacama desert near La Rioja in October 1990. Photo:Ian Thomson.

Caleta Buena. Nearby was the Junín Railway, built in 1894 with 108km of track. To reach the coast this railway also made use of an inclined plane, built in 1924, worked by gravity and 1,230m long. The locomotive stock included two Fairlies built by the Yorkshire Engine Company in 1906, and in 1930 Hudswell Clarke supplied a 1-C-1 diesel of 330hp, which at the time was the most powerful direct-drive diesel locomotive in the world. These two railways may have had a physical connection with each other, and possibly came under the same management before closure, which had taken place by 1946.

Arica - La Paz and Arica - Tacna

North of Pisagua is a stretch of territory without railways, and it is a five hour bus ride from Iquique to the town of Arica, a port with some 45,000 inhabitants, and the starting point for two international railways, serving Peru and Bolivia. The more important of these is the metre gauge Arica-La Paz Railway, opened in 1913. It has rack sections in Chile and is more fully described in Chapter 2. Connecting with it at Villa Industrial, near Puquios, was an industrial line owned by the Compañia Nacional de Azufre which extended about 32km to Tacora, site of the sulphur mine. It is understood that there were three locomotives which were fired first with llama dung and then, when pressure had been raised, by a moss like root called yareta. This line closed many years ago, but at Vila Industrial sections of mixed gauge track, ruined buildings and ore cars can be seen, together with the hulk of one steam loco, believed to be a Hanomag 0-8-0T.

The other railway is standard gauge and links Arica with Tacna in Peru, a distance of only 62km. When built the whole line was in Peruvian territory and it is described in chapter 10.

The north of Chile is rarely visited by railway enthusiasts, and indeed the interest lies mainly in the past, but intriguing relics can be found, as Mr Durrant discovered in 1977 at Taltal. Passenger services are nowadays non-existent, but while the mineral traffic is also but a shade of what it was in the past, many sections of railway remain open, including some of the early electrified industrial sections. The area contains many "stuffed and mounted" steam locomotives, and climatic conditions are such that these are in a better state of preservation than many elsewhere.

For a much more detailed background history of the northern network and full locomotive details, 'Red Norte' by Ian Thomson is highly recommended and has greatly amplified the information I originally had on this area of Chile.

Berrio, and then travel over the Antioquia Railway via Medellín to the station of A. López, from where the Ferrocarril del Pacífico continued along the valley of the river Cauca to Cali. This railway was built by the state, and work commenced at the Pacific ocean port of Buenaventura on 15 September 1915. This difficult section is 173km long, and has gradients of 4 per cent. From Cali there is a branch southwards to Popayán (159km) completed in 1934. The Ferrocarril del Pacífico totalled 759km, including two short branches (Pradera 14km and Santander 22km) and the Armenia branch, which had been intended as the main line to Bogotá, the railway holding a concession to build a 140km link between Armenia and Ibagué, on the Girardot-Tolima-Huila Railway. This section, which would have given Bogotá more or less direct rail access to the Pacific, was proposed in 1913, but requires considerable engineering works, including a 4,720m tunnel. The project was once again revived in 1946, but was dropped when the decision was taken to build the longer but more useful Atlantic Railway. There was, however, a link of another sort between the railways serving Bogotá and those reaching the Pacific, as will be seen in the next paragraph.

At Armenia, the FC del Pacífico made an end-on connection with the Ferrocarril de Caldas, which parallels the Pacífico line to A. López northwards, meeting it again at Cartago, and continuing to Manizales. This railway was built between 1915 and 1923 and was taken over by Pacífico in the 1940s. At Manizales a 72km aerial cableway crossed the mountains to Mariquita, a station on the La Dorada Railway, and this offered the Bogota-Pacific coast link mentioned in the previous paragraph. It was built around 1913 and carried all kinds of merchandise in 500kg capacity vagonetas. Latterly, coal had been the principal commodity carried, but the cableway is now closed. Common carrier cableways of this type are unusual, but there were two in Colombia, and others have existed in Spain and Eritrea. The Dorada Railway was a British concern. Its line, built between 1881 and 1907, extended from La Dorada on the Magdalena River via the headquarters at Mariquita Ambalema, a distance of 111km. The company was nationalised about 1957, and an official handout

issued at the time supplies detailed information on this railway. The first locomotives recorded were two Alco 2-6-0s of 1898, and in 1905 Hudswell Clarke supplied two 4-4-0Ts and two 0-6-0s, works numbers 730-3. In 1909 Alco supplied a further 2-6-0 and then a series of 2-6-2s between 1913 and 1920. In 1938 Hawthorn Leslie supplied four 4-8-0s and 1937 saw the arrival of two Beyer Garratts. There were two small railcars, a six seat Wickham of 1935 and twenty-two seater bogie car from Walker Bros in 1939. Most coaching stock was from the Gloucester Carriage and Wagon Co., but some third class coaches came second hand from the USA. From Ambalema a section of line was built on towards Ibagué between 1919 and the early 1930s, and this was owned by the department of Tolima until nationalisation in the 1940s.

The Tolima Railway was built to link Ibagué with Girardot, and work started at Flandres, just across the river from Girardot, in September 1893. Ibagué, 77km distant, was reached on 7th January 1921. The railway also pushed southwards to Neiva, capital of the department of Huila, reached in 1938. Meanwhile the Magdalena River was bridged in 1930, and the system retitled Ferrocarril Girardot-Tolima-Huila. It will be recalled that this railway was to link Bogotá with the Pacific, but the Ibagué-Armenia section was never completed. It was on this railway that Kitson-Meyer articulated locomotives were used, the last of which was withdrawn in 1958.

The Ferrocarril de Girardot linked the Tolima Railway with Facatativá, on the way to Bogotá, a distance of 132km but some 2,400m higher. The railway was yet another to be commenced by Francisco J Cisneros, who seemed fated to start many Colombian railways, only to see the concessions pass to others after a few years' work. In this case construction started in June 1881, and Cisneros built 33km before others took over and completed the line in 1908. The railway ascends the mountainside by means of a switchback between kms 83 and 86, with grades of 4½ per cent, and in steam days it must have been an exciting journey. At Facatativá, connection is made with the Cudinamarca Railway to Bogotá, but until 1924 transhipment was necessary as the railways to the capital city were of metre gauge.

No. 249 Ferrocarril de Caldas—Departamento de Caldas-Colombia

An old postcard view from the author's collection showing a mixed train on the F.C. de Caldas, a 69 km regional railway later incorporated into the F.C. del Pacifico.

The Magdalena Bridge at Girardot built by Armstrong Whitworth and opened in 1930 linked the F.C. Girardot with the Tolima and Huila systems.
Period postcard view courtesy of Jim Horsford.

Bogotá, the capital city of Colombia, is situated on a high plateau, the Sabana, at 2,600m above sea level, and access to the coast many miles away has always been a problem. The first railway from the capital was built across the Sabana to Facatativá between 1882 and 1889, and was originally entitled FC de la Sabana, and later FC de Cundinamarca. It was built to the metre gauge, and converted to 3ft in 1924. The line was extended in 1932 from Facatativá to Puerto Salgar, on the Magdalena river below Girardot. This is the route taken by traffic over the Atlantic railway, and it too has steeply graded sections down the mountainside. One of the first locomotives of the FC de la Sabana was an 0-4-0T 'Cordoba', built by Porter in 1875 and for many years displayed on the station at Bogotá. It was later moved to the Railway Employees club.

The metre gauge line from Bogotá to Barbosa has already been mentioned, and was entitled Ferrocarril del Norte. Another metre gauge railway, the FC de Nordeste, was built from the capital for some 300km to Paz del Río, and originally it had its own tracks parallel to those of the Norte for some distance out of Bogotá. When the gauge of both railways was converted in 1953 one track was made to suffice as far as the point of divergence at La Caro. The Nordeste was built by a Franco-Belgian concern in the 1920s and the last 30kms or so between Belencito and Paz del Río are actually the property of the steelworks there, although the rest of the railway became part of the nationalised system.

Acerias Paz del Río operate a modern steelworks which was opened on 13 October 1954 and they soon electrified at 25kV ac the Belencito-Paz del Río line, and a short branch, some 38km in all. This section is worked by six Bo-Bo-Bo electrics obtained from Alsthom about 1956 and it is heavily graded. In 1994 it was reported that there were some ten pairs of trains a day, some with a coach attached for local passengers. General Electric provided

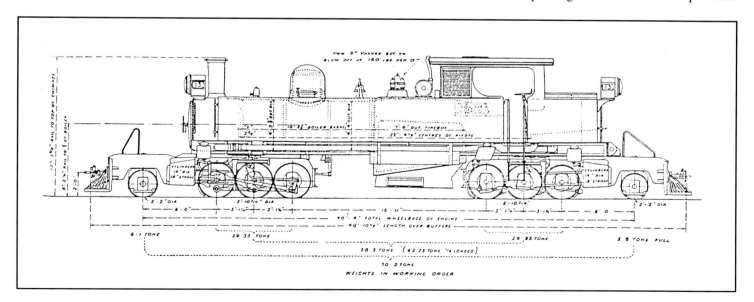

Kitson-Meyers saw considerable use on the railways in Colombia. The drawing above shows one of the F.C. Cundinamarca locos which were based on the F.C. Girardot 0-6-6-0T design but modified by the C.M.E., Mr. P.C. Dewhurst, to include the addition of leading and trailing pony trucks. They were built to handle trains between Bogotá and Palanquero with a maximum 1 in 33 grade.

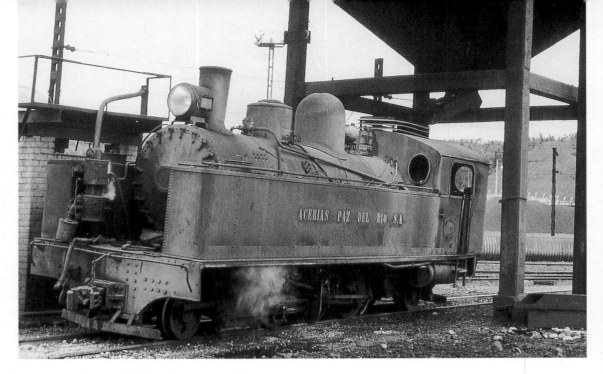

The F.C. del Norte had a series of 2-6-2Ts built by Tubize in 1931, an unidentified example of which was seen in industrial service at the Acerias Paz del Rio S.A. in November 1977.
Photo: Chris Skow
Trains Unlimited, Tours.

The Acerias Paz del Rio had five 2-8-2s built by Tubize 1951-53, one of which was seen at Belencito shunting the yard in November 1977.
Photo: Chris Skow,
Trains Unlimited, Tours.

seven 4-wheel diesel electric locos between 1957 and 1973 but four larger 1,500hp 0-4-4-0DE came from the same builder in 1989, eliminating steam traction. In 1978 there had been a roster of eleven steam locomotives, all built by Tubize (Belgium). Five modern 2-8-2s came in 1951/53, but the six 2-6-2Ts, built in 1931, were originally in service on the FC del Norte, having been built for the metre gauge and later converted. An Alco 2-4-2ST of 1921 is preserved here. In December 1993 steam had been withdrawn from use but some locomotives were still complete, although others had been scrapped. In the area are limestone/ironstone and coal mines which have, or had, 3ft gauge railways, some electrified, some underground. At least two of these are connected to the steelworks by aerial ropeways.

Another railway from Bogotá was the Ferrocarril del Sur, at one time British owned and entitled The Southern Railway of Colombia Ltd. It was commenced in 1896 and extended to Salto de Tequendama (31km). A branch to San Miguel was closed in the 1930s and the line was converted from metre gauge in 1952. finally, the FC del Oriente, commenced in 1917, extended only 25km from Bogotá to Usme, and was closed in 1934.

The multitude of companies forming the railways of Colombia were by 1960 welded into an integrated system of unified gauge, totalling 3,436km. The administration was divided into five regions but regrettably the unification of the 1950s was not followed up and an official report in 1978 stated that 50 per cent of the 169 strong locomotives fleet was out of action. The line between Medellin and La Felisa was damaged by floods and landslides in 1976, breaking the only rail link between Cali, the Pacific coast port of Buenaventura, and Bogotá.

Before the building of the Atlantic Railway there was of

necessity much autonomy within physically unconnected regions, and stock was lettered and numbered accordingly. Today, regular steam traction has been eliminated (although until the late 1980s locomotives survived at Flandres (Girardot) and worked a daily shuttle between the depot and station, over the Magdalena river bridge), but this improvement came too late to save much of the passenger traffic, lost to fierce road competition. When I visited Bogotá in 1970 no timetables were published, or even displayed in the very pleasant little terminal station there, and information on services was hard to come by.

Colombian Railways, particularly the Girardot Railway, were great users of Kitson-Meyer articulated locomotives, the first three of which were built for the Girardot Railway in 1909. They were 0-6-6-0Ts, as were a further sixteen supplied between 1912 and 1921. In 1927-8 Kitson supplied six 2-6-6-2Ts, four going to the Girardot railway and two to the FC de Cundinamarca, with one more to the latter line in 1929. The final Kitson-Meyers were two massive 2-8-8-2Ts built by Robert Stephenson in 1935, again for the Girardot Railway, and these represented the final develop-

ment of the type. The same railway also had a 2-8-8-2T simple expansion Mallet built by Baldwin in 1935, a huge superheated machine weighing 131 tonnes in working order. Despite these powerful articulated types, most of the traffic between the 1920s and 1950s was worked by various series of 4-8-0s, which accounted for some 60 per cent of the train-kilometres, freight and passenger, worked over the principal railways.

The steam locomotive stock of the Colombian National Railways as at 13th August 1957 was listed in a very detailed article on the system published in the Railway and Locomotive Historical Journal (USA) for April 1967. At that time types of loco in service included Baldwin 2-6-0s of 1919-22, several classes of 2-6-2s, mostly built in the 1920s, a few Baldwin 2-8-0s and Tubize (Belgium) 2-8-2s of 1924 and 1951. There were also the various series of 4-8-0s, Czech, American and Belgian built, and a series of American 4-8-2s dating from 1944-48. Still in stock were the two Kitson-Meyer 2-8-8-2Ts of 1935, five of the earlier Kitson 2-6-6-2Ts and three of the earliest Kitson-Meyers, built in 1909, 1914 and 1920, one of which was being used by the

Three unusual metre gauge articulated locos were built by Sentinel for Colombia in 1934 and one was tested on the Belgian SNCV in the Ardennes, as shown in this view taken from 'The Locomotive' magazine. Each axle was powered by a two cylinder compound engine fed from a Woolnough water tube boiler operating at 38.5 atm (375 psi). The operating history and fate of these locos in Colombia remains a mystery.

military engineering section of the army for training purposes. Although in stock in 1957, all the above Kitson-Meyers were withdrawn the following year. The two outside-frame Garratts of 4-6-0+0-6-4 wheel arrangement, built by Armstrong Whitworth in 1924 for the FC del Pacífico do not figure in the list, but one of the two La Dorada Railway Garratts mentioned earlier is shown. Tank engines were only six in number, 0-4-0T and 0-6-0Ts, plus a Baldwin 2-4-2T which is now displayed on a plinth at Flandres depot, Girardot. By 1961 (in which year the Baldwin Mallet was withdrawn after a boiler explosion), the steam stock had dwindled to 225 and by 1971 only a handful were in service.

Dieselisation commenced in 1949 when Wickham supplied four diesel-mechanical railcars, put into service around Cali and in the Bogotá area. They were followed in 1951 by a 5-car diesel electric set which operated between Bogotá and Ibague. When the Atlantic Railway was built, dieselisation started in earnest, Sweden supplying 28 lightweight diesel-hydraulic railcars and trailers to work the passenger service. As mentioned earlier, these proved so popular that later 10 or 12 coach locomotive hauled trains were required. The first diesel locomotives appear to have been a pair of diesel electrics supplied from America to the FC de Antioquia in 1946 and one of these is recorded as surviving into the early 1990s as works shunter at El Corzo diesel depot. This report, in "Locomotives International" issue 30 (9/95) suggests that this may well be the oldest diesel locomotive still at work on the national railway systems of Latin America. The FC del Pacífico received five Alco/GE Co-Bo-Co diesels in 1952 and the FC del Antioquia four 1,000hp BoBos from Austria in 1956.

General Electric Bo-Bos and Co-Cos followed in the 1960s, after a pair of Alsthom 1150hp Co-Cos had been ordered in 1957. A later series of GE U10B type Bo-Bos were built in Spain between 1968 and 1973 and at 88 units formed by far the largest class ever to be put in to service in Colombia. The last new locomotives received were some Co-Cos from GEC, four were delivered in 1986 and another four were ordered in 1987 but it is not known if these arrived or if the order was cancelled.

If the above information implies that all was well with the National Railways it certainly did not remain so for long. Natural disasters, competition (air/bus/road for freight) and lack of funds caused the FCN to go into liquidation and most remaining passenger services were suspended. In 1992 infrastructure and operation were split, the former being placed in charge of an organisation entitled "Ferrovias" and the latter "Soc. Colombiana de Transporte Ferroviario SA (STF)", operating on a commercial basis.

Baldwin 4-8-2 no. 68, built 1945, sets off with the Bogotá - Neiva service that had for twenty years been hauled by Kitson 2-6-0+0-6-2s. Photo: Guillermo Dîaz.

By this time many locomotives were unserviceable and rehabilitation of the network, even partially, is a massive task.

At the time of writing it is thought that only a few local passenger services are operated, and the latterly once weekly Bogotá-Santa Marta "Tayrona Express" is suspended, a far cry indeed from the 10/12 coach trains mentioned earlier. One bright spot is the intermittent operation, since the 1980s, of steam hauled tourist trains from Bogotá (an to a lesser degree elsewhere) and a few steam locomotives remain serviceable for these. It is under- stood that in 1993 STF bought five locomotives and 176 wagons from the White Pass Yukon railway in Alaska, presumably for use on the Bogotá-Santa Marta link.

Finally, it is worth mentioning that in 1923 there was a project to link Villamizar on the Cúcuta Railway with the river Magdalena by means of an aerial cableway. Work began in 1925 and by 1929 the cableway was open between Gamarra (on the river) and Ocaña (47km). The extension to Villamizar was never built though there was a road link, and the cableway is now

F.C. de Nariño no. 6, one of seven such 2-6-2s built by Škoda in 1928. Two went to the F.C. de Antioquia, three to the F.C. Girardot and the remaining two to the F.C. de Nariño.
Photo: Škoda official.

Steam and diesel were both in action at Bogotá La Sabana station in 1964. No. 96 makes a dramatic departure, passing 1957-built General Electric class U10B Co-Co no. 328. Photo: Guillermo Dîaz.

closed.

The other isolated railway was the 3ft gauge FC del Nariño, situated in the south-west of Colombia linking the Pacific port of Tumaco with El Diviso (126km). The first section was opened in 1927 and the last part, linking Agua Claras with Tumaco, between 1937 and 1944. It had been intended that the line would reach the capital of the department, Fasto, but the whole railway was closed in the 1960s.

The only previously known industrial railway, apart from the steelworks system already described, was between the station of Apulo on the Girardot Railway and the Dimante Cement works, a distance of four kilometres. Former sugar plantation systems, of which the largest was Ingenio Sincerín, with some 40km of track, are now closed.

Colombian railways are probably the least frequently visited in South America, although many routes are highly scenic, with spectacular engineering features. Gauge standardisation, and the linking up of the isolated sections, appears to have been achieved a few years too late to be of real benefit to the nation. Since then road improvements have taken their toll of the traffic available, though a new standard gauge line has been built in the province of Guajira. The El Cerrjon Coal Railway links the mines there with the port of Bahia de Portete, near the Venezuelan border, and is 150km long, worked by eight General Electric Bo-Bo diesels.

The state railways in Colombia have been declared bankrupt and are stated to have closed, however, the real situation in 2000 is that a new organisation, the Sociedad Colombiana de Transporte Forroviária SA has been formed and is now operating passenger services under contract on some lines around Bogotá and Girardot. The freight situation on these routes is not known.

A 30-year concession for operation and maintenance of the Atlantic Railway has been granted to an international consortium knwon as Fenoco. This covers the main line from Bogotá to Santa Marta, Puerto Berrio to Medellín, and branches from Bogotá to Belencito and Lenguazaque, and Espinal to Neiva, a total of about 1500km.

ECUADOR

Baldwin 2-8-0 no. 46 climbs away from Alausi with a couple of boxcars travelling over the Guayaquil and Quito Railway on 9th October 1979. No. 46 was built in 1946, works no. 71582.

The second smallest of the South American states, Ecuador has a population of around 11,700,000, the density being the highest in South America, at 39 per square kilometre, with a growth rate of 2.7% per annum.

The Guayaquil and Quito Railway

The first railway in Ecuador, and indeed the only one of any importance, was authorised in 1861, although construction did not commence until 1871. Work on the Guayaquil and Quito line commenced simultaneously at two points, Yaguachi and Sibambe, both situated towards the Guayaquil end of the line. Finance proved difficult, but the National Bank of Ecuador granted a loan in January 1873, enabling locomotives and equipment to be purchased. Within two years Yaguachi to Milagro (12km) was

opened to traffic, but further progress was painfully slow, and in 1873 the driving force behind the enterprise, President Garcia Moreno, was assassinated. In 1880 a new group formed, which promised completion in four years, but this proved to be an over-optimistic assessment, and little further progress was made during this period. By 1890 the line had reached Duran. One would have thought it more logical to start out from the coast and work inland, but this does not appear to have been the case. From Duran a connection was made to Guayaquil by ferry, this lasting until a road bridge was completed in the 1970s, however, no sooner had this section been completed than floods washed away the track, bankrupting the contractor. After political troubles had delayed reconstruction an American company took over and, backed by the government of Eloy Alfaro, work was pushed ahead until in

1902 Sibambe was reached, 130km from Duran, but only after many problems finding a route up the western slopes of the Andes. The first rails had been laid to the 3ft gauge, but when the American company took over, 3'6" was standardised upon.

Financial troubles apart, construction of the 452km G & Q presented enormous difficulties for the engineers. From sea level at Duran the line ascends gently at first and at Bucay, 87km, the altitude is only 300 metres, but a stiff climb up the gorge of the river Chanchan brings it to 1,462 metres at Huigra (116km). Next comes the most spectacular section of all as the railway is faced by a perpendicular ridge of rock over 300 metres high rising from the river gorge. Sibambe is the junction for a branch southwards to Cuenca (145km) completed in 1965, but seeing very little traffic. Sibambe to Alausi is only 12km and this is the steepest section between any two stations on the line. The average grade is 1 in 23.3 and it includes a double reversing switchback, the famous "Devil's Nose", and a series of hairpin curves below Alausi village situated at an altitude of 2,347 metres.

Continuing towards Quito there are gradients of 1 in 18, in fact such grades apply at a number of places on the mountain section between Bucay and Palmira, over which 78.5km section the line climbs 2,994 metres, resulting in an average gradient of 1 in 26.6. After Palmira (3,236 m), the track undulates across desolate moors and drops to Riobamba (230km and 2,764 m), reached in 1905. From Riobamba the summit of the line is reached At Urbina (263.8km and 3,609 m), and further undulations include a drop to 2,570 m at Ambato and then a rise to 3,547 m at Cotopaxi (393km). Here is situated the highest active volcano in the world, at 5,896 metres.

From Ambato there was formerly a railway which was intended to extend to the river Curaray, a tributary of the Amazon, which was intended to open up the eastern slopes of the Andes and Amazon basin lands in eastern Ecuador. Contracted in 1905, the railway had only covered 25km to Pelileo by 1922 and it never got any further, the track later being lifter for use elsewhere. It was worked by two Baldwin 2-6-0s built in 1914, which later became G & Q numbers 5 and 6. The final section of the G & Q

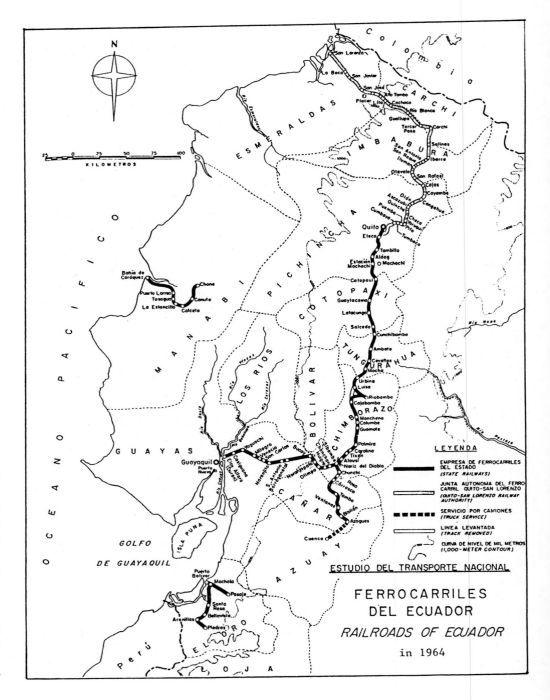

to Quito (425km and 2,777m) was opened on 25th June 1908.

Early motive power included two two-truck Shays, used in the construction work but withdrawn soon afterwards; two Baldwin 0-6-6-0 Mallets built in 1905 but not a success and also soon withdrawn; eight Baldwin moguls built 1900/01, and eight Baldwin 2-8-0s built in 1906. More 2-8-0s came later, all from Baldwin and the last in 1953, many lasting until quite recently. Generally speaking, the 2-6-0s worked between Duran and Bucay and the 2-8-0s on the mountain section between Bucay and Riobamba. It is many years since steam was to be found in the Quito area. Another successful type was a batch of three Beyer Garratt 2-6-2+2-6-2s built in 1929, which were withdrawn in the 1960s. In 1970 came a batch of ten Alco design 1,250hp Co-Cos

Baldwin 2-6-0 no. 14 leaves Bucay bound for Durán on 11th October 1979. No. 14 dates from 1901 (works no. 19347) and is not superheated. Boiler pressure is 175 lbs., driving wheel diameter 4 foot, and the loco has a tractive effort of 20,160 lbs.

Climbing the curves to Alausi is more modern motive power in the form of one of the ten Co-Co hood units built by Euskalduna in 1969. Their arrival reduced the number of operational steam locos required to just ten.

built by Euskalduna in Spain under licence. These replaced many steam workings, but by no means all.

The railway has a long history of railbus use, mostly ancient machines with locally built bodies. In the 1950s ten 230hp units were received from Ferrostaal and these seat 38 passengers - a purely notional figure as many more usually travel on the roof luggage rack! Tourist agencies are now taking up rail travel over the spectacular sections and some railcars have been upgraded for their use. Latest additions to the diesel fleet are ten Alsthom Bo-Bo-Bo diesel locomotives built in 1992 and these have taken over from the Euskalduna ones and more or less eliminated regular steam working, however, some steam is retained for tourist work-

ings and no doubt appears from time to time on other duties.

Services over the G & Q are often partially suspended due to washouts and landslips. For many years recently there was no service over the whole line, which was broken beyond Alausi, and what traffic there was at the Quito end was handled by railcars. For this reason nothing about passenger services is included here as the situation is liable to change, either for better or for worse!

The G & Q was nationalised in 1944 and a new railway was built from Quito to San Lorenzo (373km) in 1957, giving the capital an alternative outlet to the sea. Work on this section had started as far back as 1926 but little had been achieved until in 1951 a French consortium was engaged to complete the task. This

One of the older and more exotic "autoferros", Ferrocarriles Equatorianos railbus no. 204 of the Sibambe - Cuenca branch. Photo: David Ibbotson.

before diverging to go their separate ways, and it is surprising that they were never reconstructed to a unified gauge. By 1966 railcars were still handling some passenger traffic, the bananas presumably having found some other means of transport. It is possible that when the eastern line was converted to 3'6" gauge, second hand material was supplied from the G & Q and on display at Duran now is an Alco 0-4-0T said to have come from there. Both railways were closed by 1974.

Sugar Estate and Industrial Lines

There have been quite a number of sugar estate railways in Ecuador, in particular along the G & Q line between Duran and Bucay. Some 6km from Naranjito station is the Ingenio San Carlos, with both 3'6" and 600 mm gauge tracks. Their "broad" gauge steam consisted of an O&K 2-4-0T of 1913 and a Glover 2-6-0 of 1919 (nos. 6 & 7) and on the 300mm gauge they had small woodburning tender locomotives, an 0-4-0, two 0-4-2s and two Porter 2-4-0s of 1924. Most of these were still in existence, derelict, into the early 1990s, when it was reported that there were also 19 diesel locomotives, five "broad" gauge and 14 narrow, all stored. One of the Porter 2-4-0s is preserved on display. At Ingenuo Valdez, near Milagro, steam had given way to diesels by 1994 and the two oil fired Baldwin tender engines were out of use. One, 'Dolores', of 1922 is plinthed here where the gauge is, surprisingly, 3 ft. Diesel operations were reported here in 1992. Derelict at the nearby Luz Maria Ingenio in the early 1980s was Decauville 0-4-2T San Nicholas, fitted with a 4-wheel tender.

Finally, the Anglo Ecuadorian Oilfields Railway has been listed in 'World Railways', but I have no further information on it. Another obscure line was the Guayaquil Customs Railway, of 4 ft gauge, which ran along the old river front to a Customs House near the current railway jetty in Guayaquil, to which wagons are ferried for loading from Duran, a practice which may have ceased by now. An 0-4-0ST locomotive from this line is said to be preserved inside the main gate of the new docks.

3 ft gauge 0-4-0 'Dolores' of Ingenuo Valdez mill, Baldwin 55298 of 1922, is now preserved on a plinth.

No. 44 tackles the gradient over the mountain. This 2-8-0 is another Baldwin product, works no. 70891/1944.
Photo Richard Pelham.

THE FALKLAND ISLANDS & SOUTH GEORGIA

The Falkland Islands are included in this volume for reasons of geographical completeness. Administratively they are still a colony of Great Britain, but the islands are the subject of a long standing territorial claim by Argentina, the assertion of which, by force, in 1982 led to a fierce but brief war between the two countries.

The existence of railways on the Islands, however, originates in a much earlier conflict, the First World War. Trade between Britain and South America - primarily coal outwards and meat on the return leg - was of much greater importance in the early years of this century. In 1914 this seaborne trade was crippled by the presence of a squadron of German cruisers, commanded by Admiral Graf von Spee. The Royal Navy forces sent to counter this threat were woefully inadequate and on 1st November 1914, in the first major naval engagement of the War, von Spee's force annihilated the British squadron, sinking the armoured cruisers MONMOUTH and GOOD HOPE with massive loss of life.

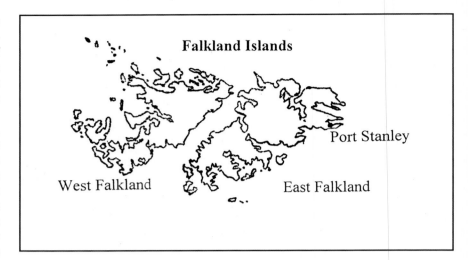

Nemesis came in turn for the German forces in the form of two powerful modern Battle cruisers INVINCIBLE and INLEXIBLE, despatched by the Admiralty to wipe out the humiliation of the earlier defeat. Lacking precise information as to the Germans' whereabouts, the British commander Admiral Doveton Sturdee called first at the Falklands to take on coal before proceeding round Cape Horn. By a bizarre co-incidence Von Spee had decided to raid Port Stanley at the same time that Sturdee was replenishing his supplies. On detecting the Battle cruisers' silhouettes, von Spee turned tail, but was pursued and within hours the SCHARNHORST, GNIESENAU and two light cruisers were sunk. Sturdee, painfully aware that he could have been caught napping in Stanley Harbour (and where the outcome of the battle could have been radically different), telegraphed the Governor: "We wish to convey our thanks for the early warning of the approach of the enemy due to the good look-out kept at Sapper Hill."

This incident demonstrated the need for improved communications, and arrangements were made by the Admiralty for a powerful spark transmitter to be built at Moody Brook to the west of Stanley. This type of transmitter required formidable power supplies: two Babcock and Wilcox boilers provided steam for the three dynamos, the boilers themselves needed large quantities of coal, hence the need for a light railway to convey material, equipment and fuel to the transmitter site from the Navy jetty some 3 miles away on the northern shore of the harbour opposite Stanley.

The contractors to the Admiralty were Marconi and Co. with the construction being sub-contracted to Holland, Hannen and Cubitts, a London-based firm with roots in the railway contracting industry. About 200 labourers were employed and despatched to the Falklands where by the end of May 1915 stors and materials were unloaded from the steamer ISMAILIA. The stores included two 2ft gauge "Wren" class locomotives, works nos 2388 and 2392 built by Kerr Stuart, ex-works on 3rd March 1915. By the beginning of June over half the length of the railway

cutting had been completed and the track was laid and was being worked for about a mile. This was creditable progress as this was the depth of the Falklands winter. There was a slight delay caused by a labour dispute but on 2nd September 1915 the Governor was able to report that 3 out of the 3 miles of railway were complete, allowing one of the 'Wrens' and four stone crushers to be redeployed onto other work. Four months later, the major construction had been completed.

The contractors then withdrew leaving a team of an Engineer-in-Charge, one artificer, two experienced stokers and eight stokers to run the equipment; the latter complement giving some indication of the amount of coal the railway had to transport.

An interesting aspect of the running of this railway was the use of wind power. Some of the wagons with seats were equipped with a mast and sails so that they could use the prevailing wind to run back from the transmitter to the port. They would all be attached to the first train of the morning and then remain at the transmitter when the loco returned, providing transport for later in the day without the need for the engine to make a special trip.

However, the invention of the wireless valve soon made the transmitter obsolete, and the large generating capacity was no longer required. The railway fell into disuse in the second half of the 1920s and the two locomotives seem to have been simply discarded, however, there is evidence that sections of the railway remained in 'unofficial' use for moving wool wagons between sheep shearing stations and loading piers.

The 1982 war brought the Falklands to the world's attention and an influx of military personnel to the islands. Remarkably it was found that much of the railway route under Wireless Ridge survived. Also, due to the lack of a scrap market on the islands, the two Kerr Stuarts too had survived, buried under a massive pile of junk. The effects of seventy years sea air had reduced them to little more than hulks, but they were later removed to container storage while plans were discussed to either repatriate them to Britain, or preserve one or more of them on site, as a memento of this small but fascinating railway.

One of the Kerr Stuart 'Wren' class 0-4-0ST by the loading point. The date is unknown, but the photo may have been taken during construction of the line as the blocks in the background appear to be sleepers.
Photo courtesy of Prof. R.A. Smith.

By the time this photo of the Falkland Island Express was taken some improved protection for the driver had been added to the cab. Coaching stock has been mounted on what looks like the chassis from some of the tipper wagons used during construction. The ship half hidden behind the engine is the hulk of Brunel's 'S.S. Great Britain'.
Photo courtesy of Prof R.A. Smith.

South Georgia

To complete the story mention must also be made of railways on South Georgia. This remote island is a 'dependency' of the Falklands and early in the century was the centre of a whaling industry. In 1912 seven whaling stations were in operation on the island. At that time the whales were brought to the stations for cutting up and processing. Huge quantities of coal were needed to power the machinery needed,and to move this, narrow gauge rail-ways were installed at most of the stations.

Most of these lines were hand worked but at least one was locomotive worked. This was operated by Ocean SA of Narvik, Norway, between 1909 and 1920, at Ocean Harbour, formerly New Fortune Bay. The remains of what appears to be a Krauss 0-4-0T survived, in heavily cannibalised condition,and tipped on its side,at Ocean Harbour in 1982. The railways are believed to have closed by 1966.

THE GUIANAS (Guyana, Surinam, Guyane)

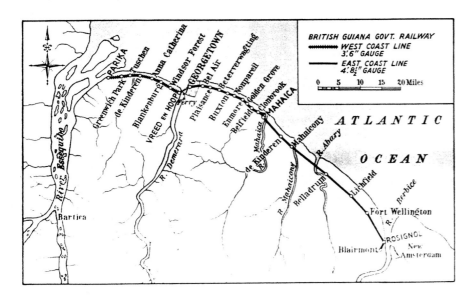

The British Guiana Government Railway

Under this heading are comprised three territories: the independent state of Guyana (until 1966 British Guiana); Dutch Guiana, better known as Surinam; and French Guiana (Guyane), since 1946 regarded as a 'Department' of metropolitan France.

Guyana is about the size of Great Britain, but it has a population of only 800,000. Communications with the interior are difficult, and the only two public railways were both on the coastal belt, where the terrain is relatively flat. Many watercourses present problems, as does flooding, as much of the land is slightly below sea level.

The first railway in South America was built in British Guiana, work having commenced on the standard gauge Demerara Railway from Georgetown to Mahaica, 24km, in August 1847. There was a disastrous trial run in January 1848, when two wagons being pushed by a locomotive were derailed after collision with a cow, a director and an employee being killed

in this accident. The railway was opened to general traffic for the first 9km in November 1848 but it took a further two years to construct the next 7km. Thereafter the line crept forward in fits and starts, and was opened throughout on 31st August 1864. The East Coast Railway, as it later became known, was extended in 1900 from Mahaica to Rosignol, on the opposite bank of the Berbice river to New Amsterdam, making a total route mileage of 97km.

The railway was single track, with twenty-five intermediate stations situated on average 5km apart. Latterly, there was hardly any freight but passenger traffic was quite brisk; in 1962 more than 2½ million passengers were carried, accounting for four-fifths of the total revenue. The Demerara Railway Company was taken over by the Government in 1922, and amalgamated with the Government owned and operated Colonial Steamer Service, under the title of the Colonial Transport Department. Five years

Guyana: A works photo of the standard gauge Demerara Railway 0-6-0ST no. 5 'Georgetown', built at the North British Atlas Works (16331/1904).
Courtesy of Uwe Bergmann.

100

Guyana: One of the 4-6-4T built in 1946 by the Hunslet Engine Co., works nos 3386 and 3387.
Courtesy of Keith Taylorson.

Guyana: Postage stamps were issued which featured an unidentified 0-6-0ST, possibly the loco constructed at the Georgetown workshops in 1946, no. 36 "Donkey".

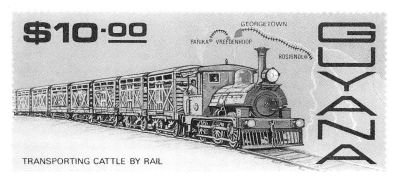

Guyana: Drewry 0-6-0DM no. 22 departing from the terminus station at Vreed-en-Hoop.

later this was amalgamated with the Harbours and Pilotage Department to form the transport and Harbours Department, responsible also for the West Coast line which will be described later. In 1970 the railway was cut back to Burma, 59km from Georgetown, and complete closure took place in 1972.

Motive power on the East Coast Railway has included a Sharp Stewart 2-2-2T perhaps aptly named Centipede, and a pair of Neilson 2-4-0Ts of 1857. Then followed an unbroken line of loco-motives from Sharp Stewart: two 0-4-0Ts in 1860, numerous 0-6-0Ts between 1863 and 1878, some 2-4-2Ts in 1899 and rather surprisingly, another 2-2-2T "Eza" in the same year. This machine was reported as still active in 1954. Locomotives by North British (two) and Hawthorn (one) came next, followed by a pair of fine 4-6-4Ts from Hunslet in 1923 and an 0-6-4T in 1931. Two more 4-6-4Ts arrived from Hunslet in 1946 and the last steam locomotive put into service was an 0-6-0ST built locally from parts of condemned locomotives in 1946. One of the 1863 0-6-0Ts Victoria remained in use until 1956, and a few years before closure one oil-burning 4-6-4T was still active, and probably remained in service to the very end. In 1948 equipment was obtained from the Bermuda Railway, and this included two diesel electrics built in 1942. It has been recorded that a petrol driven inspection railcar was used by HRH the Princess Royal when visiting the colony in 1953. In 1955 three Bo-Bo diesel electrics came from General Electric of the USA and these then worked most of the passenger trains, backed up by three six-coupled Drewry diesel mechanical locomotives also supplied in 1955. Some of the more modern passenger stock was built by the Gloucester Carriage and Wagon Co.

The other public railway in Guyana was known as the West Coast line. It was of 3'6" gauge and extended from Vreed-en-Hoop, on the opposite bank of the Demerara river facing Georgetown, to Parika on the Essequibo river, a distance of 29km. This line was built from Vreed-en-Hoop to Greenwich Park between 1897 and 1900, and extended the additional 4km or so to Parika in 1914. The original motive power consisted of four 2-4-2Ts by Sharp Stewart (three) and Hawthorn (one), built between 1897 and 1900. These lasted until 1955, when they were replaced by four 204hp diesel mechanical locomotives from the Drewry Car Co., similar to those supplied at the same time to the East Coast line. Owing to the nature of the road bed, maximum speeds were low; ballast was of sand, seashell and burnt earth, with a permitted axle load of only 10 tons. The West Coast line was closed down in 1972.

Apart from these two public railways, there are known to have been sugar plantation railways at Blairmont, near Rosignol, and Port Mourant, beyond New Amsterdam, and there was also the metre gauge Essequibo Railway, extending from Wismar (105km inland from Georgetown on the west side of the Demerara river) to Rockstone on the Essequibo river, a distance of 30km. This line was used for timber haulage and to serve the diamond fields and also had a passenger service, but is no longer in existence having closed in 1957.

On the opposite bank of the Demerara river to Wismar is Linden (formerly Mackenzie) where the works of the Demerara Bauxite Company serve the largest bauxite deposits in the world. There are some 80km of 3ft gauge railway, operated under the title of the Demba Railroad, using diesel locomotives. A 1957 Railway Gazette Map showed a 2ft 6in gauge line running from Mackenzie to Three Friends, but whether this line was ever built is not known. Near the Venezuelan border is a standard gauge railway built as recently as 1959 by Manganese Mines Management Ltd to transport ore from Matthews Ridge to a shipping terminal on the Kaituma river. Now Government owned, this railway is 48km long and diesel operated.

Surinam

Surinam (Dutch Guiana) had its first public railway built because gold was discovered at Dam, 173km from the capital city of Paramaribo. This metre gauge line opened in 1905 to Republiek, in 1906 to Kwakoegron, in 1908 to De Jong, and finally reached Dam in 1911. At first there was a steam driven cableway across the Surinam river but this was replaced by a ferry in 1923. However, the section beyond the river had regular services withdrawn in 1930, although the track remained in place and in 1959 was still used by the local population, travelling on hand-propelled trolleys! As the line ran through the streets of Paramaribo, Dutch pattern tram locomotives were provided as motive power, the first batch consisting of six 16 ton engines built by Borsig in 1904, plus two small 8½ ton four coupled conventional tank engines for the Kabel - Dam section. These had to be taken apart to be sent across the cableway and reassembled on the other side of the river. Later locomotives included two 18 ton Krauss tram engines built in 1908 and a Breda (Dutch) 0-4-0T of 1916.

The railway jogged quietly along until by 1957 busy road conditions caused the closure of the in-town section at Paramaribo. In 1961 the railway was further cut back from Paramaribo, terminating at Onverwacht, 26km from the capital. About the same time the construction of a dam and consequent lake made it necessary to close 16km between Bronsweg and Kabel. On the credit side, though, and prior to these closures, an international airport has been developed at Zanderij, beyond Republiek, and this helped to generate some traffic. In 1954 the

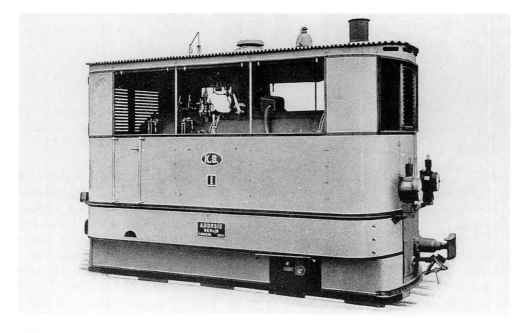

Surinam: Locomotive no. 1 of the metre gauge Koloniale Spoorwegen was an 0-4-0T tram engine supplied by Borsig in 1904. Five further such locos were built in the same batch, works nos. 5339 to 5344.
Photo courtesy of Uwe Bergmann.

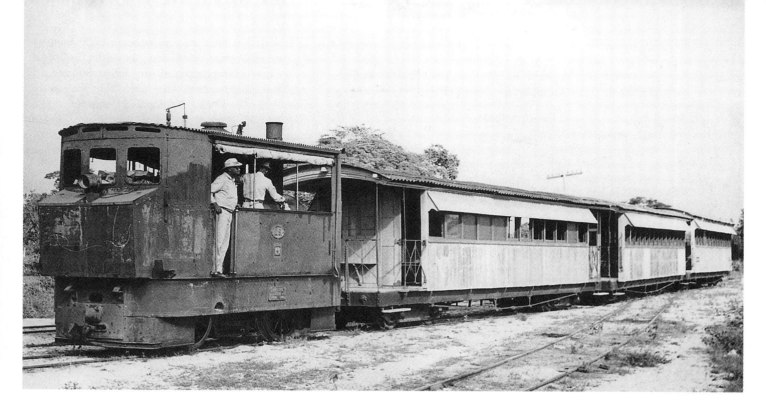

Surinam: The Koloniale Spoorwegen tram locos were still in use in 1967 when no. 4 was seen on a passenger service. It has gained a fuel bunker and is running with part of the skirting removed. Due to the tropical location the coach windows have permanent sunshades and the loco crew is wearing 'whites' as if for a game of cricket! Photo: G. Todd.

railway received a trio of three-car diesel train sets from Linke-Hofmann-Busch of Salzgitter, West Germany, and in 1959 these usually worked the thrice-daily passenger service between Paramaribo and the airport, and also twice weekly to Kabel, on which days one of the local workings had to be steam hauled. The railway also transported aviation fuel and carried material for road and dam construction. When visited in 1967 by Mr J G Todd (whose notes published in Modern Tramway have provided most of the information quoted) there were steam trains running thrice weekly, with a railcar set in use on the other days. He saw no sign of the other two railcar sets, but suggests that they could have

been sold to bauxite or sugar companies operating railways, details of which follow. Five of the original six Borsig tram engines were still serviceable in 1967, as was the 1916 built 0-4-0T. All were wood-burners.

It will be noted that this metre gauge railway was the first (and indeed only) public railway in the colony, but in about 1900 a standard gauge railway to serve a gold mine was built on the Morowijne river (which forms the frontier with French Guiana). This line had been abandoned in 1927 and is believed to have used second-hand American equipment, including a Baldwin locomotive built in 1878. There is an illustration of what was

Surinam: A works photo of one of the 0-4-0WT that worked on the Kabel-Dam section of the Koloniale Spoorwegen, no. 8, supplied by Arnold Jung in 1905, builder's no. 820. Courtesy of Uwe Bergmann.

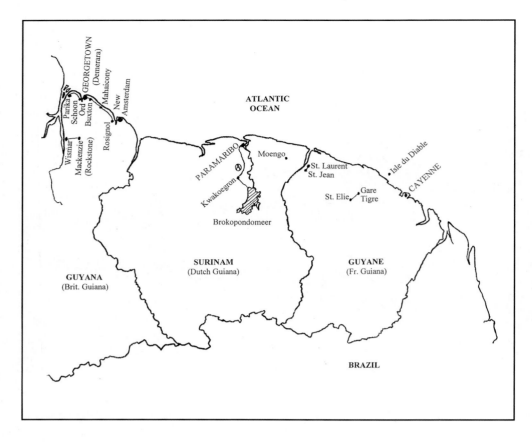

later another concern had taken over and completed 20km which were later repurchased by the Société des Gisements de Saint-Elie who had by 1898 completed 33½km of 500mm gauge track between Saint-Elie and Gare Tigre (Saint Nazaire). Lack of capital and climatic difficulties saw the workforce reduce from 475 in 1906 to 200 in 1919, in which year the company went into liquidation, after having produced, or probably more accurately after having officially recorded production of 13 tons of ore over a period of 41 years!

For some years local prospectors took over until in 1923 the Société Nouvelle de Saint-Elie et Adieu-Vat was formed and by 1926 was operating the railway once more. The original 5kg rails were replaced by heavier (9kg) track and a small steam locomotive was acquired, but is reputed never to have seen service. Mule traction was in use from the earliest days until well after World War II when, incredibly, man power took over with eight teams of four men each operating eight trips a day! It is claimed that they could move over a ton per team, while the mule only hauled 300kg! In 1956 the new company failed and gold prospecting reverted, as it were, to very individual private enterprise. The railway remained, however, in sporadic use, and a local grocer even managed to motorise a trolley for his own use! There have been plans to revive mining on a commercial basis, but the railway is no doubt too far gone to be of much use, but at least one line remained in use in 1996, with human traction. I must confess that I was in total ignorance of the existence of this line until reading of it in "La Vie du Rail" early in 1982, and all information above comes from this source and is duly acknowledged. Incidentally, the remains of the locomotive are illustrated in this article, but buried in deep jungle and quite unidentifiable.

The only other railway thought to have existed in French Guiana was a 600mm gauge line owned by the penal settlement of Chantiers Chavino, linking Saint Laurent de Maroni with Saint Jean, on the river which forms the frontier with Surinam. It is probable that this line closed many years ago, but the following description of it appeared in 1927:

"The line has two or three wood-burning locomotives but these are rarely used as the railway is a prison line running to the penitentiary and the prisoners are made to propel the cars." But economy was tempered with humanity as the quotation continues "Very few passengers and little freight are carried." Readers are invited to read the famous escape story "Papillon" by Henry Charriere, for a description of this railway.

No rail operations are believed to have remained as this book goes to press.

probably this machine well overgrown by jungle vegetation in "Railway Wonders of The World" where it is stated that the railway was abandoned (before completion?) because of the difficult territory in which it was being built.

Other railways in existence in 1959 included the Marienburg Sugar Estates system to the east of Paramaribo, thought to have been of standard gauge and using two and four-coupled steam and diesel locomotives. At that time there were some workmens' passenger trains on the system. The Surinam Aluminium Company (Suralco) had a 13km line, thought to be of 3'6" gauge, from Moengo to the river Cottica, worked by American diesel locomotives hauling big bogie wagons and with three passenger coaches for staff use. This was closed due to guerilla activity. Also, the Billitonmaatschappij, a bauxite railway of unknown gauge, had a short line from a mine near Onverwacht to Smalkalden on the Surinam river. The public line between Onverwacht and Brownsweg was last reported as active in 1975 and the railway finally closed in 1988. In 1996 it was announced that the Onverwacht - Republiek route was to be re-opened for tourist trains using one of the Breda 0-4-0Ts. It is not thought that this actually happened and there are no passenger services and probably no freight either in Suriname as at November 2000.

Guyane

French Guiana has never had any public railways but in 1873 gold was discovered some 100km inland from the Atlantic coast, and a company formed to exploit it. At first mules brought the gold to the river Sinnamary, and canoes transported it to the coast, but in 1882 a light railway was proposed and construction began in 1884 The mining concessionaires of Saint-Elie and Dieu-Mer were jointly involved but gave up after building 3½km. Two years

PARAGUAY

Paraguay is one of the smallest of the South American countries, with an area of 157,000 sq miles and a population of about 5½ million. It is one of the two landlocked states of the continent but has a slight advantage over the other, Bolivia, in as much as the Atlantic ocean can be reached by river boat from the capital and many other points in the country.

Independence from Spain was achieved in 1811, but a period of almost total isolation from the outside world followed until in 1840 Carlos Antonio López became President and opened the frontiers to trade and commerce. In 1853 his son, Francisco Solano López, visited England and appointed the British firm of John and Alfred Blyth as Consulting Engineers. In 1854 the President authorised construction of the railway which today bears his name, but unfortunately he died in 1862, within a year of the first section being opened. The Blyth's representative in Paraguay was J W Whitehead who, as well as being responsible for the first stages of railway construction, was Director of the Arsenal, shipyard, foundry, and sawmill. The line was built to 5'6" gauge by British engineers and was to extend to Paraguari (72km), with branches to serve the Arsenal and docks in Asunción, a military camp at Cerro Leon (60 km), and blast furnaces at Ybycui. Locomotive trials took place between May and August 1961 and then came the official opening over 6.4 km to Trinidad, reported as taking place on either 21st September or 21st October 1861. Exactly 87 years later the locomotive which was reputed to have worked the first train was presented to the Nation, when the following ceremony took place in Asunción. The description is taken from an official 1948 report (which favours October as the month in question):

'On the morining of the 21st, "Sapucai" (as the loco was named) was duly unloaded from the flat-car upon which she was brought from the township of Sapucay, where she had been refurbished in a livery of light brown with gold piping, and placed on a special length of broad gauge track laid for the occasion into the terminal station. Two trains were formed up in the yard, ready for the ceremonial and historical entry into the station. "Sapucai" headed one of these with old two-axle coaches. Because of the condition of her boiler, "Sapucai" could not make her last journey under her own power, but it was arranged that her "voice" be heard again by means of a carefully concealed oxygen cylinder. She was decorated with ribbons coloured with the red, white and blue of the Paraguayan flag, and carried on her smoke-box door the Paraguayan coat-of-arms, flanked by the flags of Paraguay and Britain. There were 700 guests, including the President of the Republic, and the Police Band was in attendance. All the locomotives present whistled as the veteran, quietly and imperceptibly pushed from behind, sounded her whistle and moved into the station; in the cab rode Florentin Torres, 70 years old, who remembered the locomotive during her working life'.

The early locomotive history of the Asunción to Villa Rica Railway is unclear. 'Sapucai', mentioned above, is now preserved as a 4-2-2T at Asunción. It is thought to be the original locomotive imported by Blyth in 1858/59, a Fairbairn 2-2-2T similar to L&NWR (UK) types and to a

The imposing Asunción terminus with 'Sapucai' on display. Since this picture was taken in 1968 the loco has been moved inside, under the canopy and a road has been driven across the point where the photographer is standing.

locomotive preserved at São Paulo, Brazil. It is not known when, or why, it was converted to a 4-2-2T, but the Arsenal made a new connecting rod for this locomotive in 1862. It is recorded that two 'line' locomotives were received in 1861 and two locomotives were blessed by the Bishop on the official opening day, but apart from the fact that three existed then, we have little information on the other two, thought to have been 2-4-0s.

Francisco Solano López succeeded his father on 10th September 1862 and the railway opened to Aregua (29.5km) on 25th December of that year. The exact date it reached Paraguari is uncertain, but certainly the railway was completed by the end of 1864. In 1865 came the disastrous War of the Triple Alliance. Paraguay fought against Brazil, Argentina and Uruguay, lost, and had her population decimated up to the extent of 90% of the male population. Some British contract staff died in the conflict, as did President López at Cerro Cora in 1870. He is remembered as the 'Paraguayan Napoleon', a national hero who is perhaps better known in Europe for the excesses of his Irish mistress, Madame Lynch (about whom a number of books have appeared which give a good picture of life in Paraguay in the early days of the railway).

The railway was totally destroyed (as were the Arsenal, ship-yard and blast furnaces), and only the 'small' locomotive survived plus some locally built rolling stock. Thee first class carriages were sent to Buenos Aires as trophies, a rather short-sighted move as material was soon being imported in the opposite direction to get the railway going again! The occupying Brazilian army got to work at first (no doubt in their own inter-ests), later arranging for the line to be worked by an Argentinian contractor. Finance for reconstruction was a major problem and very little progress was made until the occupying forces with-drew after a peace treaty was signed in 1876. During the period of occupation locomotives, and presumably rolling stock, had been brought in by the Brazilian army and these included E.B. Wilson 571/1856, an identical 2-2-0ST to the one preserved at Luján, Argentina, a Sharp Stewart 2-2-0, and a Sharp Stewart 4-4-0, all imported in 1869. There were also two 2-4-0Ts built by John Jones of Liverpool in 1860 and all of these were ex-Buenos Aires Western Railway, presumably having come all the way by river steamer. In those days this was the best way for both travellers and freight to reach the Atlantic coast, despite the long journey time involved. It would appear that Brazilian forces were mainly respon-sible for post-war administration, while material needs were met from Argentina.

Between 1876 and 1886 the railway was privately owned. It then passed to the Government, but was sold to a British company, the Paraguay Central Railway Co. Ltd. in 1889. This is a rather simplified version of complicated events but during this period work was in hand to extend the railway to Villa Rica and plans had been made to reach Encarnación. In 1888 four 4-4-0s were supplied by Hohenzollern, Germany and the following year four 4-6-0Ts arrived from Black Hawthorn, reflecting the new British ownership which was to obtain all future motive power from the UK.

Villa Rica was reached in September 1889 and at the same time work was progressing on the extension to Encarnación. David Angus became the resident engineer in 1889 and has writ-ten of his experiences in the country (and other parts of South America) in his book referred to in the bibliography. A change of Government in 1890 led to financial problems which delayed

further extension but Yuti was reached in August 1891, at least this was the proud claim of the contractors, actually Yuti was about 15km further on across a river yet to be bridged!

The workshops at Sapucai were built in 1892/93, resulting in improved maintenance, as there had been no suitable facilities since the Arsenal had been dismantled some 25 years earlier. More sources of traffic appeared during the 1890s when 'colonies' were set up in the region, one consisting of immigrants from Australia. The Tebicuary Sugar Mill was also built during this periond and soon had its own railway network, to be mentioned later.

Gauge Conversion

Completion of the railway to Encarnación was still some years away at the turn of the century but in Argentina rails were push-ing towards the opposite bank of the Upper Parana river at Posadas. Unfortunately, although there was plenty of 5'6" gauge in Argentina the railways reaching out towards Paraguay were (exceptionally) of 4'8½" gauge and it became obvious that for the Paraguayan system to prosper unification was essential. A gradual conversion of the railway was undertaken between 1910 and 1913, by which latter date Encarnación had been reached and train ferries were in place. Through passenger and freight traffic to Buenos Aires was now possible, although readers of the Argentinian chapter will note that another river passage was needed in that country, not just a 'bank to bank' crossing but a veritable sail along the river between Ibicuy and Zarate. Both have now been replaced by bridges - road/rail bridges which see far more road than rail traffic, having come too late to be of real use to the declining railway systems. At Encarnación, the ferry berth had to be built beyond the town and track ran along the main street to reach it, wagons and passenger stock having to be winched down a slope onto the ferry boats, which were wood burning paddle steamers built in Britain 1911-15.

Standard Gauge Locomotives

Having reached the gauge conversion we can now turn our attention to the new locomotives needed. The last broad gauge machines placed in service included a Sharp Stewart 0-6-0 built in 1895 for Spain and received in 1898, four Hawthorn Leslie 4-4-0s 1899-1904, and two 2-6-0s from the same builder, 1906/7. One of these, regauged, is reputed to have survived until 1943, and possibly one other was regauged, but the rest were scrapped. The standard gauge changed little until second-hand Argentinian types started to arrive in the 1970s. Even so, some of the earlier types remained in service until at least 1999. Nos 1-6 are 2-6-2Ts built by Hawthorn Leslie, the first four in 1910 and the other two in 1913. These are usually to be found with tenders and are used for shunting duties. Nos 10-12 also came from Hawthorn Leslie, typical industrial 0-6-0 side tanks, two built in 1910 and the other

in 1913, and these were out of use by the time of my first visit to Paraguay in 1968, two being seen derelict at Asunción. The main line locomotives came from North British and are 2-6-0s, numbers 51 to 60 and 101 to 104, all built in 1910 except for the present 101, which arrived in 1913. There was another 101, built in 1910 and apparently replaced within three years, although I do not know the fate it suffered, possibly lost at sea?

The foregoing fleet kept the railway going until 1953, when nos. 151 & 152 arrived from the Yorkshire Engine Co., 2-6-0s which were the last new locomotives to be obtained, although latterly Argentinian machines have been bought second hand. A passenger coach noted in 1968 also appeared to have been converted from a Sentinel steam railcar, a Garratt appeared briefly from Argentina but is not thought to have seen service and may in fact have been bought as scrap, and there were also rumours of a

The standard gauge international mixed train at Paraguari on 26th August 1968 with North British built 2-6-0 no. 53 being prepared for departure. The fireman is up on the tender sorting out his wood fuel as the driver oils round the locomotive. All the Paraguayan steam locos were wood fired and to cope with the volume of fuel required for a long run a bogie wagon has been coupled behind the tender. Note the hinged buffers resting on the running plate.

The last two locomotives built new for Paraguay were a pair of 2-6-0s nos. 151 and 152, supplied in 1953 by the Yorkshire Engine Co. No. 151 seen at Asunción in December 1981 was still at work in the 1990s.

visit by an Argentinian diesel, but for many years now the system has been able to claim to be the only national railway in the world to rely exclusively on wood fired steam power.

Post-Conversion Railway Building

But we are running ahead of history. The main line was completed over the 376km between Asunción and Encarnación in 1911 and the train ferries were in service by 1913. The broad gauge was lifted soon afterwards by the removal of the extra rail laid to accommodate material of both gauges, at least on the earlier sections; I am not sure if the broad gauge tracks actually reached Encarnación and if they did there would have been little point in their continuation to the ferry berth at Pacú Cua. In 1913 a scheme was considered to build a branch from Borja (later named San Salvador) roughly half way along the main line, to Iguazu on the Brazilian frontier and the site of a superb waterfall and potentially a great tourist attraction, full exploitation of which has only flourished in the latter 25 years of the 20th Century. When visited on my honeymoon in 1968 access from the Argentinian side was quite primitive and involved individual negotiation of boat hire to reach the best viewpoint. In the 1980s a visit to the Brazilian side was much more 'tourist friendly' but the natural wonders are still awe-inspiring and nobody visiting the area should miss it. Sadly the branch line never reached Iguazu, petering out at Abai, 64km, in 1920. It was sustained, at least until

relatively recently, by Fasardi Ltda., who had a 750mm gauge line extending some 34km and posessing three steam locomotives.

Paraguayan Narrow Gauge

Back along the main line we have already mentioned the sugar mill at Tebicuary. To work its standard gauge connection it has two tramway locomotives, built by Borsig in 1910, which came second hand from Buenos Aires where they had worked wagons along the streets to the market. There were also some 40km of metre gauge serving the canefields and stock included O&K 0-8-0s and a 2-8-2. To the best of my knowledge this material still exists, although inactive for many years now.

The only other railway between Asunción and Encarnación was situated a short distance from the latter town, at Carmen del Parana, and was an 18km long 600mm gauge line owned by Christopherson. At one time there was a steam tramway in Asunción serving the suburb of San Lorenzo but apart from this all other railways in Paraguay are, or more accurately today, were situated on the Paraguay River. The only public railway, built in 1910 to the metre gauge, extended 50km between Concepción and Horqueta and was entitled the Ferrocarril del Norte. There were projects to extend this line to the Brazilian frontier at Bella Vista but these never materialised and the railway has been closed for many years now. In 1970 some Orenstein & Koppel 0-6-0WTs were reported derelict at Concepción and I was told in 1981 that

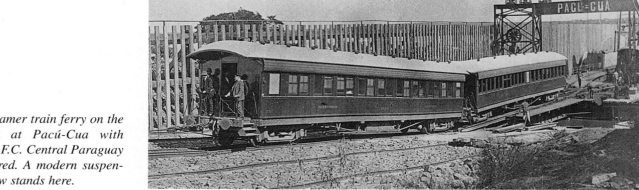

The paddle steamer train ferry on the river Parana at Pacú-Cua with coaches of the F.C. Central Paraguay being transferred. A modern suspension bridge now stands here.

4-6-0 no. 237 stands beside one of the two former Buenos Aires steam tram locos latterly used for the standard gauge connection to the Tebicuary Sugar Mill. The 4-6-0 in the photo is also of Argentinian origin, having been built by North British in 1910 for the F.C. Entre Rios and obtained by the FCPAL from the F.C. General Urquiza in the 1970s. The photo was taken on 2nd December 1981.

Hanomag metre gauge 0-4-0WT 'Tebicuary' (4992/1906) on the Tebicuary Sugar Mill railway.

a locomotive from the line is preserved in a park there. Situated some 312km to the north Asunción, this railway was extremely difficult of access from the capital by road, most traffic making use of the Paraguay River, an interesting but very slow means of transport.

The other lines along the Paraguay River were mostly built to transport quebracho hardwood, (the raw material of the tannin industry, also used in chemicals and in the manufacture of dyes), or to serve Mennonite settlements whose only means of communication with the outside world before the coming of aviation was the river. Travelling up the river from Asunción via Concepción to Horqueta, as can be done if one is willing to endure sufficient hardship, the first railway was located at Puerto Ibapobo, 760mm gauge, extending 32km to San Antonio. Next came Concepción to Horqueta, already mentioned, and then Puerto Pinasco, metre gauge, 108km with quebracho traffic, and US owned by International Products. This line closed about 1967 and in 1970 seven steam locomotives remained in existence, one being used to lift track sold to Puerto Casado.

The railway from Puerto Casado extended 159km westwards into the heart of the Chaco and was of 760mm gauge. It once had a weekly train on which passengers could travel, although it mainly existed for quebacho transportation. The interesting selection of motive power included a Henschel 0-6-2T of 1926 and two 2-8-2s from the same builder in 1926 and 1935. A Borsig 0-6-0WT of 1904 came from the Puerto Sastre system and the only non German machine was a Manning Wardle 2-8-2WT of 1916. Puerto Casado is about 210km north of Concepción by river but could be reached by Air Force flights (which carried passengers) from Asunción. This railway was visited by an enthusiast group from the UK in the 1970s, when a short

Carlos Casado S.A. operated the Puerto Casado 760mm gauge line for quebracho hardwood transportation. 0-6-0WT no. 5 'Don Carlos' was seen on a visit in November 1983. Photo: David Ibbotson.

Also on the Puerto Casado system in 1983 was no. 6 'Maria Casildo', an 0-6-2 with a makeshift tender converted from a bogie wagon. Photo: David Ibbotson.

trip was made on the remaining few kilometres of track still in use.

A little further up the river is Puerto Sastre, where the 91km railway was of 750mm gauge. It was closed about 1960. Finally, at Puerto Guarani was a 760mm gauge line extending westwards for 92km from the river and owned by the Forestal Company, which also had quebracho lines in the north of Argentina. This railway had two O&K 0-6-0WTs.

Accurate information on the facscinating but highly inaccessible railways came mostly from old issues of 'World Railways', and apart from the group mentioned above I know of no enthusiasts having visited them and indeed at the time they were operating it would have been virtually impossible to do so.

The Standard Gauge up to 1999

Let us now return to the standard gauge, which until 1998 still existed more or less as it was when I first saw it in 1968, and

indeed well before that. Apart from the two 1953 built locomotives, everything else, including the British built wooden bodied passenger rolling stock, appeared to date from the gauge conversion. One notable change had been the nationalisation of the railway in 1961, when it was renamed the FC Presidente Carlos Antonio López, in honour of its founder.

Passenger figures for 1965 are quoted as being only 415, with the track in such poor condition that passenger trains were limited to 12mph and freight trains to 6mph (Economy of Paraguay, J Pincus 1968). The timetable for 1963 shows a journey time of 12 hours but when I rode the line in 1968 this had been extended to 16 hours and the service reduced to a through train in each direction on alternate days. The speeds quoted above seem remarkably slow but the track was certainly in very bad condition, our (international) train suffering derailment of freight wagons coupled behind the passenger stock. After some delay, these were just left behind, no doubt in the knwoledge that no other traffic would pass that way until the following day!

In 1968 I thought that the railway was on its last legs, but over 30 years later little had changed apart from the introduction of ex-Argentinian locomotives and carriages. The completion of the 3km long bridge physically linking (at last) the railway with Argentina in 1990 came too late to have any effect on traffic as by then the Argentinian system was also in difficulty. In the 1970s to early 1980s projects abounded, with headlines such as 'Paraguay plans 376km electrification' and 'Paraguay studies $66 million revival package'. These studies included linking the system with Brazil by extending the Abai branch to the frontier at Caballero/Punta Pora where it would link up with the metre gauge Nordeste of Brazil, possibly requiring the Paraguayan system to be converted, at least in part, to metre gauge, while an optimistic statement in 1973 suggested '600km of new railway line, reconstruction of the existing 440kms', and terminated with 'Low cost electricity is likely to be available soon, the new lines could be electrified from the start'. Sadly this is the story of most South American railways, grandiose projects which never see the light of day, whatever money that is forthcoming being spent on roads.

Bad weather caused serious problems in 1997, but most of the system was still open apart from a break between Carmen and Encarnación, where six locomotives were trapped. Regular services consisted of a daily (except Sunday) local Ypacarai - Asunción, plus a Sundays only "Tren Recreo" from Ypacarai to Sapucai and return. In addition there was a Tuesday only mixed train Villarrica - Coronel Bogado, returning on Thursdays. Freight traffic was non-existent, apart from the conveyance of wood for locomotive fuel on the Abai branch as far as José Fassardi.

By the end of 1999 economics and motor vehicle competition had finally caught up with the railway and virtually no trains were running, the very existence of railways in Paraguay being held in the balance.

Inside Sapucai works in 1981 4-6-0 no. 286, one of the locos obtained from Argentina, is supported on jacks and receiving attention.

PERU

Peru is the third in size of the South American countries, over twice as large as France, with a total area of 506,000 square miles and a population of 24 million. It may surprise British readers to learn that Peru was visited in 1817 by Richard Trevithick, who obtained a concession from the Viceroy to build a railway from Cerro de Pasco to Oroya in connection with a mining enterprise with which he was associated. The outbreak of the War of Independence brought this scheme to naught, but in 1926 another Englishman, John Beggs, approached the new government of Simón Bolivar with a similar scheme, again without success. After further false starts, work began on 10th June 1850 on a railway linking the port of Callao with the capital city of Lima, reached on 17th May 1851. This short line presented no construction problems and was a purely interurban link which later succumbed to tramway competition and was taken over by the Central Railway in 1934.

The Southern Railway (F.C. del Sur)

The story of the two principal railways in Peru, the Central and the Southern, is bound up with the career of Henry Meiggs, who was born in New York State in 1811. After participating in the Californian Gold Rush he arrived in Chile in 1855 and was instrumental in building the mountain section of the Valparaíso to Santiago line, after which he came to Peru and commenced work on the Southern Railway in 1868. As in Chile, he contracted to

complete the line (to Arequipa) within a period of three years, or pay a monthly penalty, and work started on 27th May 1868. Despite some labour trouble, the first train ran on 24th December 1870. This section, from the port of Mollendo to Arequipa is 171km long, and by Arequipa the railway has already climbed to a height of 2,329m. Before the first public train reached Arequipa work was proceeding onwards and upwards towards Juiliaca, 302km from Arequipa and 3,825m above sea level. On this

Motive power for the Southern Railway of Peru's Mollendo to Arequipa line included some superheated Alco 4-6-0s built in 1907 of which number 82 is shown here.
Photo: author's collection.

A surviving example of the highly successful 'Andes' class 2-8-0, a type which appeared as a number of different designs as it was developed and supplied by various builders.
F.C. Central no. 206 was built by Beyer Peacock (6830/1937), and was seen at Lima station during November 1976.

section is the highest point reached on the Southern, 4,470m at Cruzero Alto. The next section to be built was Juiliaca to Puno (48km) completed in 1876 and linking Lake Titicaca with the coast. This lake is in reality an inland sea of around 3,500 square miles, situated at an altitude of 3,818m (12,500ft) above sea level. There is a steamer service from Puno to Guaquí in Bolivia, operated by the 'Inca' and 'Ollanta', which sail once weekly overnight, taking 11 hours. The steamers were built at Hull in 1905 and 1929, sailed to Peru, and were then dismantled and carried over the Southern Railway to the lake, where they were reassembled and have remained in service ever since. A tourist agency now operates a hydrofoil service across the lake. The

Guaquí - La Paz Railway in Bolivia was owned by the Peruvian Corporation, as were the lake steamers and the Southern Railway, and many tourists used this route between the two countries, often travelling over the Southern Railway from Puno to Cuzco. Much Bolivian freight traffic also uses the Southern route to Peruvian coastal ports although it is by no means the shortest route to the sea, and involves the extra maritime section across the lake.

Returning to Juiliaca, the other branch of the Southern Railway extends to Cuzco, reached in 1907 after the railway, and most others then operating or under construction, had been taken over by the Peruvian Corporation. This section is 328km long, and reaches heights in excess of 4,000m.

The Peruvian Corporation

The Peruvian Corporation, which has operated six railways with a total length of 1,708km was formed in London in 1890 because large sums of British capital had been invested in Peru against the security of the Tarapaca nitrate deposits, lost to Chile after the war of 1879-82. To protect the interests of those involved, claims for outstanding payments were waived against certain exclusive concessions, which included the right to operate certain railways, and all commercial services on Lake Titicaca, at first for a period of sixty-six years, but later granted in perpetuity. The two principal Peruvian Corporation railways were of course the Central and the Southern, both of which were uncompleted when it was formed. The Corporation remained London based until in 1956 the ordinary share capital passed to Peruvian Investment and Finance Ltd of Toronto. In May 1971 the Peruvian Government placed an embargo on the Corporation for non-payment of a loan from the World Bank for railway modernisation, as payment had been guaranteed by the government in case of default by the Corporation. The Industrial Bank of Peru acted as executor and on 30th November 1972 held a public auction of the Central and Southern Railways, lake steamers, remaining equipment of the Pascomayo Railway etc., the reserve price being just over £8 million. In theory anyone could buy, but as expected only the government was interested, and the railways and lake steamers were handed over to the recently established National Railways Company, a state corporation now known as ENAFER. The Guaquí - La Paz railway in Bolivia, owned by the Peruvian Corporation, was not included in the auction (it could prove embarrassing for one nation to own a railway situated in the territory of another) and it was incorporated into the Bolivian national system.

Because of unsatisfactory conditions at the port of Mollendo, the Peruvian government financed construction of a line from the new port of Matarani, a short distance away along the coast, to connect with the Southern Railway at La Joya, a distance of 62km. This railway was opened on 6 January 1951, and a postage stamp issued to commemorate the event depicts the inaugural train hauled by No 80, an Alco 4-6-0 of 1907. Although the property of the government, the line was always worked by the Southern as part of its system.

The motive power supplied for the opening of the original line to Arequipa was American built 2-6-0s, followed by 4-6-0s and in the early 1900s some 4-8-0 two-cylinder compounds, all of American construction. Quite a number of the locomotives were assembled in the well-equipped shops of the railway at Arequipa; Brian Fawcett quotes a roster of 46 locomotives in 1908, of which 32 were "built" at Arequipa. The roster in the 1951 World Railways is very similar at 48 machines, the largest classes being seven Alco 4-6-0s of 1907, ten Alco 2-8-0s of 1906 and ten 4-8-0 compounds of 1906. Other locomotives included four 0-6-0Ts from Hunslet in 1927-8 and three 2-8-0s from Beyer Peacock in 1937-9. These latter machines were similar to the famous "Andes" type on the Central, and further examples were supplied in 1946 and 1950, together with some 0-6-0Ts from Hunslet and the Yorkshire Engine Company between 1948 and 1952. Also in 1952 two of the Central Railway Garratts were borrowed for trials, but were not successful, and soon returned northwards. Dieselisation commenced in 1956, with six Alco DL 500 Co-Co diesel electrics derated from 1,800hp to 1,320hp in view of the

altitudes at which they had to work. They were followed in 1958 by a DL 531 Co-Co of 900hp and in 1961-2 by six DL 543 Co-Cos with an output of 2,000hp. These were followed in their turn by eleven DL 535B Co-Cos supplied in 1963-4. In the mid-1970s Canadian built DL 560 units have been supplied, along with 500hp DL 532D heavy-duty shunters, and these have been shared between the Southern and Central Railways. It will be noticed that the "road" engines are all American designs, but there are also some 344hp diesel shunters supplied by the Yorkshire Engine Company in 1964. Railcars have included Wickhams built between 1936 and 1953, and two by Saurer in 1968. All operations are now dieselised and the principal passenger trains are made up of lightweight bogie stock supplied by Cravens during 1952-8 or Romanian built in 1975. Latterly there was a daily service overnight between Arequipa and Cuzco, and through trains at least twice weekly to Puno (daily except Sundays at certain times of the year).

Cuzco - Santa Ana Railway

From Cuzco, ancient capital of the Incas and today a city of some 120,000 inhabitants living at an altitude of 3,500m above sea level, the 3ft gauge Cuzco - Santa Ana railway extends to Quillabamba (172km), serving en route the Inca ruins at Machu-Picchu, one of the incomparable tourist sites of South America and certainly the only one to be reached by the majority of visitors over a narrow gauge railway! The line was projected in 1905 and built in 1921, but has never reached Santa Ana which is situated well beyond the railhead. Quillabamba, 42km from Chaullay, was only reached in 1980. The railway was government owned from the outset and is now part of ENAFER. Trains leave from San Pedro station in Cuzco, climb up the mountainside, two double zig-zags offering a magnificent view of the city. There are special tourist workings for Machu-Picchu, and regular services to Quillabamba, nowadays diesel hauled, although some steam still survived into the 1980s for freight working and in reserve. Steam locomotives retained latterly were mostly 2-8-2s, and included two Baldwins of 1926, Henschels of 1950/1/5 and a Baldwin 4-6-0, which was usually station pilot at Cuzco. During the final few years of steam some locomotive exchanges took place with the Huancayo-Huancavalica line, which will be described later. The modern diesel locomotives came in the 1970s from Canada and there are some Ferrostaal railcars of 1966.

Railways in the South of Peru

Before proceeding northwards along the coast towards Lima, brief mention may be made of other railways in the south of Peru. The Tacna to Arica line (62km) is one of the shortest international railways in existence. The railway is of standard gauge and owned by the Peruvian government. Passenger workings are made with home-built vehicles based on lorry chassis; freight trains appear to have ceased, but to work them three steam locomotives were retained, two of which were American 2-6-0s of 1908, which came from the Ilo Railway in 1954. The other is ex Southern Railway No 93, an Alco 2-8-0 of 1914. Retained for special holiday workings was a British built 4-4-0 thought to have come from Hawthorns in 1855. Although appearing to serve no real transport function, this railway has miraculously survived intact. A thrice-weekly passenger service, operated by a railcar, ran in 1997 and the surviving steam stock was displayed in a ramshackle

A Cuzco & Santa Ana passenger train runs southbound alongside the Urubamba River near Santa Teresa behind diesel no. 484. This class DL 532B Co-Co hood unit was built by Montreal Locomotive Works in 1974.
Photo: Chris Skow,
Trains Unlimited, Tours.

'Museum' alongside Tacna station.

Between this railway and Mollendo is the small port of Ilo, from where a government-owned standard gauge line formerly extended to Moquegua (101km). Henry Meiggs was involved with the building of this line which was completed in 1872 but not in service until a year later. It was destroyed by Chilean soldiers in the War of the Pacific (1880) and not reopened until 1909, when it was state operated. More recently the line had been managed by the Peruvian Corporation until taken over by ENAFER in 1972 and it was finally closed down in 1976. It is known that two 2-6-0s went to the Tacna-Arica line in 1954 but not what operated the line thereafter. Before reading a 1995 publication on Peruvian Railways I was under the impression that it had been replaced when in 1956 work started on the 213km Ilo-Toquepala-Cuajone Railway.

The first part of this new railway opened in 1959 and as it is of standard gauge it would seem probable that the earlier tracks were used, at least in the Ilo area, although it may of course have

been built to a separate loading terminal. Owned by the Southern Peru Copper Corporation the section to Cuajone, opened in 1976, reaches 11,033ft above sea level and includes the longest tunnel in South America, 14.7km. Copper reserves here are estimated at 450 million tonnes. General Motors diesels handle all traffic and with an axle loading of 35 tonnes, this line must bear little relation to the government railway it replaced.

In contrast to this modern operation, just before Mollendo is reached a narrow gauge line formerly extended inland from Ensenada to Pampa Blanca. There were some 20km of track, built in 1895 by the owner of the "Pampa Blanca" sugar estate, at first to serve the cane fields but later, in 1905, to reach Ensenada, over which section passengers were carried. American built "Porter" steam locomotives were used but this service was withdrawn when the port of Matarani was developed. In 1944 the company had bought a 24 passenger railcar and later a German diesel locomotive for sugar cane traffic and as late as 1962 they built themselves a small locomotive which on closure in 1968, was donated,

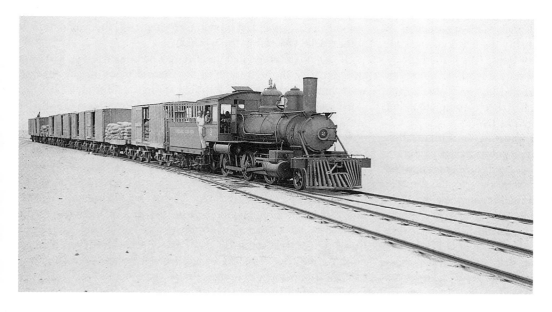

F.C. Tacna - Arica 2-6-0 no. 2 is seen entering El Hospicio with a freight train from Arica on 24th August 1955. The loco had been built by Baldwin (32983/Oct 1908), and until the year before this photo was taken had been working on the Ilo Railway.
Photo: Author's collection.

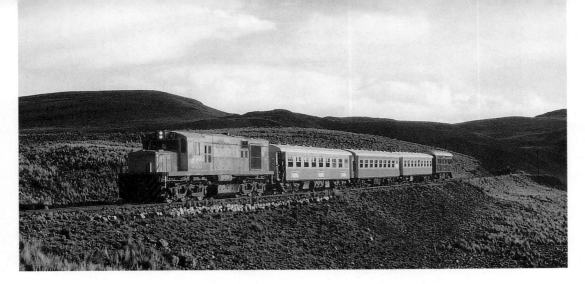

ENAFER Co-Co diesel no. 553, an Alco RSD 14 built in 1961, heads east near Saracocha over the former Southern of Peru line with a passenger train in August 1997.
Photo: Chris Skow, Trains Unlimited, Tours.

with an open passenger coach, to the Club Internacional de Arequipa. It is not proposed to go into detail, or indeed always mention, such mainly industrial railways, but this line should not be confused with the La Ensenada Chucarapa railway of 600mm gauge and extending some 20km which ran from La Ensenada station on the Southern Railway to the Hacienda Chucarapi, was built in 1922 and authorised to carry passengers in 1924.

It is a long way northwards up the Pacific coast from Mollendo and Matarani to the next railway to be described, a standard gauge line which linked Pisco with Ica (74km) opened in 1871. It was later taken over by the Peruvian Corporation but closed in the 1950s. About half way between Pisco and Lima was a 3ft gauge line built in 1872 linking Cerro Azul with Cañete (10km), serving sugar and cotton plantations, and slightly to the south of this Chinca Alta was formerly connected with Tambo de Mora (11km) by a passenger carrying line which was still operating in 1953, but closed soon afterwards. It originated in 1898.

The Central of Peru Railway

We now come to Lima, the capital city of Peru, and the nearby port of Callao. Greater Lima contains over 15 per cent of the country's population and half of the town dwellers of Peru now live in Lima and Callao. A 45km 3ft gauge line built in 1918 formerly extended from the capital to Lurín but this government owned railway closed about 1960 and two of the locomotives went to the Cuzco - Santa Ana line. At the beginning of this chapter reference was made to the Lima-Callao Railway, opened in 1851, and this brings us to what is probably the best known of all South American railways, the Central of Peru. This is the railway which made Henry Meiggs famous; he started work on it on 20th January 1870 and when work stopped in May 1878 due to the outbreak of war with Chile 141km had been completed, but Meiggs did not live to see this as he died in 1877.

When work started on the Central Railway, the Lima-Callao line was already in existence, but Meiggs got round its exclusive concession by building a private line between the capital and the docks. Later, the original railway was taken over by the Central, but by then tramway competition had made redundant the local passenger service, once worked half-hourly by 2-6-2Ts. Some 26km of track in the Lima-Callao area, mostly yards, were formerly electrified at 550V and worked with small B-B shunters built in 1923-9, but this installation was dismantled on dieselisation in 1965. At Callao is Guadalupe depot and works where even today one or two steam locomotives survive, including the last "Andes" 2-8-0 and a pair of tank engines. From here it is but a short run over the now single track main line to Desamparados station, Lima, from where the daily passenger train leaves for Huancayo. The Central formerly had a 37km branch from Lima to the seaside resort of Ancón, over which a passenger service was operated with railcars, but this closed in 1966, as did the government owned North Western Railway (to be described later) with which it connected at Ancón.

The first part of the journey from Lima towards the mountains is relatively easy, 40km up the Rimac valley to Chosica, where there is a locomotive depot formerly inhabited by the mountain section Garratts. Climbing commences immediately after Chosica and soon the first reversing section is reached at Tornamesa. The line ascends steadily, with tunnels, bridges, viaducts and further zig-zag reversals until at Chicla (141km) an altitude of 3,734m has been reached. This is where work stopped in 1878, a few months after Meiggs' death, and was not restarted until after the formation of the Peruvian Corporation in 1890. Beyond Chicla are further double zig-zags, with superb views, and by Casapalca (160km altitude 4,360m) we are nearing the summit of the main line, which is in the Galera tunnel at 4,782m above sea level. Until 1955 the highest point on the railway was on the Morococha branch at La Cima, near Ticlio, where the track reaches 4,818m, but in that year a short 1km branch was built from La Cima to the new Volcán mine, and this reaches 4,829m. Since closure of part of the FCAB Collahuasi branch (see chapter 4) this is the highest point reached by rail in the world.

It will be observed that the Morococha branch appears to offer an alternative through route to the Central main line but in fact, with three zig-zags and a terminal station at Morococha, it is a slow journey. The branch was built to Morococha (14km) in 1902, but the link between there and Cut-Off (18km), although now part of the Central Railway, was built by the Cerro de Pasco Corporation in 1921. This concern was American owned, and from Oroya on the Central Railway (222km, altitude 3,726m) their main line runs part Lake Junín to Cerro de Pasco and Goyllarisquisga, while they also work the Pachacayo-Chaucha line (80km), which separated from the rest of their system by 40km of Central track. This branch is known as the Yauricocha Railway, and was built during 1942-8. Chaucha is the highest point on the C de P (4,724m) and from there an aerial cableway extends to the copper ore deposits at Yauricocha.

Beyer-Garratt 2-8-2+2-8-2 no. 123 (Beyer Peacock 6627/1929) was photographed brand new in 1930 prior to entering service on the Central Railway of Peru. The four locos of this class proved very capable but unbearably hot for the crew to work on. Later on they were renumbered from 122-125 to 140-143, and no. 123 was transferred to the Southern Railway.
Photo: Brian Fawcett, Author's collection.

But we will return to the Cerro de Pasco Railway later. The final section of the Central, from Oroya to Huancayo (125km) was built between 1905 and 1908, and in comparison with the rest of the railway it presented no engineering difficulty, following as it does the Mantaro river valley. There used to be a local passenger service over the 45km Jaula-Huancayo section, once worked by a Sentinel-Cammell steam railcar and later by diesel mechanical railcars, but this succumbed to road competition.

The Central started out with American 2-6-0s, the first two built by Rogers in 1869-71, and these were followed by the 90 class 4-6-0s from Alco (Rogers successors) in 1906-7. Also in 1906-7 came the first 2-8-0s from Alco and this wheel arrangement soon became standard, even though the next batch, from North British in 1908, was not a success. The later "Andes" 2-8-0s of series 200 were to make the type famous, and in 1935-36 nine were supplied by Beyer Peacock, with a further eight in 1950-51. Other types tried included some 4-8-2s from the Yorkshire Engine Company but these were prone to slipping until rebuilt into 4-8-0s between 1939 and 1942. Alco supplied some 2-8-2s in 1931 and four 2-8-2+2-8-2 Garratts came from Beyer Peacock in 1930-3. The suburban 2-6-2Ts and some 0-4-0Ts and 0-6-2Ts for shunting completed the steam roster, which in 1951

The zig-zag reversing station at Ticlio, 4,758 metres (15,610 feet) above sea level, photographed by the author on 6th November 1976 when travelling in the Andes. The train was headed by Co-Co diesel no. 613.

Central of Peru shunting engines at Guadalupe:

Left: 0-4-0WT no. 20 was supplied by Beyer Peacock in 1913 and seen at the depot in January 1970.

Below: 0-6-0T no. 35 was a Yorkshire Engine Company product of 1952, formerly F.C. del Sur no. 23. It was still active on shunting duties in March 1972.

stood at fifty-one machines, all oil burners. Some diesel shunters had been supplied before the war, but main line dieselisation did not commence until 1963 when three Alco diesel electrics of 1,200hp, type DL535, were received. They were followed by a total of 15 Co-Co DL 560s of 2,400hp, supplied in 1964-6 and more recent orders have been shared with the Southern Railway. Smaller diesels in stock in 1972 included a General Electric Bo-Bo of 300hp, and 0-6-0 and 0-8-0 Hunslets of 1939 and 1950-52, varying from 150 to 500hp. Some of these came from the Paita-Piura Railway in the far north, in 1959 and 1963. In 1972 no. 20 an 0-6-0WT (Beyer Peacock 1913), no. 30 an 0-6-0ST

(Bagnall 1929), and no. 35 another 0-6-0ST (Yorkshire Engine Company 1952) remained at Guadalupe depot, Lima, along with "Andes" type 2-8-0 no. 206, built by Beyer Peacock in 1937. Number 206 has survived to the present day.

While in this area mention may be made of the Callao Port Authority, now dieselised, but formerly worked by a fleet of 0-4-0STs built by T Green in 1901-8 and later joined by some American 0-6-0STs in 1928. No 10 (T Green 1903) is displayed on a plinth just outside the entrance.

The Central is very vulnerable to landslides, washouts and other disasters caused by the violent weather conditions in the mountains at certain times of the year. When I first visited Lima in January 1970 the railway was closed for a week and I was unable to travel on it and visitors in February 1972 found the same situation, although it was working the previous month and

again in August, when Norman Forbes found that six red 12 wheel passenger coaches from the Canadian Pacific Railway had arrived in Callao. These were too heavy for the Central Railway mountain trains, which use quite modern lightweight stock, and were destined for the Cerro de Pasco Railway, replacing even older American built stock. They were later gaily painted in red (first) and blue (second) while the Central stock has changed from green to the standard ENAFER livery of orange and yellow, used for all diesel locomotives, railcars and passenger stock. One imagines that after such total closures of the railway mentioned above, the backlog of mineral of traffic was immense, but despite the great expense of keeping such a railway open there is no other alternative means of transport capable of handling the bulk traffic it carries, and the future should be secure for freight at least.

Smart operation was a feature of the Central in steam days.

Superb co-operation between dispatchers and crews, combined with locomotives in tip-top condition, reduced crossing delays on this heavily trafficked single track to a minimum which would have been the envy of any sea-level railway. When the gradients, zig-zags etc. are taken into account, the operation must represent a peak unsurpassed anywhere in the world.

The arrival of diesels, with their unvarying power and braking characteristics enabled the already slick operation to be even further improved. In steam days, all freight ran as "extras" with crossings ordered by the dispatchers as expedient. (It is one of the peculiarities of the Central that it was a British-owned railway, operating under the North American system of train orders, but using the Spanish language). Now, all services run according to timetable and can be relied upon almost to the minute.

Uphill, the diesels climb at an unvarying 25km per hour and the pauses at the reversing points are no longer than the time it takes the engineer to flick from "forward" to "reverse". Downhill, speed is 35-40km per hour, which the engineer maintains by sensitive adjustments of the dynamic brake. He keeps a steady 30lb on the straight air brake, just enough to keep the brake shoes warm, and has the automatic air brake ready, although it is sparingly used in normal running. Reversing stops are just as short as on the uphill trip, although downhill a brakeman has to drop off the end of the train and hold down the spring safety switch, normally set for the uphill direction, by sitting on it as the train sets off downhill, then leap aboard the front of the locomotive as it passes. There is no caboose on a Central train - the trains are severely restricted in length by the reversing sidings - so that the conductor and his two brake men ride on the car tops in the traditional American manner. Making one's way along the narrow catwalk on a swaying, bucking boxcar in the freezing Andean night is an experience better imagined than experienced.

Inside Huancayo shed on 8th December 1981 were F.C.H.H. nos. 107, 104, and 108. The 2-8-0s 107 & 108 were built by Hunslet and they had previously worked on the F. C. de Trujillo before being transferred to Huancayo. They were works nos. 1795/1936 and 3413/1947 respectively. The loco in the middle, no. 104, was one of five 2-8-2s supplied by Henschel and distributed among several of the 3 ft gauge Peruvian lines (Henschel 26483/1951).

Another of the Henschel 2-8-2s, no. 109 (works no. 26403/1950). This locomotive had previously worked on the F.C. Lima - Lurin as that line's no. 12, but was transferred upon closure and was in action at Huancayo when seen on 6th November 1976.

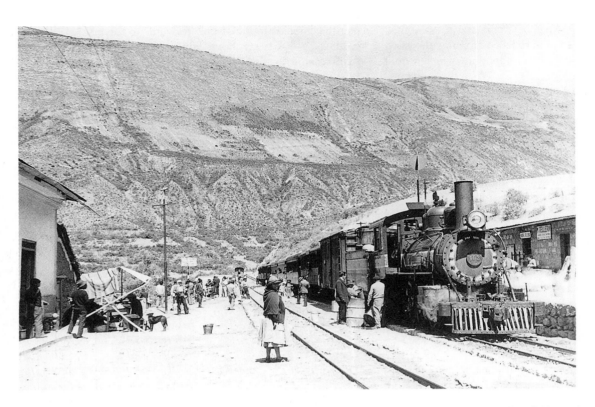

Baldwin 2-6-0 no. 103 pauses with a van and eight coaches at Manuel Telleria station on the F.C. Huancayo - Huancavelica. The loco was supplied in 1920, works no. 54262.

If my account, enlivened by the preceding paragraphs contributed by Mr J Todd, of such a famous railway seems fairly prosaic, I would like to refer readers to Brian Fawcett's book "Railways of the Andes", which is highly recommended. Bradford Barton published an album of Andean railway photographs which includes fine views of the Central in steam days, illustrations of the Sentinel railcars etc.

Huancayo, inland terminus of the Central Railway, is capital of the Junín province, and has a population of about 110,000. It is situated at an altitude of 3,621m above sea level. From here a government owned 3ft gauge railway, now part of ENAFER, extends for 128km to Huancavelica. Construction commenced in 1908 but progress was slow and by 1926 only about 35km had

been laid. At first the line follows the valley of the river Mantero but then it parts company with the road to Ayacucho (originally intended to be its destination), and crosses the mountains, offering spectacular views and serving small Indian communities. There are some fierce gradients, which can be heavy going for the daily passenger train, which takes between six and seven hours in contrast to the railcar timing of 3½ hours. The railway has been dieselised for some years now but was at least partially steam worked in the 1980s. The depot at Huancayo housed in 1981 a Baldwin 2-6-0, the last of three supplied in 1920/24, two Hunslet 2-8-0s built in 1936 and 1947, and a 2-8-2 built by Henschel in 1951, the sister engine of which was transferred to Cuzco. These railways have much in common, including vacuum brakes and

The nameboard on Huencavelica station proclaims that it is situated at Km 128 and stands 3,680 metres above sea level. The author photographed 3ft gauge railcar no. 26 there on 10th December 1981.

identical clearances and axle loadings. In fact, it was originally intended that the two should link but it is roughly 850km by road from Huancayo to Cuzco, a spectacular if highly uncomfortable journey (and highly dangerous in the days of "Shining Path" guerilla activity, when the area was out of bounds to tourists), which in practice can take several days. Thrice weekly buses are advertised to do the trip in 48 hours but in bad weather lorries are more likely to get through, and are always willing to carry deter-mined passengers who must be impervious to discomfort and intense cold at night!

At Huancayo the narrow gauge terminates in the Central Railway yard, but passenger services have now been cut back to the local station, Chilca, and no longer traverse the dual gauge section which is laid in the middle of the street containing the local market. In 1981 railcars started from Chilca station, but the train left from the adjacent locomotive shed yard, presumably to save shunting the stock into the station, where it is apt to cause traffic congestion, the station being situated in the street! The inbound working does terminate in the station, the locomotive usually continuing up the street to deliver vans to the Central Railway station yard.

The Cerro de Pasco Railway

Returning along the Central Railway to Oroya, we will now take a look at the Cerro de Pasco Railway, which rightly deserves the title bestowed on it by Brian Fawcett "railway on the roof of the world" as Oroya (3,726m) is its lowest point. The Cerro de Pasco mines had been in operation long before the railway came and they had been visited by Richard Trevithick in 1817, bringing by mule train some steam pumps for use there. At this time it was silver which was being mined, and the rich copper ore was thrown aside as useless, as indeed it was without facilities for bulk trans-portation and processing.

After gauge disputes, a short narrow gauge line was built to carry ore from the Cerro mines to a smelting centre at Pasco, and the title of this company was adopted when the standard gauge line was built in 1904, Henry Meiggs had been granted a conces-sion for this railway in 1877, but with his death and the Chilean war, this had lapsed, and the South American Development Company finally built the railway. In 1915 the Cerro de Pasco Copper Corporation was formed and this organisation ran the rail-way until nationalisation of the mines in the 1970s. The line is now entitled Ferrocarril de Centromin.

It was a very American outfit which like the Central, soon settled for 2-8-0s and two (Alco 1902) were acquired immedi-ately, along with four 2-6-0s from the same builder. 2-8-2s were also tried, and locomotives were for many years coal-fired as the Corporation had its own mines. This coal was poor stuff though, and ultimately the example of the Central was followed and oil firing introduced. Up to the early 1950s the C de P had been an all-American outfit, but when they came to buy new steam it was not available in the USA, and so they went to Beyer Peacock for ten of the "Andes" 2-8-0s, as supplied to the Central. These were delivered in 1954-7, but despite this new influx of modern power, dieselisation took place soon afterwards with General Motors 1,310hp units and 800hp shunters. Some of the modern steam locomotives were on loan to the Central for shunting around Callao in 1972 but in 1976 one stored in a shed at Oroya was claimed to be the last in existence.

The Cerro de Pasco Railway had several feeders, all of narrow gauge, two of them connecting with the standard gauge quite near to each other and to Cerro de Pasco itself. One was the FC de Shelby opened in 1922 and owned by the French Compagnie des Mines de Huaron, producing lead-silver-zinc ore. This line was 30km long and of 750mm gauge. Nearby at Ricrán was the FC Minas Ragras-Ricrán, built in 1928 and owned by the Vanadium corporation of New York. It was 29km long and of 3ft gauge. Also of this gauge was the government owned line striking off in the opposite direction to the other two and entitled FC Tambo del Sol a Huachon. This was commenced in 1950 as the first part of a grandiose scheme to reach Pucallpa, on the river Ucayali, well towards the Brazilian frontier through an area at the time quite devoid of roads. The distance is around 400km but the railway appears to have petered out after some 70km and as nothing more has been heard of it closure would seem to have taken place.

Some Connections to the Central of Peru Railway

Returning down the Central Railway to Lima, we leave the present for the not so distant past when the Ancón branch was still in service. At Ancón the standard gauge terminated and the 3ft gauge government owned North Western Railway extended northwards parallel with the coast via Huaral (8km branch to Chancay on the coast), Huacho (56km branch inland to Sayan) to Barranca (198km). Motive power on this railway, which closed in 1966, included six North British 4-8-0s, four of which were built in 1911 and the other two in 1923 and 1925. At Chancay on this line was a 20km metre gauge railway owned by the Empresa Ferrocarril Muelle de Chancay, now defunct, while at Barranca was the 600mm gauge FC de Supa a Barranca, a 46km line opened in 1903 and closed in the 1950s, which linked the port of Supe with Barranca and the sugar plantations. Also at Supe was the FC Supe-Hacienda San Nicolas, a 3ft 6in gauge agricultural line opened in 1901 and operated in conjunction with the 600mm line with dual gauge track in Supe. Travelling northwards up the coast there was another agricultural line of the same gauge and 48km long at Samanca. Other sugar cane lines may well have existed in this area but all have been closed for some years now.

Slightly north of Samanca is Chimbote, with a fine harbour and until the disastrous earthquake of 1970 a rapidly developing town of some 200,000 inhabitants. From here the 3ft gauge government operated Santa Corporation Railway (formerly a Peruvian Corporation line) ran to Huallanca (138km) and Quires,

offering fine views as it climbed up the Santa valley. Passengers were well catered for with daily trains to Huallanca taking five hours, and a weekly railcar taking only 3½ hours. Cars were also transported to Huallanca which was not easily accessible by road from Chimbote. The first section of the railway was built by Henry Meiggs in 1872, and the line reached Huallanca in 1924. With passenger and coal traffic from the anthracite mines of the Chuquicara valley the railway was doing well when destroyed by the earthquake . Two of the four diesel locomotives in stock went to the Cuzco-Santa Ana line in 1970. The first steam locomotives on this line were a pair of 2-6-0s from Cooke in 1872, followed by five Rogers 2-6-0s of 1875, in which year a Baldwin 2-2-4T named Emilia and classified as an inspection loco, was received. The first diesel came from Hunslet in 1939.

Travelling northwards again, the next railway was at Trujillo. It closed in 1966 and was latterly the only 3ft gauge line operated by the Peruvian Corporation. It extended from Salaverry via Trujillo to Ascope and with branches it had a total route length of 76km. Nearby, linking Chicama and Puerto Chicama, was the 3ft gauge sugar plantation system of the Empresa Agrícola Chicama Ltd, with 196km of track and sixteen steam locomotives, including a number of 2-8-2s and some 0-4-0 fireless. In 1975 there was a Sundays only passenger service to the beach but most of the rest of the system had been lifted. There were other sugar factories in the Trujillo area with 3ft gauge systems and one or two locomotives are preserved on display, for example at Chiclin and Laredo.

At Pascasmayo was the standard gauge Peruvian Corporation railway to Chilete (105km) with a branch from San Pedro to Guadalupe (26km). The first part of this railway was opened in 1871 but it closed in the 1950s. Near Chiclayo, a town of about 160,000 inhabitants, were two lines which survived until fairly recently, both of which are of exceptional interest. The first is the Empresa del Ferrocarril y Muelle de Eten, which formerly operated between Puerto Eten, Chiclayo and Ferreñafe, with a branch

Ferrocarril Y Muelle de Eten no. 7 is a Baldwin 0-4-2ST built in 1903. In November 1977 it was in the shed at Puerto Eten alongside one of the other two locos of the same type.
Photo: Chris Skow, Trains Unlimited, Tours.

from Chiclayo to Patapo, 67km in all. These standard gauge lines serving sugar plantations have been closed, but to serve the wharf at Puerto Eten tracks remained until recently together with an incredible assortment of motive power. This included a 4-4-0 of 1871, an 0-4-2 and an 0-4-2ST of 1890-1, all by Rogers, and a 4-4-0 plus two 0-4-2STs by Baldwin in 1910, 1913 and 1903 respectively. After closure of the main line this concern was retitled Transportes y Embarques del Norte, but locomotives were in steam only once or twice a month when vessels called at the wharf.

Nearby, the Ferrocarril y Muelle de Pimentel connected the port of Pimentel with sugar plantations inland by means of 43km of 3ft gauge track, and their locomotive roster included a 2-4-2, some Baldwin 2-6-0s, the oldest dating back to 1876, two Alco 2-8-0s and a 2-6-0 from the Trujillo line. There were also German built 2-6-2s, and two Hudswell Clarke outside frame 0-6-0s of 1951. This railway once had three 0-4-4-0 Fairlies built by the Vulcan Foundry in 1873. Despite the large locomotive roster, operations were only sporadic and dependent on a vessel being in port, although prior to the mid-1960s there were passenger services over the line.

Running into Puerto Eten was a 600mm gauge sugar line owned by the Hacienda Cayalti, with fifteen locomotives built by John Fowler and Baldwin. Opened in about 1903, the line lasted until 1969. The Hacienda Pomalco, near Chiclayo, also had a railway system connecting with the Pimental Railway, and this was unusually of 700mm gauge, motive power including Baldwin 4-4-0s of 1878 and a 2-6-0 of 1875. There were also other lines of a similar nature in the region, all now defunct.

Between Chiclayo and the next railway at Piura is a vast area of shifting sand, the Sechura desert, now gradually being made fertile by irrigation projects. Piura was founded in 1532 (before Lima), and is the provincial capital with a population of 120,000. The port for this cotton growing area is Paita, and the two towns were formerly linked by a 105km standard gauge railway operated by the Peruvian Corporation. The railway was completed between 1876 and 1887, and motive power included Baldwin 4-4-0s of 1874/6, an Alco 4-6-0 of 1908 and a Baldwin 2-8-0 of 1921. The first diesel came in 1939, and in fact bore the next Hunslet works number to the one on the Chimbote line. Further diesels arrived in 1950/1, when the railway received a 204hp 0-6-0 and two 500hp 0-8-0s, all from Hunslet. The old 4-4-0s remained in existence until closure took place in the late 1950s and early 1960s.

Two railways north of Paita, towards the Ecuador border, were an 11km line of 750mm gauge between Puerto Pixarro and Tumbes opened in 1909 and closed in the 1930s, and Negritos to Talara, 93km - 760mm gauge, the former government owned and the latter the property of the International Petroleum Company of Canada and closed when the company was expropriated in 1968.

The Situation in 2000

Perurail SA operations have been taken over by Sea Containers Ltd., also known for operating the famed 'Orient Express'. Railcars are run from Cusco to Machu Picchu (up early in the morning, back in the afternoon) and the Cusco-Puno-Arequipa line actually has an increased locomotive-hauled public service. The Railroad Development Corporation has taken over operation of the Lima - Huancayo route and the former Cerro de Pasco lines, but passenger trains have been or are about to be withdrawn. ENAFER still runs public services Tacna-Arica and on the Huancavelica branch.

"La Joya" was built by Rogers Locomotive Works for track inspection duties on the Southern Railway of Peru and was illustrated in "The Engineer" of 31st December 1869. Up to this time inspection trolleys were all hand powered - on a railway climbing from the coast up to an altitude of 14,668 ft.

An additional benefit of introducing steam power was that a wagon with materials and tools could be towed and up to ten people could be seated on water tanks that were built up into benches.

URUGUAY

Uruguay is the smallest of the South American republics, with an area of 72,170 square miles, about the same as England and Wales together, but the population is only a little over the three million mark and two thirds of the inhabitants are town dwellers. The country has 193km of Atlantic seaboard and the principal river is the Uruguay, forming the frontier with Argentina for a distance of 435km, the first 322km of which, to Salta, are navigable all the year round. Altogether there are 1,247km of navigable waterways and these were the principal means of communication before the coming of the railways.

The Central Uruguay Company

The first railway projects in the country date back to the 1850s, when lines were proposed from Montevideo to Colonia (1853) and Rio de Janeiro (!) in 1855. Nothing came of these schemes and the first concession granted, on which work was subsequently begun, was for a standard gauge line from Montevideo to Durazno, which was authorised on 4th October 1866 and begun on 26 April 1867. The first locomotive, named General Flores, arrived later the same year, and was soon joined by General Artigas, who had the honour of hauling the first train on 1st January 1869 over the 16km section from Saladero de Naza (Bella Vista) to Las Piedras. These first locomotives were 0-6-0STs built by Manning Wardle in 1867, and were followed by other British types, including two Manning Wardle 0-6-0s and some 2-4-0s from Sharp Stewart, Beyer Peacock and the Vulcan Foundry, most

Montevideo main station in October 1995 with a special train to Minas standing behind Beyer Peacock N class 2-6-0 no. 119 (5399/1910). The loco is actually carrying the identity of sister engine no. 120.
Photo: David Ibbotson.

of which bore names.

Despite political troubles, the line reached Durazno in 1874, but soon afterwards the local company failed financially, and in December 1876 the Central Uruguay Company was formed in London to take over operations. This concern continued the line to the Brazilian frontier at Rivera, 565km from Montevideo, which was reached on 4th February 1892. Meanwhile in 1886 the company acquired a line extending westwards from 25 de Agosto, the first section of which had been opened to San José on 15th May 1876. This line had been worked by the British owned FC a Higueritas and the Central Uruguay set about extending it, as the Central Uruguay Western Extension Railway, to Puerto Sauce (1900) and Colonia (1901). The Western Extension Railway also

reached Mercedes, on the Río Negro, from Mal Abrigo on 14th December 1902. In 1889 the Uruguay North Eastern Railway was acquired, and extensions were built via Nico Pérez to Melo (reached 1909) and Treinta y Tres (reached 1911).

By the turn of the century the Central Uruguay Railway had acquired quite a number of 2-6-0s, mostly from Beyer Peacock, a few 4-4-0s for passenger work, and three 2-8-0s, which were subsequently converted to 2-8-2s, one as a tank engine. From the Uruguay Western Railway came some Baldwin 4-4-0s built in 1889, the first non British built locomotives taken into stock. By 1937 the Central Uruguay Railway, consisting of the Central, the Eastern, Western and Northern Extensions Cos, and the North Eastern Railway, was the largest railway in the country, with a

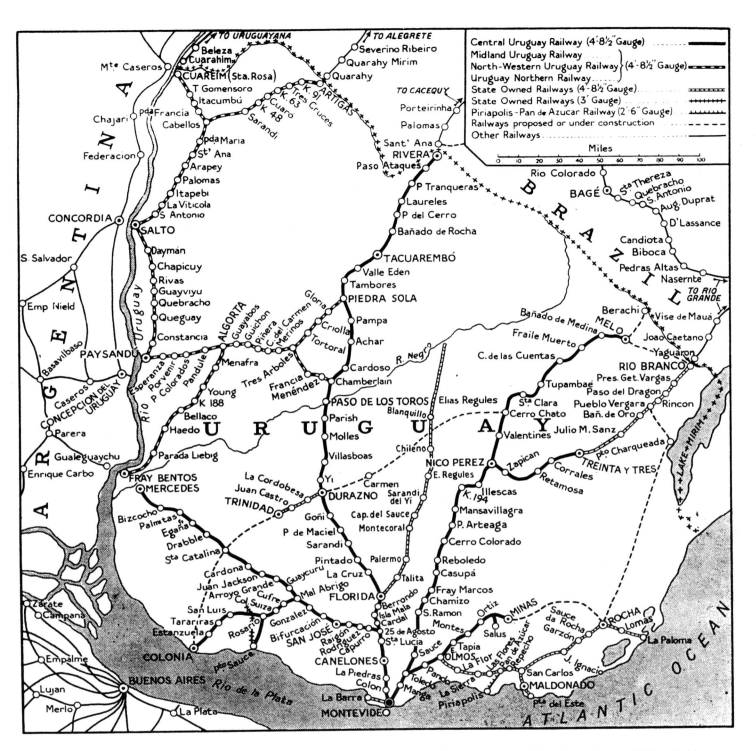

Central Uruguay Railway (4'-8½" Gauge) ....
Midland Uruguay Railway
North-Western Uruguay Railway } (4'-8½" Gauge)
Uruguay Northern Railway
State Owned Railways (4'-8½" Gauge) ....
State Owned Railways (3' Gauge) ....
Piriapolis - Pan de Azucar Railway (2'-6" Gauge) ....
Railways proposed or under construction ....
Other Railways ....

Miles
0 10 20 30 40 50 60 70 80 90 100

system of 1,561km operated with 91 locomotives, 111 carriages, 2,165 wagons and 70 brake vans. Furthermore, it had acquired a controlling interest in the Midland Uruguay Railway. The fine terminal station at Montevideo is still in use, as are the principal works of the company at Peñarol, in the city suburbs.

Along the extreme western border of the country, the river Uruguay had sufficed for communication, at least to Salto, but above this point were impassable rapids and in 1868 a line was authorised to bypass this obstacle, work commencing in 1872. After a short section had been opened the company failed, and was taken over by the North Western Uruguay Railway which reached Cuareim, on the Brazilian frontier, on 13th April 1887. At

first the river was crossed by ferry, but in 1897 a bridge was proposed and built by a London company bearing the grand title of Compañia del Puente Internaciónal del Cuareim. It opened on 3rd June 1915, and carried dual gauge track, the connecting Brazilian system being of metre gauge, while all the main lines in Uruguay have always been of standard gauge.

The Midland Uruguay Railway

There is also a branch off this line from Isla de Cabellos to Artigas (117½ km) which was originally a separate undertaking, also British, the Uruguay Northern Railway. Opened in 1891, this small concern had a motive power stud of five locomotives. For a

A.F.E. 2-6-0 no. 92 was in steam at Paysandu in October 1993. Beyer Peacock built no. 92 in 1906, works no. 4750. Photo: David Ibbotson.

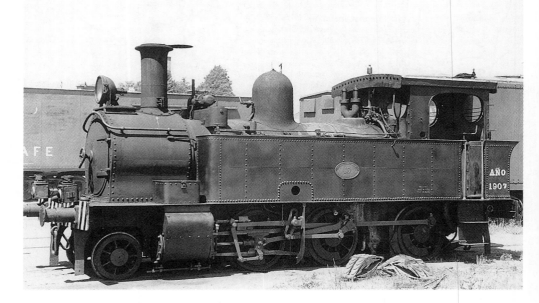

B class 2-6-0T no. 15 was built by Hudswell Clark in 1906, works no. 788, and was still in occasional use for shunting in 1993.

few years the North Western was isolated from other railways, its traffic outlet being by river from Salto, but in 1884 another British company, the Midland Uruguay Railway, promoted a line from Salto via Paysandú to Paso de los Toros, on the bank of the Río Negro, which was reached in 1889. Here the Midland made connection with the Central Railway main line from Montevideo towards Rivera. In 1911 the Midland opened lines from Algorta to Frey Bentos (of corned beef fame), and from Tres Arboles to Piedra Sola, and with its headquarters established at Paysandú the Midland took over the working of the Salto based Northern and North Western Railways, although the former was still legally a separate concern in 1946, by which year the Midland group had been acquired by the Central Uruguay Railway.

The Midland locomotive stock, which stood at twenty-four locomotives in 1935, consisted mainly of Beyer Peacock 2-6-0s, while the North Western brought them some Hunslet four and six coupled tank engines, and a 2-4-0T they had built themselves at Salto, which is now displayed at a museum in the town as the only locomotive ever built in Uruguay!

Ferrocariles y Tranvías del Estado

Most of the early locally financed lines fell into difficulties and became part of the British systems, but in 1915 the government formed the State Railways, entitled Ferrocariles y Tranvías del Estado, to promote a number of lines, mostly extensions of existing railways which presumably the companies were unwilling to build. These lines were mostly isolated from each other and included Durazno to Trinidad (48km) built in 1915, and the Uruguay East Coast Railway Ltd, between Empalme Olmos and Maldonado (114km) which was purchased in January 1919 and extended 7km to Punta del Este in 1930. In the same Atlantic coast area the short isolated Rocha to La Paloma (30½km) line was also acquired in January 1919 and later connected with the existing Montevideo-Maldonado line by the construction of a 72½km link opened in March 1928. Later State Railway construction included Florida to Sarandí del Yí (117½km) opened in July 1933, Sarandí del Yí to Blanquillo (51½km), opened December 1939, and Treinta y Tres to Río Branco, on the Brazilian frontier (122km) opened April 1936. Here an international bridge over the river Yaguarón offers road and rail connection with Brazil, the

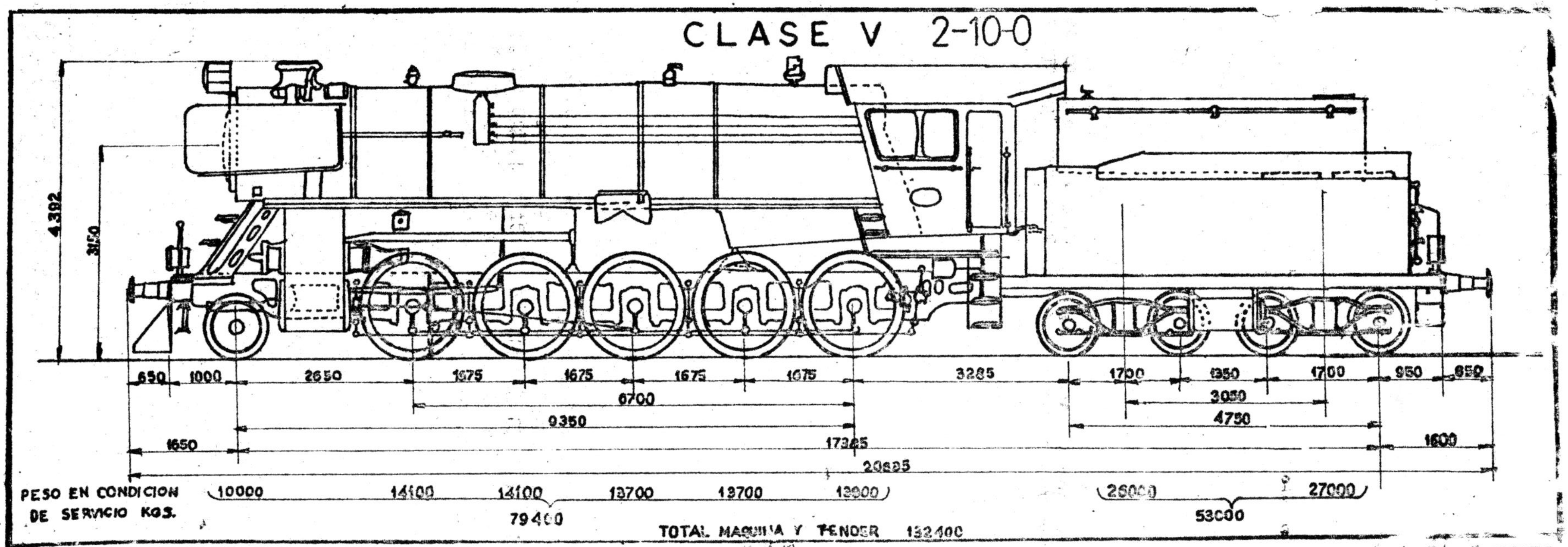

CLASE V 2-10-0

MAQUINAS Ns. 156 al 160 fabricadas por HENSCHEL & SOHN – 1950

Potencia: 890 HP

2 Cilindros: Diám.: 530 mm
Carrera: 660 mm

Fuerza de tracción a 85% de presión en la caldera: kg 16.069

Ruedas Acopladas: ϕ 1525 mm

Peso Adhesivo: kg 69.400

Ruedas Portantes: ϕ 914 mm

Superficie Total de calefacción: 150.72 m²

Ruedas Ténder: ϕ 914 mm

SERVICIO TECNICO
de nuestra Asociación

Como anunciamos previamente, comenzamos en este número la inclusión de material técnico informativo para brindar a nuestros lectores información detallada sobre diferentes aspectos de los sistemas de transporte por riel en nuestro país.

TECHNICAL SERVICE

As previously announced, we begin in this issue the publication of technical material for giving our readers a detailed information about the rail systems of transportation in our country.

The Henschel 2-10-0 design for Uruguay.

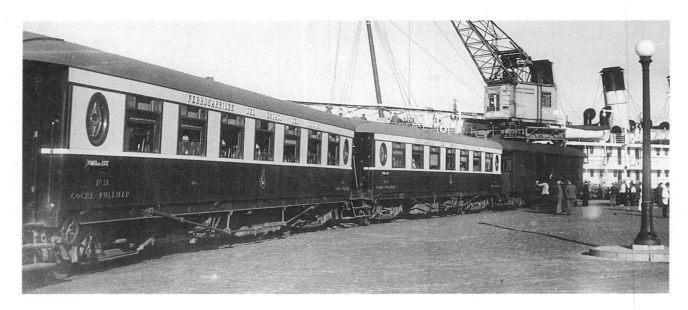

Until the 1950s a de-luxe service ran from Montevideo to Punta del Este using Wagons-Lits type vehicles, seen here alongside the night steamer from Buenos Aires. Photo: R. Bisagno, author's collection.

single rail track on the bridge having the metre gauge laid inside the standard gauge to enable trains of each country to cross into each other's territory. In 1946 an extension beyond Blanquillo was being constructed but it has made little progress and by 1953 had reached Km 329.

The State Railways also absorbed, in 1915, the Ferrocarril y Tranvía del Norte which had a horse-drawn tramway system in Montevideo and a connecting 20km railway to Santiago Vásquez. This line, built in 1874 to supply Montevideo with meat from the slaughter houses by the Santa Lucia river, received in the same year two 0-6-6-0 Fairlies from Avonside. In 1925 the tramway system was abandoned, and the railway was apparently taken over and electrified by the German owned company, La Transatlántica, but closed in 1957.

Most of the State Railway tender engines were 2-6-0s, although they had a varied selection of tank engines, the majority built by Hawthorn Leslie and Beyer Peacock. Motive power on the railways of Uruguay, which are relatively easily graded, has always been of modest dimensions. For example, in 1926 the Central Railway had 83 2-6-0s, 24 2-8-0s and 27 4-4-0s on its books and on most other lines Moguls predominated, with quite a large number coming from Beyer Peacock. In fact, of 246 loco-motives supplied to the standard gauge railways, no less than 109 were 2-6-0s, and there have never been any 4-6-0s of 4-6-2s in the country. 129 locomotives were supplied by one builder, Beyer Peacock. The Central also had some 4-4-4Ts from the Vulcan Foundry in 1913/15 but very little new steam was supplied in the 1920s and 1930s. The only post war steam locomotives were five Henschel 2-10-0s built in 1950; the only ten coupled machines in the country.

Nationalisation of the British companies took place in 1948, and full integration came in 1952, when 2,975km of track were taken over to form the Administración de Ferrocariles del Estado, comprising the Central Railway, the Midland and the State Railways. The Cuareim International Bridge Company was also taken over with the railways.

Diesel Traction in Uruguay

The railways of Uruguay made considerable use of diesel rail-cars before World War II, and indeed some pre-war examples of American and Hungarian manufacture remained in service until quite recently, notably the Ganz single and articulated units dating from 1938. The first main line diesel electric locomotives came from General Electric and Alco in 1951/54, the former numbered 1501-47, and the latter 1601-3, all Co-Cos. There were also some smaller General Electric Bo-Bos supplied in 1951 and followed by a batch of main line Alsthom Bo-Bos in 1965, Nos 801-825. Some Japanese diesel hydraulic shunters came in 1963. Seven three-car diesel trainsets were supplied from Austria in 1952 but suffered from breakdowns and were relegated to use as coaching stock. More recently Ganz have supplied 15 three-car sets (1977) and about the same time four diesel shunters came from General Electric. Refurbishing of the main line diesels also took place in the mid-1970s with the aid of a World Bank loan and not before time, as a report on the situation in 1972 recorded only 18 out of 75 main line diesel locomotives as being serviceable. In this year services reached an all time low and it was possible that the rail-way system would be totally abandoned but wiser councils prevailed and improvements, albeit not as drastic as required, were made. The only modern passenger rolling stock at that time consisted of sixteen units supplied by Allan of Rotterdam about 1954 and some newer first class stock from Fiat Concordia, Argentina. In 1982, second hand material was purchased from Western Germany, including 23 railbuses and trailers, 15 passen-ger coaches and 5 diesel shunters.

Stock figures at the start of 1993 were given as 24 Alco and 18 Alsthom diesel electrics, 7 diesel hydraulic shunters and 4 steam locomotives, while in November of that year delivery was taken of 10 GEC (Canada) 1,800 hp diesel-electrics. Railcars and multiple unit stock were not mentioned, although it was stated that refurbished Brill railcars of 1936 were still in use! A far cry from the days when a luxury Pullman express comprised of Wagon-Lit type cars imported from Europe linked Montevideo with the fashionable resort of Punta del Este, a service withdrawn

A modern passenger train of the Uruguayan State Railways pulls into the station at Montevideo in October 1996 hauled by Bo-Bo diesel no. 916. The locomotive was built by the Hungarian firm of Ganz.
Photo: Chris Skow courtesy of Trains Unlimited, Tours.

in the early 1950s.

Developments From the 1970s-1990s

New railway construction in the 1970s concentrated on linking Mercedes with Frey Bentos via Ombucito, completed in 1979, a 27km long section needed to provide easier access to the north-west but delayed by the need to bridge the Río Negro. Other improvements in this area included a direct link between the Frey Bentos line and Paysandú and, just north of Salto, a 14km line to reach a new dam at Salto Grande on the Uruguay river. When opened in 1976, this link was the first new railway construction to be completed since 1953, and the line was later extended across the dam to link up with the Urquiza Railway in Argentina, also of standard gauge. A ten year track improvement programme was

also authorised which should have seen renewal of two-thirds of the existing network by 1990.

Sadly, this brief flourish of railway enthusiasm was short lived as more and more passenger traffic was lost to the fast, efficient long distance services of private bus operators. With losses mounting, it was decided by the Government late in 1987 to withdraw all passenger services and this was effective from January 1988. Freight operation continued over parts of the system, although many lines were closed completely, but during the 1990s a slight passenger revival took place. The first service reinstated seems to have been a daily railcar between Tacuarembo and Rivera in 1993, and in 1994 outer suburban services restarted out of Montevideo to 25 de Agosto, basically morning and evening only. Montevideo and Rivera were linked soon afterwards (once

AFE railcar no. 116, a Brill product of 1934, arrives at Montevideo in November 1977.
Photo: Chris Skow courtesy of Trains Unlimited, Tours.

a week) but this service was soon withdrawn.

In the September 1997 edition of the Argentinian magazine 'Rieles' (Rails), it was confirmed that at that time there were four daily trains between Montevideo and 25 de agosto, these all working to the city in the mornings and returning late afternoon, apparently well used by city workers. As in 1993, Rivera was linked with Tacuarembo once daily with an average loading of 60 passengers per train. Some track has been renewed, mainly the Rivera and Blanquillo lines, but other sections have been lifted and the active locomotive stock was quoted as 30, including the 10 GEC (Canada) diesels. Also mentioned in 'Rieles' was the 'Tren de la Costa' project, really a light rail linking Tres Cruces (Montevideo) with El Pinar 27 km along the coast, with park & ride facilities for city workers and the added bonus of serving popular seaside resorts.

Harbour and Dockside Railways

The only other standard gauge railway in Uruguay is operated by the National Port Administration at Montevideo. In the 1950s they had 25km of standard gauge, plus 4km of 900mm gauge track, with a stock of ten steam (including one narrow gauge), three petrol locomotives and two diesels. By the late 1960s only four steam locomotives remained, two 0-6-0Ts from Orenstein & Koppel in 1912 and two 0-4-0Ts from Linke-Hoffman in 1926, plus two General Motors diesels built in 1949, which were the first diesel locomotives imported into Uruguay. More recently a General Electric diesel built in Spain under licence in 1972 has been added to stock and at the last count two steam locomotives remained in reserve. In 1977/78 a "children's train", now preserved, was operated round the docks on Sundays using homemade "toastrack" style coaches and hauled by a British 0-6-0ST, "La Manicera". One each of the O&K and Linke-Hoffman locos are also now preserved. One or two locomotives were also displayed outside the main terminal station in Montevideo. At one time there was a 2km standard gauge branch to a sugar factory at Montes, which had its own locomotives, but nothing further is known about this.

A special passenger train for a visiting party on the 600mm gauge sand quarry system owned by Indare. The locomotive is no. 25, an 0-4-0T built by Henschel (25818/1950).
Photo: David Ibbotson.

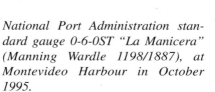

National Port Administration standard gauge 0-6-0ST "La Manicera" (Manning Wardle 1198/1887), at Montevideo Harbour in October 1995.
Photo: David Ibbotson.

Narrow Gauge Railways

A state owned narrow gauge railway, which closed sometime in the early 1950s, formerly extended from marble quarries at Puntas de San Juan to Puerto Sauce (40km). It was of 900mm gauge and it is probable that the Port Authority had the 4km of 900mm gauge track at Puerto Sauce connecting with this line, although confirmation of this is needed. A passenger carrying railway of 750mm gauge was opened in 1909 to link Pan de Azucar (on the Olmos-Maldonado line of the then Uruguay East Coast Railway), with Piriapolis on the coast, a resort developed by Don Francisco Piria, the railway being originally known as the FC Piria. It was some 15km long and carried passengers as well as serving marble quarries in the area. In 1926 it was reported to be worked by Orenstein & Koppel built locomotives, being taken over by the State some time in the 1940s and closed on 14th December 1958, when the stock was still quoted as six locomotives plus 14 coaches and wagons.

Finally, in the 1980s another narrow gauge system was discovered in Uruguay. It was of 600mm gauge and is owned by Indare SA of Boca de Rosarío, accessible from Colonia. There was a "main line" about 5km long and some 15km of sidings, including an 8-track marshalling yard. The object was to carry sand from a quarry to a point on the Río de la Plata from where it was shipped across to cement plants in Argentina. The locomotives were all 0-4-0Ts, and were originally wood-burners, although many were later converted to oil firing. Builders include Jung (1927 and 1928), Henschel (1928 and 1950) and Neumayer (works no. 5 of 1923). There were also some derelict Orenstein & Koppel machines but even towards the end some dozen locomotives were serviceable at any one time. The railway was only active when ships were loading, which caused disappointment to several visitors, but those fortunate enough to arrive at the right time could find several locomotives in steam at once.

One or two group visits were arranged to this railway before closure in the early 1990s, but this purely industrial line does not appear to have featured in "World Railways" and its existence appears to have been unknown to European enthusiasts for many years. It therefore comes as something of a surprise to learn that it has reopened! Operations started over the first few hundred metres from the loco shed to the river in January 1999 and the lifting bridge and a further 2km are to be brought back into operation presently. All the locomotives extant at closure still survive.

Kerr Stuart 3'6" gauge 2-6-2T 'Orinoco' was built for the British-owned Venezuela Central Railway, works no. 1038.

earlier. There are a number of Baldwin products, and probably the oldest exhibit is a Tubize 0-6-0T of 1889.

From Valencia to Puerto Cabello a British company built a 55km railway, again of 3'6" gauge, and this included a 4km Abt rack section between Las Trincheras and El Palito. This line, the Puerto Cabello-Valencia Railway, was built in 1886-7, before the Gran FC de Venezuela, with which it connected at Valencia. Some of the locomotives were built by Beyer Peacock. In 1946 the company was in liquidation, being nationalised soon afterwards and closed in 1959. With the construction of these two railways a link of unified gauge extended from Caracas towards the narrower gauge Bolívar railway. In 1939 the Government decided to close the gap and had the 3'6" gauge Palmasola to El Palito railway (55km) built by a Danish firm. This line opened on 22 March 1942 and was worked with Puerto Cabello-Valencia Railway stock. It was closed about 1954 when the new standard gauge railway was being built from Puerto Cabello to Barquisimeto (173km).

Railway Construction Since 1950

All the railways described so far formed a continuous link, and before considering the many isolated lines a few words on Venezuelan railway policy are needed. It will have been noted that the government followed a policy of buying up the foreign railways but took little interest in them until a grandiose plan was published about 1950, proposing the closure of all existing lines and their replacement, over a period of twenty years, by a standard gauge national system, the first phase of which envisaged the building of 2,424km of main lines and later 1,800km of secondary routes. The only tangible result of this plan was the building, between 1954 and 1957, of a new standard gauge railway linking the coast at Puerto Cabello with Barquisimeto, via San Felipe, the total distance being very similar to that of the old Bolívar Railway, which was then closed. The new railway is diesel operated and started out with two and three car Fiat diesel trains supplied in 1957 and 1960 for the passenger services. Another standard gauge line was also built at Guanta, but this will be dealt with later in geographical sequence.

Thereafter no more was heard of the National Railway Plan until 1972-4 when a new scheme was proposed, suggesting an equally comprehensive network which has never materialised, apart from certain bulk mineral carrying facilities. Improvements were proposed to the Barquisimeto line, with several industrial branches, diesel locomotives and shunters and wagons to be bought, plus new railcar sets for the passenger workings. In 1983 the 110km Yaritagua-Acarigua-Turen line was partially opened, and it is understood that passenger traffic is worked from Acarigua via the junction with the earlier line through to Puerto Cabello. In 1991 the remaining 40km to Turen were said to be awaiting track laying and the railway is intended principally to

carry general merchandise and agricultural traffic. Incidentally, it was reported late in 1960 that the Venezuelan government had made arrangements to purchase three lightweight diesel trains from the New York, New Haven & Hartford Railroad, but no news of these arriving in South America followed. Another priority of this plan was the construction of a 90km phosphate line from the Riecito mines to the petro-chemical processing plant at Moron, a line due to make physical connection with the existing railway near Puerto Cabello. By 1991 this railway still "lacked track" but ultimately it is intended to carry passengers over it.

Narrow Gauge Lines

Having now described the construction and closure of the narrow gauge lines around Caracas, and the one new standard gauge line so far active, we must again turn to narrow gauge lines all of which have ceased operation. Many were purely industrial, but some operated passenger services while a number of the earlier ones were built to facilitate transport from the interior to the nearest point of shipment, usually a river port. The railways now to be described were all to be found around Lake Maracaibo and the Colombian border, the one of these actually had physical connection with a line across the frontier, although in neither case was there any connection with other railways in either of the countries concerned. This was the Gran Ferrocarril del Tachira, of metre gauge and built in 1893 between La Fría and Encontrados, on the banks of the river Zulia which flows into Lake Maracaibo. A short branch joined this railway to the Cúcuta Railway in Colombia, and the total trackage involved was about 120km. The line closed about 1960 and known motive power included three 2-6-2Ts built in 1913, five 0-6-0 tender/tank engines built in 1924-28, and an 0-4-4T of 1928, all Baldwins. Some of these have survived to be exhibited in the Caracas Transport Museum.

Another river flowing into Lake Maracaibo is the Escalante, and from the river port of Santa Barbara extended the government owned railway to El Vigia, metre gauge and 60km long. This railway was built to facilitate communications with Mérida, capital of the state of this name, the onward link being maintained with mules! Now there are roads, and the railway closed some time in the 1950s. This line originally had four locomotives built by Fives-Lille, which were later replaced by three Baldwin 2-4-4Ts, two in 1926 and one in 1936, and a 2-6-2T.

Again linking Lake Maracaibo with the interior was the Gran Ferrocarril de la Ceiba, a privately owned 3 ft gauge railway extending 82km inland to Motatan. Locomotives included a 2-8-2T of 1893, an 0-4-0 of 1925, a 2-6-2 and 2-8-0 of 1926, an 0-6-0 tender/tank of 1922 (all by Baldwin) and a Hanomag 2-6-0 of unknown date. It will be noted that every locomotive recorded is of a different wheel arrangement! "World Railways" quotes the stock as being 7 steam, 5 motor railcars, 11 passenger coaches and only 32 freight cars, so it would appear that passengers were as important as freight before closure, which took place in the late 1950s.

Other lines on the lakeside, owned by petroleum companies, were the 2 ft gauge Encontrados-Bobures (34km) and the San Lourenzo-Mene Grande (17km) of the same gauge. It will be recalled that Encontrados was also served by the metre gauge Tachira Railway but it is doubtful if there was ever any connection between the two lines. A 760mm gauge line from Altagracia to El Mene was owned by the British controlled Oilfields of London company and carried 1,000 tons of freight and 4,000 passengers in 1950. All are thought to have closed by 1960, as pipelines were laid to new refineries on the Paraguaná peninsula, where the short 3 ft gauge line linking La Vela with Coro also disappeared about this time. The final (known) railway in this region is shown on a 1943 map as extending from Inciarte to Carrasquero, near Maracaibo, but in 1926 it was reported to have been abandoned in 1918!

Lines East of Caracas

It is now necessary to proceed eastwards past Caracas to a

point on the coast were the 3 ft gauge Ferrocarril de Carenero ran inland via Miguerote to El Guapo (54km). It was privately owned, with a passenger service, and was quoted as owning 7 locomotives (mostly Belgian), 7 carriages and 48 wagons before closure some time in the 1950s. A four wheel coach, which belonged to the owners of the railway, and has saloons at the extremities with a veranda in the centre (!), is being restored by the El Encanto museum line enthusiasts.

Much further along the coast in the eastern region of the country towards Guyana was the 36km state owned Guanta-Barcelona-Naricual railway, a 3'6" gauge line which had been in existence for years and was then converted to standard gauge in 1956 during the brief period of national enthusiasm for railways. It will be recalled that this was mentioned earlier as the only other line constructed under the National Railway plan. Soon after reconstruction, which slightly shortened the length of the railway, the coal mines it served closed and it has remained inactive for some years now but still intact and possibly to be reopened in the future (1991 report).

Finally, in the same region, travelling upstream along the river Orinoco, there are two iron ore lines, one of 56km linking El Pao with the river port Ciudad Guayana and the other 145km long linking Ciudad Piar (Cerro Bolívar) with Ciudad Guayana. These two standard gauge railways have no physical connection as they arrive at the river port on opposite banks of the river Caroni, a tributary of the Orinoco. These railways are operated by Ferrominera Orinoco, a subsidiary of the State owned Corporacion Venezolana de Guayana. Originally, they were owned by American companies and have General Electric 7,750hp and 900hp locomotives, the larger machines handling 108 car trains of four-axle 90 ton ore cars over 132 lb rail. A little further upriver a 52km line has been constructed to bring bauxite from Los Pijiguaos down to the river Orinoco at Gurnica and this was built by another subsidiary of the CVG. Similar wagons to those mentioned above are used and some locomotives have been transferred from those on the other two lines. This new venture commenced operation in 1992.

1990-2000 Proposals and Developments
Yet another "National Railway Plan" was published in "Developing Railways 1991" but at the present rate of actual implementation it is unlikely that any but the youngest readers will live to see much, if any, of it completed.

In 1995 a 342km scheme was announced to form a standard gauge line to run from Matanzas, through Maturin and Carapito to the already rail served part of Guarita. Iron ore would be the commodity carried. At the same time construction was said to have started on a line linking Caracas with Puerto Cabello, part of one of the earlier "Plans". Five years on it still remains to be seen if this will be completed and meanwhile 'Ferrocar' only has the Barquisimeto line available for passenger services.

But at least Venezuela has plans for rail expansion, which is more than can be said for a number of other South American States!

The Guanta - Barcelona - Naricual railway was converted from 3'6" to standard gauge and operated twin-unit Fiat railcars such as this one, numbered G-N-03 and seen in 1959 running over newly ballasted track.

BIBLIOGRAPHY

4-8-0 Tender Locomotives | D. Rock Carling | David & Charles, 1971
A Railway Engineer in Brazil | T.C. Hanson | Excalibur Press, 1989
Anglo-Chilean Nitrate and Railway Company | Donald Binns | Trackside Publications, 1995
Antofagasta (Chili) & Bolivia Railway, The | J.M. Turner & R.F. Ellis | Locomotives International, 1992
Articulated Locomotives of the World | Donald Binns | D. Bradford Barton, 1975
Central Railway of Peru & Cerro de Pasco Railway | Donald Binns | Trackside Publications, 1996
British Steam on the Pampas | D.S. Purdom | Mechanical Engineering Publications Ltd., 1977
Fairlie Locomotive, The | Rowland A.S. Abbot | David & Charles, 1970
Far Wheels | C.S. Small | Clever Hume Press, 1959
Garratt Locomotive, The | A.E. Durrant | David & Charles, 1969
Kitson-Meyer Articulated Locomotives | Donald Binns | Locomotives International, 1992
Les Locomotives Articulées du Système Mallet dans le Monde | Lucien M. Vilain | Editions Vincent, Freal et Cie, Paris, 1969
Meyer Articulated Locomotives | Binns/Koch | Trackside Publications, 1997
Narrow Gauge Rails to Esquel | Keith Taylorson | Plateway Press, 1999
O&K Steam Locomotives Works List 1892-1945 | Martin Murray | Arley Hall Publications, 1978
Origen y Desarrollo de Los Ferrocarriles Argentinos | | El Ateneo. Buenos Aires, 1946
Railway Conquest of the World, The | F.A. Talbot | Heinemann, 1911
Railway Foundry Leeds, The | R.N Redman | Goose & Son, 1972
Railway Wonders of the World | | The Amalgamated Press Ltd.
Railways of Argentina | Reg Carter | Reg Carter, 1997
Railways of South America: Chile | US Dept. of Commerce, Trade Information Series 1927-30
Railways of the Andes | Brian Fawcett | George Allen & Unwin, 1963/Plateway Press, 1998
Red Norte: The Story of State Owned Railways in The North of Chile | Ian Thomson | Locomotives International, 1997
Round the World on the Narrow Gauge | P.B. Whitehouse & P.C. Allen | Ian Allen, 1966
South American Steam | Roy Christian & Ken Mills, 1970
South American Steam | M.H.J. Finch | D. Bradford Barton, 1974
South and Central American Special | Donald Binns | Locomotives International, 1993
World of South American Steam | Roy Christian & Ken Mills, 1974

Periodicals:
Continental Railway Journal
International Railway Journal
La Vie du Rail (France)
Locomotives International
Modern Tramway
Modern Transport
Railway Gazette
Railway Magazine
Railway Scene (Sweden)
Via Libre (Spain)

137

138

With thanks to my wife Mary, seen here on the running plate of no. 104.
"What a way to spend a honeymoon!", Paraguay, 1968.

LOCOMOTIVES INTERNATIONAL
BOOKS AND MAGAZINES

Red Norte: Railways in the North of Chile

East European Narrow Gauge

The Steam Locomotives of Czechoslovakia

Forestry Railways in Hungary

The Barbados Railway (Spring 2001)

Steam and Rail in Indonesia

Steam and Rail in Slovakia

Steam and Rail in Germany

Broader Than Broad: Hitler's Great Dream

Locomotives International Magazine

LOCOMOTIVES INTERNATIONAL books and magazines are published by:
Paul Catchpole Ltd., The Old School House, Arrow, Alcester, Warwickshire, England, B49 5PJ

see more details on our web site: www.stargate-uk.co.uk/locomotives-international